RENEWALS 458-4574

DATE DUE

GAYLORD			PRINTED IN U.S.A.

SEARCHING SHAKESPEARE
STUDIES IN CULTURE AND AUTHORITY

Searching Shakespeare

Studies in
Culture and Authority

DEREK COHEN

UNIVERSITY OF TORONTO PRESS
Toronto Buffalo London

© University of Toronto Press Incorporated 2003
Toronto Buffalo London
Printed in Canada

ISBN 0-8020-8778-7

Printed on acid-free paper

National Library of Canada Cataloguing in Publication

Cohen, Derek
Searching Shakespeare : studies in culture and authority / Derek Cohen.

Includes bibliographical references and index.
ISBN 0-8020-8778-7

1. Shakespeare, William, 1564–1616 – Criticism and interpretation.
I. Title.

PR3014.C64 2003   822.3′3   C2003-903485-2

University of Toronto Press acknowledges the financial assistance to
its publishing program of the Canada Council for the Arts and the
Ontario Arts Council.

University of Toronto Press acknowledges the financial support for
its publishing activities of the Government of Canada through the
Book Publishing Industry Development Program (BPIDP).

For Susan

Contents

Acknowledgments

My thanks to the friends and colleagues who have kept the conversation going over many years: Ron Bedford, Lloyd Davis, Doug Freake, Deborah Heller, Kenneth Gibson, Magnus Gunther, Steven Hayward, John and Linda Hutcheson, Philippa Kelly, Ninian Mellamphy, Anne Pilgrim, Linda Scott, Ato Sekyi-Otu, David Shugarman, Don Summerhayes, Stephanie Taylor, and Tony Voss. Jane McWhinney is a friend who happens also to be a professional editor: she read the manuscript with care and made invaluable comments and suggestions. I thank my children, Sam and Sophie, just for being there as roommates and pals – especially during some difficult times – and I thank Brian and Nikki as well. Thanks to the editors of the *University of Toronto Quarterly, Studies in English Literature: 1500–1900,* and the *Dalhousie Review* for permission to publish chapters that appeared in different form as articles in their journals (chapters 1, 2, and 3, respectively). York University has provided financial support towards the publication of this book. I thank Bob Drummond, Kim Michasiw, and Suzanne Macdonald for easing that part of the process. Finally, I thank my wife, Susan, for just about everything.

Introduction

The essays in this book fall into three parts, each aimed at exploring an undercurrent in the plays studied. Literary criticism is always about undercurrents and implications. In this sense, it is always about irony and the matter that lies beneath and often contradicts what is merely ostensible. Attempting to lay bare this concealed but teeming life in the plays, the critic finds himself drawn into strange, dark, and exciting places by the agency of words. Shakespeare's uncanny and singular imagination carries his reader to the edges of imaginary experience, far away from the literal world that is made visible by the text but that, in reality, is merely a point of entry into the subtextual, ironic places that the text suggests. It is a world that the bold, the bad, and the unlucky inhabit as if destiny had carried them there rather than a subtle author. This world vibrates with feeling and suggestion but can always be referred back to the literal, to the words that are the critic's touchstones and lend solidity to the vague, the suggested, and the ironic.

In part I (chapters 1–4), I attempt to address issues of history, historiography, and the politics that lie beneath the surface of the narrative dramas that are always the first causes of the plays. I approach the plays somewhat indirectly here, by way of history and theory, attempting to clarify and understand the sometimes blurred distinction between history and narrative. Part II (chapters 5–7), on the other hand, is an attempt to engage more directly with the human elements of self and identity that lie deep in the three plays discussed: this part consists of readings that centre on the language of the plays' chief characters and on some implications of Shakespeare's linguistic styles. The focus here is on a different kind of history, one that moves away from history as a subject to separate histories of the subject: that is, to a focus on unofficial history, the personal and private, removed from the grand meta-historical arenas of politics and national self-consciousness to that site of human experience accessible largely through eavesdropping and voyeurism, which are the real sources and facts of life of drama and theatre. The essays of part II are about the past and mostly private lives of the characters in three tragedies. The idea of 'history' is reconfigured to include the ordinary lives of Shakespeare's far-from-ordinary characters. All three chapters take as their starting point the question of how the simple past (amorphous, unmediated, and untheorized) informs and influences the present. In them I explore and analyse how individual and collective consciousness of the past – or the lack of it – affects each play as a whole. In part III (chapters 8 and 9) I continue to explore the relationship between life as presented in the plays and the boundaries that contain them. On the one hand, there is the literal boundary containing the subject under investigation: on the other, there is the hypothetical boundary that dramatic sensationalism both acknowledges and, in the hands of Shakespeare, explores and challenges.

In chapter 1, 'Tragedy and the Nation: *Othello*,' I address historical questions of nationality and nationhood as they are represented in *Othello*, a play in which the word 'nation' is, in fact, used only once. However, the implications of the dark stranger haunting the lives and the very homes of the Venetians of that play make issues of nationality and cultural difference a virtual obsession for most characters. The resistance and the violence and pain always accompanying the search for nationhood and its concomitants, like consensus, on matters of culture and issues of uniformity and conformity are carried in this play by the weight of social and individual tragedy.

In chapter 2, 'History and the Nation: The Second Tetralogy,' I attempt to come to grips with the various ways in which the last three plays of the tetralogy – but *2 Henry IV* especially – absorb, remember, and represent the murder of Richard II. The murder is staged for the audience in the first play. It then becomes an obsessional issue in the following plays as it is remembered and used by succeeding political interests in the process of forging the English nation. But it never goes away and seems, in the subsequent plays, to contaminate the idea and reality of nationhood, despite the attempts of the successor kings to distance themselves from its terrible and spectacularly violent reality. Each successor play represents the murder of Richard variously, seeming only in *Henry V* to have resolved the complex problem. It is in the second part of *Henry IV*, however, that the ambiguities and contradictions are most vivid and problematic, and in that play they reveal themselves through fragmented verbal and dramatic structures, leaving the world in a limbo of uncertainty.

In chapter 3, 'Slave Voices: Caliban and Ariel,' I attempt to move one step further in the post-colonial analysis of *The Tempest*, in which Prospero is taken as an exemplar of European domination and imperialism. It is my contention that the post-colonial context that has been invoked in discussions of the play circumvents or submerges an even more brutal reality – the reality that Caliban and Ariel are more than colonial subjects: they are actual slaves between whom and colonized subjects there is a sharp and significant difference. The slave's subjection is always enforced, as it has been throughout the world and throughout history, by the constant and enforceable threat of disabling violence or death. The history of slavery is older and more universal than that of colonization; this chapter provides a context for such assertions.

History is a core concern in chapter 4, 'The Scapegoat Mechanism: Shylock and Caliban.' I attempt here to propose that it is not merely inevitable that these two characters themselves are historical subjects, but also that today it is difficult, and even morally problematic, to read Shakespeare's Jew and his Slave as though the concentration camps and the institution of slavery never happened; to read them purely historically, that is, and to concomitantly obscure the terrible consequences of a marginalization that in Shakespeare is *relatively* benign. I attempt thus to link Caliban and Shylock to the subsequent histories of their nations or kinds by an examination of the contemporary contexts of marginalization described by the plays and to link that context to a larger and more catastrophic history, a history as old as social experience. My inspiration here is the work of René Girard, who has written compellingly about the origins, functions, and effects of scapegoatism.

In part II the starting point is the proposition that within each play there exists verbal and visual evidence of a past that precedes the opening scene; that is, several of the characters in each of the plays advert, allude, or refer to a life that existed in the past – a fictional personal history, in other words. I have been interested to explore the extremely different ways in which that past is constructed in the three plays examined in this section. Chapter 5, 'The Self-Representations of *Othello*,' for example, represents an attempt to understand the potent dramatic effects of Othello's own obsessive references to his private history, a history that strongly determines much of the behaviour and action in the drama. Othello is unable, even (or especially) in his last moments, to separate his present from his past, and he seems to use that past to fashion and direct and understand the self he has created from his pre-play memories and fantasies.

In *King Lear* (chapter 6, '*King Lear* and Memory'), on the other hand, we are exposed to very little of the pre-play lives of the characters. Indeed, there is evidence here of a searching for evidence of the past, of the kind of evidence upon which Othello so heavily depends. The searching, however, offers almost nothing in the way of comfort or consolation. I argue, on the contrary, that to some extent the evident loss and corrosion of memory seem to produce some of the cruelty and violence of the play. A family or a nation in which memory has become as tainted, deformed, and desiccated, as seems to be the case in this play, is in danger of losing its moorings.

In chapter 7, 'The Past of *Macbeth*,' the focus is on the curious omission or the simple, but no less strange, absence of the past in that play. Shakespeare gives us characters who possess almost no personal history. The life that precedes the beginning of the drama, though powerfully and indisputably implicit, is hardly mentioned, and it is as though the urgency of the business of the play demands a total concentration on the present. When the past is given presence in the play, it usually possesses the force of a nightmare that jolts its subjects back to the terrible reality of the here and now. The protagonists seem to know enough to avoid it as they bury themselves in the present in dreadful anticipation of the uncertain future that they have forged. Their histories and history itself bring suffering and affliction. But here, as in the two previous chapters, particularized pre-play life as well as its absence assume a large burden of the drama.

In the third and last part of the book I continue the practice of close reading, but apply it more widely, including in each chapter discussions of several plays relevant to the theme of each. Chapter 8, 'Messengers of Death: The Figure of the Hit Man,' deals with the phenomenon of the hired assassin as a messenger figure in the plays. The hit man is a messenger of a special kind, but, while weapons are his metier, he uses words as well. Like all messengers, he is placed in a contractual and subordinate relationship to his employer as well as a relationship of an equally complex kind with his victim. These relationships are usually more fraught than they first appear. The message of death adds to them permutations and subtleties quite different and more charged, no doubt, than those between the employer of the more conventional messenger by mouth or paper. Killing by messenger brings the suborner of murder, the messenger's employer, into strange and often unforeseen dangers. In this chapter I attempt to relate the hit man to the more typical messenger as well as to analyse the ways in which the issue of violent death affects the social relationships in which it is imbricated.

Chapter 9, '"noseless, handless, hack'd and chipp'd": Broken Human Bodies,' is an attempt to deal with the way in which torn and mutilated bodies have the dramatic capacity to fascinate and repel, arousing feelings of disgust while they simultaneously carry a strange kind of allure for the audience. The allure of the disgusting is a powerful tool for the dramatist, who can use it to galvanize an audience. Human partibility is one of the most powerful sources of disgust, and it is exploited with fascinating force in the plays. There is, too, the question of the imagined mutilation of the human body in *The Merchant of Venice*, which holds up the idea of the pound of flesh as a persistent, but only imaginary, human body part to great dramatic effect almost throughout the play. The effect of the imagination upon the audience is to compel a kind   of vicarious complicity in some of the play's more sadistic fantasies. The dramatist's use of disgust and the audience's virtually uniform response to the disgusting remind us of the shared and common experience of the same work of art in some of its more emotional moments.

The subjects of these last two chapters are situated somewhere on the boundaries of experience. The assassin lurks on the fringes of society, half hiding himself and half hidden by the shadows that seem natural to his marginal status. Equally, the cutting up of live human bodies is itself an activity that belongs on the margins of human practice, always bathed in the foul but enticing aroma of disgust. In this exploration of marginality, the chapters belong firmly to the book as a whole; for the theme that unites this book is the idea of the boundary, that literal, imagined, constructed, or figurative extreme of the Shakespeare experience, where life at its richest and most intense is made almost to seem normal.

Quotations from the plays are taken from the Arden Shakespeare, general editors Harold F. Brooks, Harold Jenkins, and Brian Morris.

PART I

CHAPTER ONE

Tragedy and the Nation: *Othello*

I

A nation is, among other things, a collectivity of people made aware by its history of the possibility of its own extinction as an entity. The history to which such a possibility alludes is the national metanarrative that is constructed over time by the historians who have served to define the nation through their narratives. The fact that the nation can be destroyed is a crucial element of nationhood. That destruction, imagined or real, need not be violent. A nation can cease to exist as a nation when other, more powerful nations so decide. (The history of Yugoslavia supplies, perhaps, one of the most vivid examples both of the violent and of the merely political extinctions and reformations of the collectivity we call the nation.) Dramatic tragedy can be the imaginative representation of that destruction. Tragedy possesses an appropriately vast and encompassing reach; it includes a range of society in its characters, and it has a wide social and national range of catastrophic effects. It is thus an example of how society needs tragedy as a means of defining, containing, and representing itself by enforcing awareness of the fragility of national identity. The nation is a nation because it can be destroyed.

Tragedies, as representations of society *in extremis*, are products of that precise social consciousness. Their value is therapeutic and admonitory. For tragedy teaches of the constant and imminent possibility of the triumph of injustice and accident. It contains those possibilities within a form that both shelters us from and reassures us of their outsideness to ourselves and, paradoxically, of their direct and tangible relevance to and possibility in our lives. Many a nation has been defined by its leaders in precisely these fearful terms: its existence as a nation is made directly contingent upon its possible extinction. Philip Edwards has written: 'It is impossible for me to conceive of serious drama, comedy or tragedy, which is not, consciously or unconsciously, a hieroglyph of the pressures and tensions within the community outside it ... the conflicts in plays subsist on and are nourished by a nation's conflicts whether the relationship is overt or subliminal.'[1] A nation requires the means of collectively representing its destiny. Tragedy, like epic, is one of those means. For a group of people arbitrarily or voluntarily united in the purpose of preserving the group under this or that political ideology, there seems to be a need for culturally recognizable representations of nationhood that recall both the vulnerability and the durability of the nation. Other representations also figure among the national needs, but none so fully or extremely contains the national sense of value and urgency as tragedy.

The word *tragedy* is used in political contexts not merely to define unfortunate events, but also to describe the sense of ultimate disaster by which nations are transformed. An event marked as tragic is one that describes some powerful individual or group's version of the history of the nation. In other words, an event acquires the contours and the status of tragedy not by any immanent reality as tragedy but because it is a socially acceptable way of viewing disaster. Theorists of nationalism are united in the axiomatic proposition that the principle of nationalism always precedes the existence of the nation. This valuable truism helps to explain the connection of tragedy to nationhood. Because nationalism – like tragedy – is an artificial ideological construct, the nation it defines is vulnerable to fragmentation and, more relevantly, to destruction. The medieval metaphor – still current – of the nation as possessing the attributes of the human body, including mortality, strengthens the discourse of nationhood and associates it more vividly with the processes of tragedy and its representations of death and renewal. The tragedy of the individual is enacted in the historiographic reconstructions of national histories. *Othello* is both about the Moor as an individual and Venice as a nation as well as being a consideration of their interconnectedness.

On another level, *Othello* addresses a fundamental question relating to England as a nation. The English attitude towards Venice was somewhat ambivalent. On the one hand, there was widespread recognition by the English of the Italian state as a republic governed, like their own realm, by fairness and justice. Virginia Mason Vaughan notes that Venice 'had come to stand for an ideally ordered state, a model of "civility," and a mirror of what England aspired to be under James.'[2] On the other hand, as an Italian, Catholic city-state, it was regarded with suspicion and prejudice. Yet its representation as a locus of order, not least in two of Shakespeare's dramas, is an indication of its prestige as a place where order and the rule of law prevailed. By using an African, a black man whose ethnicity can in no sense be confused with that of the inhabitants of Shakespeare's Venice or, for that matter, of his England, Shakespeare considers at least an aspect of the nature of English nationalism. Liah Greenfeld makes a strong case that the England of Elizabeth was based upon a new, unprecedented kind of civic nationalism. 'English nationality at this time,' she writes, 'was certainly not defined in ethnic terms; it was defined in terms of religious and political values which converged on the rational – and therefore entitled to liberty and equality – individual.'[3] However, *Othello* vividly demonstrates that when ethnicity is made part of the equation, its concomitants tend to dominate what Greenfeld calls the 'rational' matters by which Elizabethan nationalism came to be defined. It is indeed true that Othello is accorded the civil rights of the Venetians while he is the commander of their armies and the scourge of their enemy. Once he transgresses their laws and customs, however, his ethnicity is restored with a vengeance and he is cast from the nation in a way that Iago, for example, cannot be. Vaughan's point is apposite: 'Like Cyprus, Othello can be colonized by Venice – he can be put to use. But he can never become wholly Venetian. This liminal positioning makes him vulnerable to Iago's wiles and like Cyprus, if he is not fortified, he will turn Turk.'[4]

While each nation may contain a plethora of notions of nationhood, and while its members may disagree about the meaning of the concept of the nation, at least there is vague general agreement about the category of tragedy, if not about all its ramifications and implications: it is sad, it is serious, and it usually ends badly. Thus, while within the same society there will be disagreement about the meaning of a given tragedy, there will be much greater accord about what it is that constitutes a tragedy. To some members of society *Othello* was, and for some readers it remains, a cautionary tragedy about the consequences of interracial marriage – and hence a moral paradigm for any nation that might choose to define itself through ethnic purity. To others the tragedy of the play is a social one that dramatizes the failure of society to accommodate itself to interracial marriage – and hence helps to define a nation that might value ethnic integration. In either case, everyone agrees that the play, its hero and heroine violently killed, is a tragedy. Being a tragedy, *Othello* helps to define the nation that produced it as well as those nations that have accepted and absorbed it. Part of the reason for the nearly universal appeal of the play is that it constitutes a progressive discussion of the nature of the Nation. At the moment he commits suicide, Othello most compellingly asserts his right to membership in his adopted nation. But just as he claims his right on grounds of service and desert, so it is denied him. Thus, a tragedy of self-deception continues beyond death. While Othello sees his own death as a passport to the nation, at his death his would-be comrades and compatriots begin the process of erasing him from their culture. They re-estrange him.

In his discussion of the *Henry VI* plays, Richard Helgerson explores the concept of the 'theatre of the nation,' a phrase given currency by Alfred Harbage's *Shakespeare and the Rival Traditions*. The definitiveness of Harbage's distinction between public and private theatres has been challenged in recent years, but the relation of the theatrical institution to its plays remains a valid and accepted basis for the analysis of the formation of English nationhood in the early modern period.[5] Helgerson discusses the way in which England is seen to be negotiating its nationhood and the nature and meaning of nationality through, chiefly, the agency of comedy and the history play. The Essex rebellion and the death of Elizabeth, he maintains, initiated a marked shift in generic preferences, 'as the national history play and romantic comedy gave way to satire, city comedy, [and] tragedy.'[6] The treatment of the subject in tragedy lends both a sense of renewed urgency to the subject of nationality and also, perhaps, an acknowledgment that the subject does not admit of the ready solutions so often and simplistically proposed in much historical drama, as the testing time of recent history would surely have demonstrated to Elizabethan and Jacobean audiences. *Othello* can be read as a sustained tragic meditation on the fraught matter of national identity, its conclusion a recognition of the fragility of the ideological forms from which the nation derives its sustenance. The implicit and visible ethnic differentiation that marks the play from start to finish forces Shakespeare's audience to confront issues of nationhood and questions of national identity with abruptly renewed attention.

The conclusion of *Othello*, with the Moor's erasure and Lodovico's final words, which consign Othello to oblivion and shameful history, has the effect of a failed political experiment. Until the moment when

Othello's public behaviour confirms the prejudices against him and establishes his unfitness for Venetian citizenship – when he strikes Desdemona in the presence of Lodovico – it actually seems as though he has achieved full citizenship in Venice. In the early scenes of the play, when the legality of Othello's elopement and marriage is endorsed by the Duke himself, Othello appears to have overcome obstacles to his full participation in the Venetian polity. His position as a valued member of the commonwealth is established, and his civil rights in the state have been affirmed by the highest secular authority. Civic nationalism appears to have triumphed. The collectivity that is the Venetian state appears able to absorb into itself even strangers, born outside the state, who have earned the right to citizenship. Othello's ethnic difference appears to have done little or nothing to disqualify him from that participation. He is identified with Venice and his social well-being is coeval with that of all Venetian citizens. This notion of a civic nationalism as superior and preferable to an ethnic one is a concept that, Liah Greenfeld argues, was gradually transforming the political landscape of sixteenth-century England.[7] Shakespeare has transported the concept to his version of Venice and gives the unusual and even subversive picture of a black African enjoying political and social authority in a contemporary European state. It is represented in the end, alas, as an aberration. *Othello* is Shakespeare's interrogation of the limits of the civic inclusiveness of the modern polity.

Ernest Gellner offers two makeshift but essentially sustainable definitions of the nation:

1. Two men are of the same nation if and only if they share the same culture, where culture in turn means a system of ideas and signs and associations and ways of behaving and communicating.
2. Two men are of the same nation if and only if they *recognize* each other as belonging to the same nation.[8]

That is, the fusion of will, culture, and polity becomes the norm by which the nation is identified as such. According to the first definition, Othello's much-discussed strangeness is a direct effect and function of his national difference. The second definition helps to explain the hopelessness of Othello's quest for acceptance. Gellner's view of nationalism is apposite. He regards the celebration of nationalism as a case of societies' worshipping and deceiving themselves by imposing what he calls a 'high culture' (i.e., school-mediated, academy-supervised idioms of communication) on the lives of the majority of the population; that is, imposing a dominant ideology that establishes 'an anonymous, impersonal society, with mutually substitutable atomized individuals, held together above all by a shared culture ... in place of a previous complex structure of local groups sustained by folk cultures.'[9] E.J. Hobsbawn recognizes the inevitable presence of the same phenomenon, which he describes as a universal criterion in the formation of a nation. He writes of the necessary existence of 'a long-established cultural elite, possessing a written national literary and administrative vernacular.'[10]

II

The word *nation* appears only once in *Othello*.[11] In his rage and grief Brabantio, a member of the necessary elite, is trying to make sense of Desdemona's elopement with 'the Moor.' He puzzles:

> Whether a maid so tender, fair, and happy,
> So opposite to marriage that she shunn'd
> The wealthy curled darlings of our nation,
> Would ever have, t'incur a general mock,
> Run from her guardage to the sooty bosom
> Of such a thing as thou – to fear, not to delight!   (1, 2, 66–71)

The phrase 'our nation' is vital: it is defensive and aggressive, inclusive and exclusive. It supplies clarity and logic for Brabantio and argues the primacy of reason over passion as the proper motive for action. The constructed dichotomy of the first scene – a foreign black man and a local white woman have eloped – is resolved in what look like moral terms. 'Our nation' resonates. The elopement is given wide-ranging implications, and the body affected by it is much larger than merely the family of Brabantio. The 'wealthy curled darlings' are Brabantio's version of the most eligible bachelors of Venice. They have money, looks, youth, and, presumably, appropriately high class. But most significantly, they are 'ours' – that is, they are white and, like Desdemona's father, they belong to the world of wealthy senators and power-brokers. They don't simply represent 'our nation,' they *are* 'our nation' in the sense that they define it, their homogeneity being represented as the crucial element of their nationality. This element of nationhood, the 'natural' coherence of like with like, is echoed in Iago's cruel confirmation of Othello's, 'And yet how nature erring from itself':

> Ay, there's the point: as, to be bold with you,
> Not to affect many proposed matches,
> Of her own clime, complexion, and degree,
> Whereto we see in all things nature tends.   (3, 3, 231–4)

Richard Helgerson has noted that it is in the histories and, perhaps most specifically, in the first tetralogy that the definition of nationhood includes references to the nation's poor and disenfranchised – partly, however, as a way of more clearly defining the nation as the preserve of the patriarchy. The latter, in turn, is partly defined negatively: that is, the poor are included to illustrate and foreground the authority of their masters, who really control the national discourse.[12] *Othello's* Venetian patriarchs, who define the prevailing cultural norms and practices of their nation, have no such democratic impulses. Their definition of nationhood is exclusionist in the most blatant and unapologetic way. There is no evident malignancy in their assumption of the right to define and describe their culture, but they possess absolute certainty and confidence in their entitlement to do so. Othello, by his difference, enables the 'Venetians' to discover themselves as a nation through the articulation of difference.

III

In common with tragedy, nationalism employs aggrandizement. Where in tragedy aggrandizement flows from the engagement of large character with large action, in nationalism the aggrandizement is manufactured – it is always self-aggrandizement, and no nation has managed to survive as a nation without it. Aggrandizement of the group or nation necessitates, almost by definition, the displacement or belittlement of that group or individual who may, or may seem to, challenge the primacy of the group that declares itself to be the national group. South Africa during the apartheid years under the thumb of the National Party or National Socialist Germany are two of the more egregious examples of the practice – although by no means the only ones. In demonstrating the need for the Irish in the formation of English identity in early modern England, Michael Neill notes that 'they also threatened it. For in the English mind, Ireland constituted not merely a defining limit, but a dangerously porous boundary.'[13] How much more dangerous to notions of national identity are those collectivities who live within the national boundaries of nations that, like 'Venice,' rely on ethnicity as the defining imperative of their nationhood.

In act 4, scene 1, Lodovico arrives in Cyprus with letters for Othello, summoning him back to Venice. In the exchanges of Othello and Lodovico the Venice/Cyprus dichotomy is clarified, greatly to the advantage of the former. Venice is formal and orderly:

> Lodovico. The duke and senators of Venice greet you.
>   [*Gives him a letter*]
> Othello. I kiss the instrument of their pleasures.   (213–14)

Cyprus is mentioned in an opposite context:

> You are welcome, sir, to Cyprus ... Goats and monkeys!
>   [*Exit*]   (259)

Between these moments of Lodovico's arrival and Othello's departure from the stage, Othello, enraged and confused, publicly strikes Desdemona. Lodovico tells him, 'My lord, this would not be believ'd in Venice, / Though I should swear I saw't' (237–8). There is something slightly schoolmasterly in this chiding. It very clearly identifies the authority capable of granting and withholding approbation. Venice, which would not credit Lodovico's report of Othello's violence towards his wife, is referred to as a kind of arbiter of good behaviour. 'Venice' as used here is not Venice, of course, but Lodovico's version of that segment of it that determines national standards and criteria of decent behaviour. The reference to Venice, here as elsewhere in the play, serves only to distance Othello culturally from the city. By his behaviour, the Moor is betraying what is arbitrarily represented as a national standard. Venice is and is not Shakespeare's England. Because it is Italian, the writer is freed to construct an imaginary nation without the demands and responsibilities of plausibility that would have been entailed in the writing of 'England.' On the other hand, the early modern English cultural realities are intrusively present and give familiarity and form to the textures of the nation of Shakespeare's creation.

For those who see the tragedy of Othello as a warning against miscegenation, the public striking of Desdemona produces a kind of relief. They are the Brabantios, the fathers – and mothers – who dread the possibility of their daughters marrying black and alien men. Lodovico's incredulity at Othello's blow is never put to the test: would this really not be believed in Venice, or would the information have been happily seized upon by members of the nation made anxious by the 'unnatural' marriage, by fathers dreading such an event within their own families? We do not know; but it would be naive to think of Brabantio as entirely unrepresentative. The Duke's 'I think this tale would win my daughter too' (1, 3, 171) is merely gestural, since the hero in question is a safely married man who may be flattered in this way without cost. The public striking of a wife puts a man outside the national culture. Othello's act is a terrible, visible sign that threatens a Venetian patriarchal norm: that wives may be struck in private is accepted social reality; to expose this reality in the public arena of the castle in Cyprus – or on the Jacobean stage – is to declare difference with a vengeance. Neill's point that the Irish 'figure in the English imagination ... as incarnations of "the wild man within," sinisterly seductive embodiments of the barbaric, uncultivated state to which all men, given the chance, will instinctively return'[14] may be applied with force to this contradiction between public and private realities so powerfully represented in this crucial event of *Othello*.

Striking Desdemona in public contributes significantly to the process of barbarization of Othello and hence to securing the national identity of 'Venice.' Contending within him are his barbaric, original self and his civilized, Christian, Venetian self, both visible constructs of two ostensibly complex social formations, the Moorish and the Venetian. At such times it is clear which self is in the ascendancy. But what is powerful and intriguing about the internal conflict of Othello is that it is specifically a cultural conflict that is tearing him apart. He is riven by forces that are culturally identifiable: a more or less savage – superstitious, mysterious, folkloric – culture is at war with a more or less civilized – modern, western, Christian – culture.[15] This fact is important; for this is a battle that has clear sides and clear stakes. Other tragic battles within contending subjects, like those of Macbeth, Hamlet, or Lear, are fought on the fields of morality, perception, and knowledge; in short, each emanates from a single cultural complex possessed of its own dilemmas and paradoxes. But Othello himself is a product of two nations and two cultures and he cannot straddle both. That is why his identity as a soldier signifies – he cannot be allowed, as perhaps Hamlet can, to take two sides at once. His taking of sides is a life-and-death issue for himself and the nation he represents professionally, but it remains, for all that, a choice between cultures and, by extension, a choice between nations.

Othello's choice has relevance to his vocation as a soldier. While not all entities that define themselves as nations possess militias, it is probably fair to say that all imagine themselves as ultimately having the capacity to enforce their authority as nations through the use of their militias. The militia is the means of the enforcement of social order upon which the power-holders of the nation depend. As a leading military defender of Venice, the Moor identifies himself with its power-holders. Yet while he enjoys Venice's dependence upon himself, his confidence is famously fraught with ambiguity: this is acknowledged, even before the drama begins, in his apparent recognition of the need to marry Desdemona in secret.

There is a sense in which the soldier is the opposite of the barbarian and, of course, a sense in which he epitomizes him. All military enforcement depends upon discipline and a hierarchy of command; all notions of barbarism start with the assumption of broken or absent hierarchy and disorder; the barbarian is believed to live in something like a Hobbesian state of nature – appetite-driven and self-gratifying. His practice of aggression and warfare is a given of his barbarism, as captured in Othello's enraged chastisement:

> Are we turn'd Turks, and to ourselves do that
> Which heaven has forbid the Ottomites?
> For Christian shame, put by this barbarous brawl.   (2, 3, 161–3)

The propensity for a human to be violent against his own species is as old as humanity; it is a primal form of expression alarmingly realized in the play in the public beating of Desdemona.[16] The soldier who beats his wife is betraying his discipline while simultaneously exposing its very core. Tragedy, as images of warfare constantly remind us, is the eruption into visibility of such contradictions. Othello's striking Desdemona brings into the open some of the reality of violence and injustice with which tragedy is nearly universally concerned.

IV

Othello's hand, with which he strikes his wife, with which he has held his sword and killed his enemy, with which he murders Desdemona, is the same hand with which he finally kills himself. It is, after all, this hand that has value to Venice, this that the nation hires to carry its power to Cyprus, to maintain the order upon which the nation depends for its identity:

> Zounds if I stir,
> Or do but lift this arm, the best of you
> Shall sink in my rebuke.   (2, 3, 199–201)

In some curious fashion the soldier, necessary to the nation and essential to its self-definition, is the chief agent of nationhood. To Venice, Othello is his hand – the synonym for his power to hold the nation together. When he strikes his wife he exposes another, darker side of the soldier. He is volatile, unpredictable, human, more than his hand. It is here that his redefinition begins: as he was the valued general, the iron fist of nationhood, now he devolves into little more than a highly useful immigrant worker, almost unrecognizable in the former capacity:

> Is this the noble Moor, whom our full senate
> Call all in all sufficient? This the noble nature,
> Whom passion could not shake?   (4, 1, 260–2)

V

By turning his hand against himself, Othello means to rectify the balance. His act of suicide restores the nation to itself, reproduces in tragic action the ideology of order and harmony by which the nation sustains the image and discourse of its own nationhood. In the last speech of the play, Lodovico grants Gratiano, who is Desdemona's uncle and Brabantio's brother, the fortunes that once belonged to Othello:

> Gratiano, keep the house,
> And seize upon the fortunes of the Moor,
> For they succeed to you.   (5, 2, 366–8)

There is a return here to the rule of law in the succession of Othello's wealth to Brabantio's family. The assuredness with which Lodovico passes on the Moor's fortunes bespeaks substantial authority. What remains of the Moor is his fortune, and it is absorbed into the patrician class of Venice by an act of patrician law. The act of succeeding to the fortunes of the stranger who has nearly destroyed a great house is more familiarly played out in treaties and surrenders that follow wars. It is Othello's fate to be remembered in Venice as the killer of Desdemona and the cause of the death of Brabantio. That his fortunes should revert to the survivor of that House – should be legitimately seized by him – is a reference to the hopeless foreignness of Othello, which is represented as ethnic difference throughout the play by the persistent use of the descriptive phrase 'the Moor.' Othello is officially 'the Moor': no speech in the play carries the stamp of officialdom or employs official language more fully than this phrase. His name is authoritatively erased, his ostracism a given. The explanation may lie in another play:

> It is enacted in the laws of Venice,
> If it be proved against an alien,
> That by direct, or indirect attempts
> He seek the life of any citizen,
> The party 'gainst which he doth contrive
> Shall seize one half his goods, the other half
> Comes to the coffer of the state.   (*Merchant of Venice*, 4, 1, 344–50)

While slightly varied in detail, the rule is familiar. The alien status of Shylock and that of Othello guarantee the obliteration of their names through the requirement that their fortunes be confiscated and added to those of members of the thriving classes. Shylock puts it thus:

> You take my house when you do take the prop
> That doth sustain my house.   (371–2)

The word 'seize,' used in similar contexts in each play (*Othello* 5, 2, 367; *Merchant* 4, 1, 349), suggests the violent efficacy of this enforced erasure of alien identity. The nation is almost literally restored to its imagined pristine form by the act of seizure, which seems designed to efface the memory of the offending stranger.[17]

The word 'seize,' also has the effect of negating the impulses, efforts, and motives of Othello's last desperate speech – his bid to be well remembered, to be entered into the book of national heroes. There is an irreconcilable conflict advanced in the play's two scripted endings. Othello's own desperate final speeches indicate the attempt to enlist tragedy in his own behalf. His self-consciously heroic suicide takes the form of a violent embrace of the nation he wants to call his own. The countervailing speech of Lodovico, the official voice of the nation, bids the 'object' – the spectacle of waste, murder, and destruction contained on the bed of death – be hidden from sight, eradicated from memory.

The pathos of Othello's last speech lies in the desperation of his attempt to correct the injustice and folly that have produced the surrounding wreckage. The speech is a plea to be admitted to the nation that he has betrayed by his violent and turbulent nature. The admission is to be purchased by the suicide enacted under the horrified gaze of all present. Tragedy is by definition a public mode of expression, and the form of Othello's suicide constitutes a deliberate and spectacular attempt to take control of his own history by the public performance of a ritual of nationality; acts of self-slaughter give validity to a human need to account for injustice and the arbitrary cruelties of life while preserving the social formation that produced them. Suicide inevitably, then, feeds the forces of reaction, shores up the damaged national identity, confirms its survivors as embodying a kind of consensual, residual justice. Public suicide is normally recorded as an ultimate act of courage, however necessary or unavoidable it may seem. This part is easy for Othello, whose tremendous courage is, in any case, a matter of record. His purpose in killing himself, however, is enacted in the unusual form of reaching out to the nation he has chosen while at the same time purging it of his presence. He knows that he has been grossly deceived and made a fool of by Iago, and he knows that the Venetians who surround him and look on his tragic disgrace know these things too. In his last speech he attempts to place a moralistic cast on the deed of horror that has brought him to this pass, to explain and justify himself and his history in terms of his relationship to the nation whose embrace has eluded him. Othello's desire to be well remembered can have small success within Venice. The facts of his public treatment and secret murder of Desdemona are too vivid and real to admit of much public compassion, too easily explained by his strange tempestuousness.

VI

Michael Ignatieff usefully defines the difference between civic and ethnic nationalism. Civic nationalism 'maintains that the nation should be composed of all those – regardless of race, colour, creed, gender, language or ethnicity – who subscribe to the nation's political creed.' Ethnic nationalism claims, by contrast, that 'an individual's deepest attachments are inherited, not chosen.'[18] The distinction is historical as well as merely political and philosophical. Civic nationalism is a concept associated with the modern democratic polity. And while theorists of nationalism agree that the phenomenon of nationalism belongs to the post-enlightenment world, it is possible to trace the origins and the force of both forms of nationalist ideology in the cultural products of early modern Europe.

Indeed, in *Othello* Shakespeare explores and meditates upon precisely these two distinct kinds of nationalism. He involves Othello intimately in the crucial affairs of a nation not originally his own and proceeds to interrogate the possibilities of the acquisition of nationality. In the play civic nationalism is given imaginary life. Othello, like Shylock, is offered access to the law and civil institutions of Venice. Othello goes farther by marrying into the nation, thus allying himself to it through the irrevocable bond of sexual intimacy and the institution of marriage. He gives Venice the gift of himself. But the gift is accepted only conditionally. By breaking the conditions of his national acceptance, Othello is driven back to the margins, to his origins outside the state he has claimed; his service, his excessive demonstrations of loyalty – like killing the malignant Turk for beating a Venetian and traducing the state – are as nothing now.

Shylock is a villain, but Venice has its own villains. The nation contains Iago as well as Othello, Cassio, and Desdemona. Nationhood is not a moral culture, though it often presents itself as such. Ignatieff illuminates this point: 'This psychology of belonging may have greater depth than civic nationalism's, but the sociology that accompanies it is a good deal less realistic. The fact, for example, that two Serbs share Serbian ethnic identity may unite them against Croats, but it will do nothing to stop them fighting each other over jobs, spouses, scarce resources and so on.'[19] In *The Merchant of Venice*, Shakespeare raises the question of the acquisition or change of nationality, especially in the case of Jessica. She seems to lose or surrender her Jewish identity in her embrace of her husband's Venetian one. The play glosses over the conflicts or regrets that may result from such loss. In *Othello*, because of the constant of Othello's visible racial difference, that difference is asserted more vividly while the possibility of its effacement is proposed. That possibility seems to exist primarily in the mind of Othello himself until his last moments. His desire for absorption into the nation is undercut by the universal public and vocal consciousness of his colour. While the depth of Othello's and Desdemona's love seems to have come within a hair's breadth of overwhelming the sustained enterprise of differentiation upon which nationalism necessarily depends, the almost official re-estrangement of Othello after he is dead declares the triumph of ethnicity as a basis for national identity.

VII

I took by the throat the circumcised dog
And smote him thus.   (5, 2, 356–7)

As he strikes the blow fatal to himself, Othello utters this harsh and terrible death sentence. The act is fraught with the famous self-consciousness of this hero, a self-consciousness that here achieves a new level of self-awareness. The speech act is a moment of dreadful and searing self-loathing. It self-consciously tears Othello from the Venetian culture, identifying him compellingly and, even, physically with a proven traitor to that culture. As terms of abuse go, 'circumcised dog' ranks high in the Shakespeare lexicon; it refers to the cursed religious rituals and spiritual life of the heathen and his brutal animality. Othello presents himself as the embodiment of this perverse nature, and his suicidal blow lends powerful depth of feeling to the words. The ritualized ceremoniousness of martial suicides in Shakespeare is bluntly negated by Othello's language. The heroic aggrandizement that usually accompanies such acts is crushingly reversed. No spirit of duty or honour is invoked by the Moor here, no sense that suicide offers any possibility of redemption is given form; the last lines of the speech are the precise converse of the thrust of its opening. Having bidden his spectators to remember him well, Othello then enforces upon their consciousnesses the spectacle of himself brutally killing a brute who is the more brutal for being a malignant Turk – the opposite of everything that is supposed to be Venetian. Of course, for those who have observed Iago in action, Othello's resort to this form of abuse by nationality is somewhat ambiguous, however sincerely it is meant. This violent act of assertion and negative national self-identification is a gesture of submission by which Othello hopes finally to insinuate himself into the culture that is, ironically, about to cast him off.

The act is one of ultimate self-exile. Othello's suicide casts him violently from the nation: other suicides, like that, say, of Brutus, relocate their actors firmly within the nation's core. This violence is the physical realization of his earlier recognition of the force of Desdemona's dying look, which, he says, would hurl his soul from heaven for fiends to snatch at. Othello makes his place with the fiends who here are specifically constructed as enemies and traitors to 'Venice.' The act of suicide involves the perpetrator's taking control of his own destiny by seizing the means of his own death. Instead of allowing himself to fall into the hands of the state and become subject to its laws and the sordid punishment of legal execution, Othello creates a tragedy out of his plight by forging its conclusion from the materials of narrative and performance. In doing so, he robs the nation of its opportunity to purge itself of the pollution he has brought on it. But the tragedy of Othello's crime and punishment has exposed the nation to the compelling truth of its fragility as a unit. His suicide saves the nation the task of slow and unclear justice; the act confirms national solidity by the powerful endorsement of one of its public heroes. Lodovico's summation gives Othello's suicide the contours of a tragic demise by supplying a strong and authoritative sense of closure to the tragic scene. Simultaneously, it attempts to erase evidence of the Moor's existence by the arbitrary bestowal of Othello's fortune on Desdemona's uncle:

> O Spartan dog,
> More fell than anguish, hunger, or the sea,
> Look on the tragic lodging of this bed;
> This is thy work, the object poisons sight,
> Let it be hid; Gratiano, keep the house,
> And seize upon the fortunes of the Moor,
> For they succeed to you: to you, lord governor,
> Remains the censure of this hellish villain,
> The time, the place, the torture: O enforce it!
> Myself will straight aboard, and to the state
> This heavy act with heavy heart relate.   (5, 2, 362–73)

CHAPTER TWO

History and the Nation: The Second Tetralogy

I

The past, in the figure of the murdered King Richard, haunts the protagonists of the *Henry IV* plays and prominently figures in King Henry V's prayer on the eve of Agincourt. The relation between the Richard they remember or merely imagine and the Richard of *Richard II* is fraught with emotional, moral, and ideological consequences. Richard's post-mortem power turns out to be greater than that he possessed alive and figures significantly in the various constructions of the English nation of these histories. His murder is the transforming fact and detail of Henry IV's monarchy, and it looms over and transfigures the events of Henry IV's reign. All crucial events refer to it. Richard, in death, becomes the focal point of action, the site of conflict, and the means by which the present and future are made coherent. Richard himself is a curious presence, represented in the plays in which he figures in a strangely ambivalent way. The play of Richard searches for a defining royal essence in his character, and for some of those who observe him it seems to express itself in the great moments of self consciousness just prior to his violent death. For others, Richard remains the fixed emblem of failure, a king who never achieved sufficient command of himself or his kingdom. His tragedy is, of course, coincident with the process of his failure and begins only after the loss of his monarchy has become an established fact. In the play of Richard, the king stands in a contradictory and perplexing relationship to many of his subjects. Among those close to him are his enemies as well as his friends; those who love and those who hate him stand in dangerously equal proximity to this monarch. The array of perspectives upon the beleaguered king includes, of course, that of the audience, privileged to see a private side, invisible to both his friends and his enemies.

The Elizabethan preoccupation with history was, according to Phyllis Rackin, a matter of urgent national interest, regarded both as a means of preserving peace and political stability and as a matter of national self-definition. The multiplicity of understandings of the nature and purpose of the study of history is reflected in the plays, where radically different conceptions of history and its relevance to national identity are subjected to intense dialectical pressures.[1] Richard II himself is engaged in the making of history. This is a conventional and inevitable function and by-product of monarchy, and it is the way in which, for centuries, we have been schooled to understand the historical process – large affairs under the management of large men. The notion of history as justificatory political narrative confirming and legitimizing bourgeois political ideology has been explained by Jean-François Lyotard in his pursuit of a definition of the postmodern. To Lyotard, the postmodern is the very antithesis of the presumed credulity of the political imperatives that demand acquiescence and obedience to the authority by which history is heroic, male, and seamlessly woven into master narratives. Postmodernism is the rejection of that authority.[2] The progressive and often contradictory historical revelations of the second tetralogy indicate that Shakespeare was aware of the traps and simplifications of traditional historical narrative.

The symphonic, ordered heroics of *Richard II*, and even of *1 Henry IV*, break up in the narrative dissonances and foundering of *2 Henry IV*. The almost compulsive reflexivity of Part Two, as it refers backwards to the originating tragedy of the cycle and as it somewhat cynically deconstructs its predecessor part, has the effect of separating *Henry V* from its founding history. This play's famous performability as a separate drama contributes to the impression. Graham Holderness argues that the first three plays of the tetralogy help to mark the beginnings of modern historiography, that they present 'a clear, historically informed apprehension of the political struggles of later medieval society; in particular the long struggle between monarchy and nobility which developed out of the contradictory nature of feudal order, and was arrested by the accession of the Tudors.'[3] They also chart the uneasy and sometimes violent shift from a notion of England as a medieval monarchy to modern nationhood. The 'realm,' as imagined by John of Gaunt (act 2, scene 1), with its secure sense of how things should be, describes a world before the decline of the barons, a medieval England like that described by Liah Greenfeld, 'in which the population [is] related to the polity only as occupants of the land and the king's subjects; their stake in it being of a utilitarian and accidental nature.'[4] Gaunt and Richard are possessed by a nostalgia for lost plenitude, a world in which an imaginary unity, simplicity, and certainty once prevailed, a world that, according to Catherine Belsey, 'precedes symbolic difference.'[5]

King Richard, however, is Shakespeare's deluded monarch and is not a historian. He sees himself as a participant in the master narrative of a continuous history. He adverts, refers, and alludes to his historic role. Those around him, for and against him, similarly recognize this function as the unavoidable destiny of a king. It is his self-perceived and self-produced historical role as one monarch in a political continuum that explains his appeal both to those who court his favour and to those who seek his destruction. The king is the emblem of the future, according to this narrative; he ensures its coming because he is the essential link in a lineal progress that has no predictable or apparent end and springs from a mysterious beginning hedged with myth and magic. He is the personification of continuity in the nation and thus the locus of its stability or disturbance. To and from him all things are seen to tend. Thus, his strength and weakness are rooted in the same place.

The king defines the entity we call the nation. He transcends in his person the complexities and ambiguities of geography and ethnicity and even civility – in the technical and political senses of the word. He is the nation, and thus he and his body civil must be preserved. When and however he dies, the office must still survive; for on that survival depends the survival of the organism known as the nation – this contingency has been transformed into a fixed political imperative in the minds and behaviour of the citizenry and its masters. The falsity of the ideology – and hence the falsity of the analogy, which in Shakespeare turns the ideology into a truism – was not predicted by Shakespeare but was, remarkably, demonstrated by the real event of the Civil War and its aftermath – a coherent England without a monarch. In Shakespeare, however, the English nation as an entity is dependent on and referable to its kings. The passionate anxiety of all engaged in preserving, protecting, restoring, or replacing the monarchy testifies to the continuous presence of a fear of its demise.

The context of this fear, however, is something of a paradox. Shakespeare was writing in a period of unprecedented social mobility. Under the New Aristocracy, in which noble birth was losing importance in the face of an aristocracy of ability and merit, a tentative process of democratization was under way. The old nobility, Greenfeld argues, was all but extinct by 1540, replaced by a new Henrician elite of men of modest birth but remarkable abilities.[6] This perceptible, if still exclusive and partial, tendency towards equality of condition among different social strata remained focused on the monarch throughout the century; it was he or she who symbolized England's distinctiveness and sovereignty. In Tudor England, Robert Weimann reminds us, 'those who upheld the independence of the nation supported the sovereignty of the crown; its authority was accepted not only against the claims of the Roman church but also in the face of domestic unrest and foreign invasion.'[7]

What is good or bad in Shakespeare's medieval or Tudor monarchies is always subordinated to the simple but overwhelming fact of kingship. The king simply is; his monarchy survives until his death or until he is usurped. The kind of king he was entirely depends upon his use of power and power's use of him. The king in his lifetime, while making his history, is feeding the maw of his posterity – the successors and descendants who will remember, praise, or blame him, and the writers who will reinvent him for their time. Shakespeare carries his medieval monarchs into his own centuries and uses Henry V, according to Marie Axton, to sound his own doubts, not about Henry as a person, but to suggest doubt 'about the soundness of an historical figure as basis for a Scottish claim in 1600.'[8]

II

The monarch's history-making is abetted by the ideology that has made him monarch. His place in history is assured: but how does he perceive himself filling that place? Are his motivations those of a man who wishes to be remembered in a particular way? Does he seem to care whether history records his as a good or bad monarchy or him as a good or bad king? He is, of course, always at the mercy of the historians: while it is his destiny to be 'historical,' a named part of the process, it is his chroniclers, not himself, who will make his history. Shakespeare's Richard is, in the end, a very human character, driven, it seems, by ordinary desires and hopes and by ordinary malice. He is a subject of his power very much as his subjects themselves are. Because he has enormous political power, his use of that power is always vastly consequential to others. Thus, he must be careful, but his impulses are frequently spontaneous and lead him to abuse his power. The responsibilities of office are at war with the inclinations to carry that office into spheres of life where it doesn't belong. There are at least three Richards in the play: the Richard known only as a public figure, the man his enemies fear and despise; the Richard known to and supported by his friends; and the Richard known privately to the audience through asides and through the audience's privileged view of both friendly and hostile perspectives offered publicly and privately.

Richard the king, the public man, the icon of the nation, appears most commanding in the opening scene of the play. He is surrounded by men who are implicated in the necessary deceptions of public politics. They all behave according to the dictates of form, and they flatter him by the performance of ceremonies designed to honour him and confirm his authority. In the first scene we have pure performance, pure acting on all sides; and winnowing out enemies and friends is not possible without the aid of historical information. We have a king apparently revelling in his authority, surrounded by subjects, some of whom play at being loyal and obedient. The play's first speech convincingly implies a Richard in complete control. Harry Berger Jr has noted the way in which his (deliberate?) use of the word 'boist'rous' has the effect of infantilizing (making a boy of) Bolingbroke, his hitherto unrecognized nemesis,[9] and thus by extension aggrandizing, or (to use Richard's own word) 'monarchizing,' the king. The stage belongs to Richard and he uses it to full effect. All addresses made to him in this scene allude to his royal station. His regality is in the foreground of each speech and is reinforced by his self-conscious and ostentatious use of the royal plural. While Richard here adverts to the dissension between the two contestants, he manages to keep firm control over the proceedings. Gaunt's, Bolingbroke's, and Mowbray's performances of obedience continue the illusion of a Richard in charge. It is an illusion not long sustained; but it is the canny Richard himself, the arch-actor, who observes how the two contestants are vying for his credulity,

> We thank you both, yet one but flatters us,
> As well appeareth by the cause you come,
> Namely, to appeal each other of high treason.   (1, 1, 25–7)

Later in the same scene Richard offers what may be an aside, a remark that refers to the tone of Bolingbroke's determination to avenge the death of his uncle, the Duke of Gloucester, a death that he lays at the door of Mowbray (but that, we know and learn, implicated the King himself). As he watches and listens to Bolingbroke, Richard notes: 'How high a pitch his resolution soars' (1, 1, 110). The line has a thoughtful, private quality, as though whispered or wryly observed to a trusted friend. It tells of the astuteness of the king who knows more than he tells, sees more than he lets on. So the ceremony is subverted and with it – but only momentarily – the notion that this monarchy is an example of a pure, flowing, sequential 'history' of an ordered medieval world. The possibility of Richard's words being an actual aside lends it the appearance of a line overheard only by the audience: this possibility introduces a note of irony; Richard knows things that have not been declared or revealed. A subtext of subterfuge, secrets, and lies is suddenly exposed. The human motive of simple distrust pierces the carapace of ceremony. The man who is king is shown to possess a side. The play seems to take off from this point. Its vitality depends upon the conflict of the private and public personae constructed for private and public occasion. Later in the first act the spectacle of Richard and his friends talking with malicious glee of Bolingbroke's departure provides a curious scene, one in which the sarcastic pleasure of young men almost obscures the presence of danger to the throne:

> Wooing poor craftsmen with the craft of smiles
> And patient underbearing of his fortune,
> As 'twere to banish their affects with him.
> Off goes his bonnet to an oyster wench;
> A brace of draymen bid God speed him well
> And had the tribute of his supple knee. (1, 4, 28–33)

Perhaps it is the cynicism of Richard that contributes to his undoing. So caught up and delighted does he seem in his awareness of pretence and acting that he appears to forget to wonder what it truly conceals, what danger the perceptible duplicity of his subjects offers his security. This lighthearted banter with its serious implications is a nice contrast to the vehement Duchess of Gloucester's bloodthirsty exhortation – also in private – to her law-abiding brother-in-law Gaunt to avenge his brother as, she tells him, a brother should and a real man would.

The contentions that drive the play are multifarious. Their danger lies in the secrecy and caution with which they are marshalled by Richard's enemies and in Richard's culpable blindness to them. This, at least, is Shakespeare's version of events. The moment of Richard's direst peril is the moment when, just after John of Gaunt's death, he leaves Ely House with the contemptuous parting words:

Think what you will. We seize into our hands
His plate, his goods, his money and his lands.   (2, 1, 209–10)

The place is left occupied by angry conspirators who talk of the impending return of Bolingbroke and rebellion. Belsey notes that Richard's words are absolute only on condition that they remain within the existing system of differences. Like his subjects, he is bound by the symbolic order, which allots meaning to the orders he gives. But he surrenders his absolutism by transgressing the system of differences: 'Richard-as-England has consumed England's material wealth in riot, misusing his sovereignty to mortgage the land, devouring in the name of his title his own entitlement ... Richard violates the symbolic order, and in consequence his words lose their sovereignty.'[10]

The rest is history. At the end of the play rebellion has triumphed, Richard is murdered, and the new king is enthroned. Henry's reign is doomed from the start. Or rather, Shakespeare presents his reign as doomed and supplies a heavily moralistic underpinning to the start of that reign to account for its unhappy history. Here, the play interrogates the utility of the moral and political forces that animate the drama and dominate the sequel plays. Bolingbroke's disavowal of Sir Piers of Exton is an act of double treachery, which only reifies the habit and practice of moral compromise that is to characterize his reign. On the treachery of the powerful in the two *Henry IV* plays, which continue the tradition, Paola Pugliatti makes the useful point that the way the denouement comes about 'involves an interesting exchange of prerogatives, for it is achieved by means of a double betrayal: the betrayal by John of Lancaster of the forces of rebellion and the betrayal by Hal of the forces of misrule.'[11] Political action is profoundly rooted in an apparently unavoidable duplicity and finds its historical power in compulsive hypocrisy. Stephen Greenblatt does not exaggerate when he observes of the Henry plays that in them 'moral authority rests upon a hypocrisy so deep that the hypocrites themselves believe it.'[12] Actions that lack spontaneous double awareness, such as, for example, the Bishop of Carlisle's attempted obstruction of Bolingbroke's accession, are dangerous in the extreme. From Richard's quietly ironic recognition of Bolingbroke's ambition, to Henry IV's double-dealing with Exton, the pattern of secrecy followed by lying establishes monarchy as a political practice that is *necessarily* sustained by public dishonesty.

III

So deeply embedded in the practice of monarchy is the form and habit of deception that the actors of Shakespeare's history – kings and nobility alike – themselves do not comprehend the extent to which they are involved in its convolutions. They write, record, and recall history with apparent sincerity, yet their versions of the same past events are remarkably different. The multiplicity, even infinity, of meanings to which history is automatically and eternally subject marks Shakespeare's awareness of what has more recently been described as a process of deferral. This difference arises partly because the past of *Henry IV* is fixed in the crime of murder, which calls out for revenge or expiation. Thus, the plays that succeed the reign and the death of Richard are locked in a remembered and recorded eternity. The past cannot be laid to rest if the murderer goes unpunished and dies quietly in his bed in the Jerusalem Chamber. So the past persists into the eternal present, a sore in the mind that worries the history being enacted and that shapes and forms the nation.

In *Henry IV* Shakespeare describes the inevitable process by which real events are transmogrified into myth and, hence, national consciousness – or, more accurately, into the prevailing culture's idea of national consciousness. The murder of Richard is directly apprehensible to the audience: it is observed and thus forced upon the collective awareness. The murder permeates, as well, the consciousness of Richard's posterity, both his actual and his would-be heirs. Their ambitions and aspirations are shaped by the way they relate to the murdered king. Each side in the Henry rebellions defines itself by the way in which it defines its own and its enemy's perception of that relation. It holds onto its beliefs about the other side's perceptions of the crime. The murder is passed down to posterity *as* a murder. Its witnesses – audiences, readers, onlookers – are implicated in its permutations of meaning, its subtle capacities, its effects on its perpetrators, its transformative power. To posterity the murder of Richard is merely one of history's regicides; to the witnesses of the slaying, it is an individual and unique event in which a man – guilty and innocent like all of us – is slaughtered by armed assassins. What happens in the minutes during which that slaughter occurs unavoidably becomes part of the witness's past and, thus, the means by which the privileged onlookers of the murder must measure the narrative simplifications and ideological tendencies of the inheritors of Richard's legacy. To Richard's successors the murder becomes mythology the minute it becomes publicly known. To the audience, the actuality of the murder – its visible, brutal violence – thwarts or determines the mythologizing process of history. What Shakespeare's audience sees is a man killed: what Recorded History comes to know, on the other hand, is a depersonalized version of the event and its transformation into a mythological instrument of use in the pursuit of political power. Myth is mythical because its incidents conform to familiar, recognizable patterns. The murder of a king is as old as kingship. The murder of Richard continues the familiar cycle.

The simplification and depersonalization of regicide concern the process of transformation from act to language. The murder of Richard is a vastly complex event, loaded with implications that are actual, imaginary, historical, ideological, and dramatic. There is and can be no definitive reading – or history – of the murder of Richard. It is a dramatic event that may be viewed from a multiplicity of angles and perspectives. We may choose, as critics usually have done, to view it as an integral part of a dramatic sequence or narrative. But it may be viewed, with equal validity, as a chaotic reenactment of an already mythologized event upon which an author has chosen to impose form – aesthetic, moral, or monitory. The possibilities are literally endless. The deferral of a definitive reading has no limit. However, the inheritors of Richard's story, friendly and hostile, implicated and indifferent, fulfil some kind of human compulsion in their attempts to put the murder into the forms of language. This is the eternal human trap. By giving voice to history in order simply to possess it, we unavoidably simplify it, attempting, as Belsey reminds us, 'to arrest the play of meaning. But meaning is always plural, to be able to speak is to be able to take part in the contest for meaning.'[13] The murder of Richard looms over its own future, well into the age of Elizabeth. Those close to it recognize a need to position themselves in relation to it. Nothing less than the enveloping concept of the English nation is at stake. The focus in these plays on the deceased king was a reminder to Elizabethans of their own dependence on Elizabeth as the focus of their national aspirations. The sycophancy that we all too easily read into Elizabethan literature is sometimes confused with rampant conservatism; the often obsequious language used by poets was, rather, a kind of national celebration by the poets of themselves through the agency and symbolism of the queen, just as the concentration of attention on Richard directs the attention of the English upon the central place of the monarch in both the concept and the reality of the English nation.

IV

In *Henry IV* the conceptualization is pressed in new directions. As the England of these histories is developed through the machinery of both formulated and implicit history, the creation of national identity becomes freighted with some of the contradictory impulses of history making. Imposing meaning on past events is one project of the two central plays of the tetralogy, and in them different ways of making history contend for supremacy. There is, for example, the history of Henry's predecessor, which is foregrounded many times as it is remembered by both those who were there and those who know it by report. Then there is the history contained in the dramatic reality of human character as it breathes life into the present. The first words spoken by King Henry in Part One are an example of the latter:

> So shaken as we are, so wan with care,
> Find we a time for frighted peace to pant.   (1, 1, 1–2)

The lines are redolent with allusion and painful but contingent memory, referring obliquely to the conclusion of the previous play – but they are not the stuff of history. Yet the feelings they represent and the tidings to which they allude comprise a part of the story in which the lives of those engaged in making history are intertwined. In the Henry plays, history, as recalled and recounted by the characters, is a means of negotiating with the present. The retrospective mode animates the present, and the past is a felt and perceptible force that directs and positions that present. As we may expect, Prince Hal, the omnicompetent young politician, possesses the keenest awareness of the crushing presence of the past on the present and future. His 'I know you all' speech is a declaration of precisely this recognition. He announces in advance his plan to mould the present in order to mould the future, so that when the present has become the past, its groundwork, the conditions upon which it must be read and understood, will already have been established. This is a young man who is quite simply trying to avoid the unpredictable. That is, Prince Hal's project is to manipulate and control the forces of uncertainty that disturb, distort, and deflect history from the paths of the inconvenient reality to which it must so often submit.

Unlike Richard and Henry IV, Prince Hal is more than merely aware of his assured place in history and his destined role: he is determined to direct the forces of history and bend them to his will. Hal's perspective on the past will prevail and, in prevailing, will give him the power to define the English nation in the terms he dictates. This mastering of all circumstances is his constant strategy and is what distinguishes him from his immediate predecessors. Surprise is not a reaction Hal ever shows. Apparently, there is no moment unaccounted for, no eventuality for which he is unprepared, no passion for which he does not have the right words at his immediate disposal. This general readiness, not a quality that has always endeared him to Shakespeare's audiences and critics, is nevertheless the secret of his continued successes. He thinks less about the past or the forces that have made him Prince of Wales and the future king, than he does about the means needed to prepare himself for the great day. When it comes he evinces only the most correct emotion and appropriate feeling. His life is a life's work. When he is king, and especially in the play of *Henry V*, his monarchy seems to be driven in part by retrospectivity and a sharp eye on the retrospective view of posterity.

Those around him are in a constant state of acute awareness of those traditions and their relation to them. They look back in order to contextualize the present. The first reference in *1 Henry IV* to the previous king occurs in the dialogue among Northumberland, Worcester, and Hotspur as together they ponder the cause of the present disarray of the nation:

> *Worcester.* Was not he [Mortimer] proclaim'd
>   By Richard that dead is, the next of blood?
> *North.* He was, I heard the proclamation:
>   And then it was, when the unhappy King
>   (Whose wrongs in us God pardon!) Did set forth
>   Upon his Irish expedition:
>   From whence he, intercepted, did return
>   To be depos'd and shortly murdered.
> *Wor.* And for whose death we in the world's wide mouth
>   Live scandaliz'd and foully spoken of.   (1, 3, 143–52)

The passage reeks with regret. Northumberland's remorse at having taken the wrong side renders his part the least attractive. Richard, whom we have seen bullied by him in the previous play and forced to confess to crimes and royal transgressions, has become the 'unhappy king,' as though the sympathy and 'wrongs in us' that Northumberland has latterly discovered will put a gloss on his complicity in the king's murder. The passage nevertheless supplies a useful reminder that historical facts do, in fact, exist. Northumberland actually did, in words and actions, support Bolingbroke's usurpation of Richard's crown, which no amount of ideological tampering can erase. His regret at having done so is a fascinating example of rehistoricizing that fact. But it cannot remove it. Young Harry Hotspur is equally interesting in his 'reading' of his father's new version of his complicity. He sees fit to chastise Northumberland, not, however, for participating in the subornation of the murderers of Richard but for doing so for the sake of 'this forgetful man' (158), who has neglected his obligations to his fellow murderers. Hotspur's speech, passionate as usual, does manage to take the history in interesting new directions. He is unstinting in his blame of his father, but he loses some credibility in his reincarnation of Richard, whose downfall he himself aided. This is, of course, familiar narrative, but the question of what drives the narrative in these and other directions is what fascinates. There is among the rebels and within the king himself a recognizable desire for political and personal power. The craving, however, bespeaks larger issues and larger desires, above all, the determination that the meaning of 'England' that finally prevails shall be the meaning imposed by themselves rather than that which has been stamped upon the nation by the reigning monarch.

Hotspur understands all too well the compelling force of history and the need to situate himself in relation to it. He has, on the one hand, a strong sense of the past and, on the other, a strong desire to create a favourable impression of himself in that relation. His rhetoric is provocative:

> Shall it for shame be spoken in these days,
> Or fill up chronicles in time to come,
> That men of your nobility and power
> Did gage them both in an unjust behalf
> (As both of you, God pardon it, have done)
> To put down Richard, that sweet lovely rose,
> And plant this thorn, this canker Bolingbroke?   (1, 3, 169–74)

This is both brilliant and naive. Hotspur distances himself from his friends as he embraces them. He understands the moral force by which chronicles are directed, the roles of shame and injustice in their construction. The 'sweet lovely rose' is a self-serving description, which supplies a rallying point for the rebellion but violently contradicts the actions of these three men in the earlier play. Historical simplification carries the argument: good and bad, present and future are its bases. Hotspur's bluster is a kind of protective moral covering that he places between himself and the cowardly killing of the Richard he has here reinvented. His talkativeness is a means of silencing opposition and questioning. Time and again he drives his auditors to impatience; but that impatience has the interesting and useful effect of warding off difficult and probing questions about himself. The rebels see a need to talk themselves out of complicity in the crime of killing their king. They are enraged at having been duped by Bolingbroke, 'this king of smiles' (1, 3, 243), 'this fawning greyhound' (248). The worse Bolingbroke is, the better they are. If the king is a villainous regicide and their enemy, they are, by logical extension, virtuous simply in their opposition to him. Thus, they are 'for' England, while he is its enemy. Yet it is they, the rebels, who are willing to divide England into the spoils of victory. The tripartite division of the realm, described by Holinshed and realized in the play with the aid of a map, in act 3, scene 1, runs counter to the prevailing mood of national consciousness and patriotism of Elizabethan England. The act of division effectively isolates the rebels and lends credibility to the prince's party as no amount of moralizing would have done. It is possible to see the rebels' division of the kingdom as an internal directive to the audience about the threat to the national well-being offered by those who would divide the nation.

Unlike those of the other histories, the characters of Part One seldom engage in conscious analysis of history, state, or politics. The motor of its drama is created by the psychological forces that prompt rebellion and the social aftermath that rebellion can produce; its historiography takes the form of self-justifying narrative. Northumberland's revolt is a product of envy and the perceived ingratitude of the king. Bolingbroke's version of his ascent to power is no deeper. In his crucial exchange with Hal, he remembers Richard and himself and the opposition that brought him to the throne. His speeches describe a king who degraded the dignity of his office, and he uses that perceived degradation as a justification of usurpation. The energy of the drama of Part One swirls about issues of motivation and personal and political morality. The problem of the criminal incipience of the reign of this monarch supplies a straightforward political moral. A great crime begets great consequences. This play's memory – its accumulated references and allusions to the past – has occluded the great speech of Richard II, who reminded his hearers of the history of bloodshed upon which the English Crown was founded – on 'the sad tales of the death of kings ... All murthered' (*Richard II*, 3, 2, 156–60). Its focus is on the dramaturgical mechanics of war and heroism and opportunism. History has become a simple matter of sides. Henry's description of his ascent and Richard's fall invokes a Manichean view of the past that does nothing towards finding truth but does much to vindicate him. Its purpose is served with Machiavellian efficacy, since it elicits from the wayward son apparent feelings of guilt and the famous oath of both fealty and love and the promise of redemption.

> I will redeem all this on Percy's head,
> And in the closing of some glorious day
> Be bold to tell you that I am your son   (3, 2, 133–5)

Hal's preoccupation with achieving greatness through the Crown lends most of his great speeches a forward- rather than a backward-looking quality. He predicts and prepares a future from which he will be able to look back and through which posterity will judge him.

V

Part Two of *Henry IV* is another story. Here, the impulses of history and history-making dominate the action, although the process is tainted and confused by popular and vulgar reality. As Part One devolves heavily on the personal, on issues and theories of character and the forging of historical personae, Part Two more sweepingly locates human character and action in an encompassing framework of political and historical conceptualization. This is a drama of ideas in which the difficulty of writing history within the framework of a visibly and inconveniently awkward reality is addressed. The power-brokers of this history want something more complex and ambitious than to seem ethical in the eyes of their subjects, their sons, and their posterity – they want to *be* right and to *have been* right. In pursuit of these aims they are constantly placed in the position of having to reflect on the past and to re-form their reflection into suitable, and usually self-aggrandizing,

forms. We are thus, and inadvertently, alerted to the potential unreli-
ability of any history that is written by its participants. The often
engaging triviality of Part One – Hal's mockery of Hotspur, Falstaff's
joking, Lady Hotspur's threatening to break her husband's little finger
– is sidelined in this play. There is, to put it simply, no innocence in Part
Two. Even its naughtiness is tainted by the gravity of the issues of history. The play moves inexorably to its stunning and eternally ambiguous climax as Prince Hal becomes King Henry and promptly rejects
Falstaff. Where Part One has dramatic excitement, life (comedy), death
(tragedy), and heroic action (epic), Part Two has self-reflective moral
and intellectual magnitude, which is reinforced and complicated by
the omnipresence of moral uncertainty. And it is in Hal's addressing
the questions of uncertainty and ambiguity that his difference from the
other makers of history is demonstrated. Unlike those around him,
including his father, his brother John, Northumberland, and West-
moreland, among others, Hal shows strength in his ability and willingness to acknowledge the inevitable and inherent ambiguity of political
and historical processes. While his friends and enemies argue by asseveration, Hal alone seems able to accept and abide with the reality of
moral uncertainty or relativism.

A kind of ill temper pervades the play: each of the chief characters
seems to anticipate impediment and conflict, which they pre-empt
with quick and ready aggression. Rumour's presence as prologue
establishes the sequence of lies followed by compromised and
thwarted responses; this pattern somehow becomes fixed as a condition of the structure of the play. The result is an essentially human
motive of angry pessimism, which lends the project of history-making
a bias that the characters and the play never shake. Paola Pugliatti
argues convincingly that Part Two enacts 'a process of corruption
whose seeds are already present – albeit hardly stressed – in Part One.
Various forms of sickness now attack the core ... and in the end, the
axiologies which militate against the king are defeated by a process of
pollution which changes their very nature.'[14]

What Dover Wilson really showed in The Fortunes of Falstaff was not
so much his own conviction that the rejection of Falstaff was morally
justified as it was the fact that it was foolish of readers before him not
to have seen it coming. Clearly, he saw it coming, but he equally clearly
also wanted it to be right, proper, and Christian that it did come. We
have moved away from such moral certainty and absolutism in our
reading of Shakespeare. It is interesting that Dover Wilson's reading of

the rejection is an example of the very reading of history advanced by a proponent of a rather secular notion of the 'rules' of historiography. I refer, of course, to Warwick, whose 'hatch and brood of time' speech propounds the convenient ideology of the repetitiveness, predictability, and inexorability of a comprehensible historical process.

> There is a history in all men's lives
> Figuring the nature of the times deceas'd;
> The which observ'd, a man may prophesy,
> With a near aim, of the main chance of things
> As yet not come to life, who in their seeds
> And weak beginnings lie intreasured.
> Such things become the hatch and brood of time;
> And by the necessary form of this
> King Richard might create a perfect guess
> That great Northumberland, then false to him,
> Would of that seed grow to a greater falseness,
> Which should not find a ground to root upon
> Unless on you.   (3, 1, 80–92)

Henry's response is a resounding affirmation of this view:

> Are these things then necessities?
> Then let us meet them like necessities.   (92–3)

Looking back, we can wisely predict what we have come to. The point is less banal than it might look. Warwick alludes to the complex forces that shape historical progressions. While a treacherous man must always be watched, it is also true that the 'history' in all men's lives and the 'nature' of times deceased have become something other than the things themselves – they have become language and argument. Warwick's way of understanding history repeats the notion of history as an orderly master plan, possibly presided over by a master planner. But it is not confirmed by the deliberate subversions and interstitial interventions of this extraordinary play, which constantly threatens to switch moral, political, and dramatic direction. Pugliatti makes the further interesting point that 'Warwick's idea of change taking place in time and his stress on the observer's activity also epitomises the spectator's experience, which is obviously the mirror image of the dramatist's.'[15] We are put on guard by 2 Henry IV against the transformative power of speech in a quite explicit way. The Lord Chief Justice dismisses Falstaff with words that might be an epigraph for this play: 'I am well acquainted,' he tells him, 'with your manner of wrenching the true cause the false way' (2, 1, 107).

'Wrenching the true cause' is a fine metaphor for much of the narrative pattern of this play's history. In the histories in particular, abstractions, memories, ideas, and certitudes are recovered into pure, whole, and traditional narrative forms nowhere so vividly as in the descriptions of historical battles. Shrewsbury is innocently misrepresented by Lord Bardolph as the glorious triumph of the 'rebels':

> The King is almost wounded to the death;
> And, in the fortune of my lord your son,
> Prince Harry slain outright ... Sir John,
> Is prisoner to your son.   (1, 1, 14–16, 19–20)

And then,

>   O, such a day,
> So fought, so follow'd, and so fairly won,
> Came not till now to dignify the times
> Since Caesar's fortunes!   (20–3)

That 'Caesar' is an apt example of heroic glossing over the sordid realities of war in the borrowed robes of classical precedent, transporting both the orator and the auditor to those pure and unsullied realms of nostalgic imagination where history and mythology meet.

In the beginning of Part Two, however, the resolution is entirely illusory. The first dramatic scene begins with three rapid and confusing questions as the all but anonymous Lord Bardolph and the literally anonymous Porter fire interrogatives at each other, lending the opening a ferocious sense of anxiety. The scene then violently disjoins dramatic narrative by the introduction, not of lying – of which we have a plenitude in the play – but of sheer and terrible error. Lord Bardolph lyrically declaims the wrong tidings in full view of an audience that knows the truth, and he tragically compounds the error by sowing false hope among the rebels. The circulation of false information lends potent subversive force to this drama of disaster and produces confusion and preternaturally strained emotion. Among the rebels to whom he brings this moment of misfounded ecstasy is a man – Northumberland – who must publicly carry the burden of having betrayed his own son and helped him to his grave. The scene is charged with multiguous and hopelessly muddled emotions and information, which cause the safety and certainty of conventional theatrical predictability to be radically disturbed. The audience is thrown into confusion about what it thinks and what it thinks it is supposed to think. The presence of a malevolent mischief is deeply felt by all who participate in and watch this scene as guilty and innocent parties to the rebellion are overwhelmed first by exhilarating and then shocking 'news.' The heroic ugliness of Northumberland's 'Let order die' speech, where he invokes murder and destruction upon mankind, calling on darkness to be 'the burier of the dead' (1, 1, 155, 160) is a characteristically excessive and hyperbolical example of the tendency towards disintegration that is the signature of this play.

In Part One, whether we find the subplot carnivalesque,[16] subversive of, or complementary to the monarchical plot, it is clearly and deliberately subordinate to it. The same cannot be said of Part Two, which begins in brutal and tragic error and concludes in ambiguity and disintegrity. Hal, it is true, is a kind of link with the heroic, but by any standards he is a critically compromised hero by virtue of things such as his applause for Prince John's chicanery, his rejection and denial of the most spontaneous and vital part of his own past, and, indeed, his absence from so many of the crucial scenes of the play. The whole of this first scene, more of an overture to the play than even the Induction, is a crazy vacillating career through a range of opposing emotions leading nowhere. It is the utter directionlessness of the scene that lends it strength, an extraordinary but emotionally charged pointlessness. The purpose of the scene is entirely mysterious in terms of normal dramatic expectation: nothing of the plot or story is advanced; it stands isolated as a surreal evocation of violently contradictory emotion, its connection to the drama merely temporal. The scene tells the audience nothing new. It simply reveals what everyone already knows: if you tell a dead soldier's father that his son is alive, you make him happy, and if you then tell him that he is, in fact, dead, you make him sad and exceedingly angry. It is all very well to employ the Procrustean method of criticism that insists that such a scene strikes a thematic note, but in such analysis more questions are unanswered than answered. We are left with the simple but unpalatable reality of maliciously and gratuitously produced pain.

More to the point is the way in which history is rendered unreliable, subjective, and susceptible to ideology, producing, instead of ultimate truth, a response of (healthy?) incredulity, which Lyotard recognized as the identifying stamp of the postmodern. The kind of mind – Lord Bardolph's in this case – that constructs a narrative of battle as Caesarean is a schooled, academy-forged and -mediated mind common to the 'high people' of the plays in the tetralogy. The courtiers sound remarkably alike, regardless of the side they support. Each has his own particular version of the 'truth' without being capable of particularizing that truth as uniquely his. The moral uncertainties of this play, with its alternative 'histories' of the recent events, reveal epistemological structures as heavily and inevitably compromised. Thus, while the impulse to produce what Belsey, following Lyotard, calls a 'grand narrative'[17] reveals itself constantly in the posturing and the speeches of power-brokers on both sides of the civil conflict, the play's actual narrative and moral energies tug it away from the ideological simplifications that such a narrative implies. Grand narrative is surely the impulse that motivates Northumberland's recognition of Morton, the bearer of ill news:

> Yea, this man's brow, like to title-leaf,
> Foretells the nature of a tragic volume.
> So looks the strond whereon the imperious flood
> Hath left a witness'd usurpation.   (1, 1, 60–3)

Thus do the makers of history attempt to encompass and control the material of their narratives. Northumberland's deeply felt fearful anticipation is, nevertheless, couched in the accustomed metaphors of heroic history. News, good or bad, is lifted from the realm of human action by an officially promulgated, academically sanctioned language of epic narrative. The story of Northumberland's family is presented in the speech as possessed of inherent and inevitable grandeur. The father strains to find meaning in the tragedy of his son's death. And he finds it in the precedents and rituals of rhetoric.

Disintegrity and a downward-spiralling deconstruction of the enforced codes and forms of history-making are the centres of energy of this strange play. They are most notoriously manifest in the treachery of Prince John; but criticism has not overlooked Prince Hal's complicity in the flagrant dishonesty. This is a modern world of expediency and pragmatism, and success is its highest reward, while honour and its effects are relegated to memory, to a quaint historical narrative upon which we may feed our thirst for order and old fashion, but which will do nothing to enrich our lives. Hal's crown stands squarely upon the violation done to chivalry by the deception of the Duke of Lancaster: chivalry dies in this play. The rejection of Falstaff is another of the signifiers of a monarchy centred in ambiguity and hypocrisy. And the erosion of certainties and the concomitant embrace of the 'modern' are further exposed by the evidence of cruelty, corruption and violence on the level of the street. Comic violence in the tavern is suddenly made very real and very ugly when the First Beadle warns Hostess Quickly and Doll Tearsheet, 'Come, I charge you both, go with me, for the man is dead that you and Pistol beat amongst you' (5, 4, 16–18).

VI

History proper makes its most visible and verifiable appearance in the epilogue, when Rumour traverses the boundary between fact and fantasy via his reference to Oldcastle and his unconvincing assertion that 'this [Falstaff] is not the man' (Epilogue, 32). He informs us that the narrative will continue 'with Sir John in it'; that is, he knowingly promises the delights of comedy and sex ('fair Katherine of France') as though he understands where the audience's real interest lies – not, evidently, with Henry V. Making history himself, Shakespeare, according to Rackin, 'severs the connection between his disreputable theatrical creation and its original historical namesake in order to evade censorship and prosecution. Named for the real historical Oldcastle, the character would have had real historical consequences for the players in the enmity of Oldcastle's present descendants. Dehistoricized by the name of Falstaff, he acquires the impotence (fall-staff) of fiction, but he also acquires its licence.'[18] Perhaps, of course, 'Falstaff' is a wordplay not on fallen staffs but on full staffs, and it stands for the opposite of impotence, a reading that more accords with my own feelings about him: certainly he is one of the sexier presences in the play just as, in my opinion again, Hal is one of the least sexual of Shakespeare's characters. Be that as it may, Rackin is surely right in adverting to this passage's sheer historicity, just as Shakespeare seems explicitly to be denying it. In that denial of the historicity of Falstaff and in his correction of the assumption that Falstaff is based on Oldcastle, Shakespeare, in a way, subverts his own denial.

The almost compulsive reconstructions of the past that animate these history plays reflect the persistence of a need both in the characters of his plays and in the author himself to construct something whole out of something inherently fragmented. The past is known only in bits and pieces and, by the time Shakespeare is writing his epic, has been moulded into something only partially and unsatisfactorily known. The multiplicity of versions of the same history, already a fact in the late sixteenth century, itself is an index of a restless recognition of the ultimate failure of the 'grand narrative' to be what it always purports to be – the last word on the subject. The Shakespearean project, starting with *Richard II* and continuing through three more plays, is another attempt to view that past and to reshape it yet again. The symphonic and sweeping generalizations about history and England undergo critical deconstructive scrutiny in the plays that follow, culminating in the scratchy 'unconformities' – to use Kristian Smidt's term – of *2 Henry IV*.[19]

The pristine 'England' longingly recalled in Gaunt's speech remains a barely intact but nevertheless remembered reality in *Richard II*. It is an England ruled by 'Divine Right,' a feudalism, according to Holderness, given 'cohesion and structure by the central authority of a king bound to his subjects by reciprocal bonds of fealty.'[20] But even the economic bonds that, according to Gaunt, tie the nation together in mercenary agreements appropriate to 'tenements' and 'pelting farms' are a form of wholeness. That wholeness is a conception the trajectory of the group of plays interrogates by slowly breaking it down into its component parts. For all the flaws that modern criticism has found in the person of King Henry V, his play is a celebration of the potential coherence of the English nation, bound together by civil bonds that are not – as misunderstood by Richard – the patrimony of the monarch, but rather comprise a commonwealth of many essentially and potentially equal participants. While that commonwealth is somewhat fragile and its mechanisms of coherence somewhat precarious, the idea of unity itself, its conceptual power, is given force in the play by the very threat of its fragility. Pistol supplies a case in point. Axton makes the argument that Pistol's inevitable subjection to the Welsh leek is an additional illustration of the precarious unity of the British realm. She reminds us that the so-called miracles of unity and prosperity are illusory; that whichever version of Prince Hal one sees, 'ripening or rotting, beneath the nettle leaves of Eastcheap in the earlier plays of the tetralogy ... one *is* prepared; one *sees* no miracle.'[21]

Indeed, notice of *Henry V*'s part in the formation of identity is provided in the epilogue of *2 Henry IV*: the last play of the tetralogy persistently recollects and builds upon the material developed in its predecessors. Crucial moments like the Dauphin's insults to the English king are grounded in the material of both parts of *Henry IV*, as is the failed Cambridge conspiracy. King Henry's prayer on the eve of Agincourt famously promises to expiate the deposition and murder of Richard II, thus proclaiming the connectedness of *Henry V* to the process. And the evanescence of Henry's glory is a constant theme of the drama, which together with the recollections in the epilogue of the disaster that followed in the reign of Henry VI leave us with a celebratory drama that often sounds like a warning in its scepticism about the future. Notwithstanding its political and philosophical ambiguities, the drama of King Henry V seems vividly to strive for an impression of wholeness: its dramatic impulses and political idealism seem grounded in the values of dramatic and political integrity. The ambiguity and tentativeness often seen in the character of the king and the imagery and ideology of the chorus all labour under a larger structure of order and completion. These forms are imitated in the trajectory of the narrative and the conventional and traditional forms of drama being imitated. While nationality and the nation are shown to be infinitely fragile in this period and climate of political uncertainty, they are represented as desirable and possibly even worth fighting and dying for. But one of the spiny problems with which Shakespeare invested his search for the roots of nationhood was a recognition of the complex place of history in the process.

CHAPTER THREE

Slave Voices: Caliban and Ariel

I

The construction of Caliban as a colonized native has become a truism of contemporary criticism of *The Tempest*. Meredith Skura and Alden and Virginia Vaughan have traced the history of Caliban and the way in which he has been read as monster, as villain, and, most recently, as victim. Caliban has become a cultural icon, an enabling force and a touchstone of the culture from which he derives and of those cultures that have appropriated him. Skura argues that new historicism is just one example of that large body of works that attempt to account for the exploitation of the New World by the project of economic adventurism of the sixteenth and seventeenth centuries.[1] According to this view, Prospero, far from being the divine orderer of more traditional interpretations, is the embodiment of European, Old World, cultural domination. Power over the New World Other, not the rehabilitation of Italian (or, of course, English) political turbulence, is seen as the essential part of his political mandate within the play.

Leslie Fiedler, writing in 1972, made the point: 'thanks to such political commentators as Franz [*sic*] Fanon, as well as certain more adventurous literary critics like Frank Kermode, no respectable production of the play these days can afford to ignore the sense in which [the play] is a parable of transatlantic imperialism, the colonization of the West.'[2] Another aspect of the history of the collision of the European and the 'barbaric' worlds emerges through an exploration of the inner dynamics of the play, its psychological, cultural, and linguistic constructions. The relation of Prospero to his two servants, Caliban and Ariel, falls squarely into the pattern of typical and traditional master-slave interaction. Prospero's so-called servants are more properly described as his slaves, complete with the connotations, both old and modern, that the term carries. Servants are waged labourers with rights, sometimes those of citizenship and sometimes of access to the legal system. Clearly, no part of this description fits the situation in *The Tempest*.

The institution of slavery has always been sustained by the fact and the omnipresent threat of violence. Nevertheless, it remains disturbingly true that slavery has been justified in the past by some leading intellectual figures, including the likes of Aristotle and Grotius – who saw slavery as harmonious with natural justice – and Hobbes. To Hobbes, as clearly to Prospero and a host of Shakespearean despots, political and social obligation are modelled on the subordination of the vanquished subject, who gives obedience to the victor in exchange for his life, thus producing a rationale for obedience as a *desideratum* of social stability.[3] Slavery is practised successfully only in those societies where, Orlando Patterson argues, it does *not* completely dominate the society. 'A truly vibrant slave culture, if it is to avoid the crisis of honour and recognition, must have a substantial free population.'[4] This certainly was the situation of which Aristotle wrote and that then, as subsequently, called for justifications such as that provided in *The Politics*.

G.W.F. Hegel's famous discussion of slavery – his terminology is of 'lordship and bondage' – supplies an intriguing imaginative recreation of the beginning of history in order to explain the advent of social classes: the discussion also provides an analysis of slavery and self-consciousness. Hegel proposes that this beginning was the moment when men were locked in mortal combat in the primal pursuit of the basic human need for recognition (Aristotle's *thymos*). The outcome of the battle was the division of society into two classes: a class of masters who had risked their lives for victory and a class of 'slaves' who surrendered because of their fear of death. The master's need for recognition, however, could not finally be fulfilled, because recognition by a slave would never be sufficient, coming as it did from a defeated subject: the slave was not acknowledged as fully human and thus could not satisfy what Hegel saw as the primary need of the human being. The slave, on the other hand, in totally lacking recognition or the possibility of recognition, sought evidence of his humanity outside the narrow limit of recognition. To Hegel, the slave was able to recover the humanity that he had forfeited – on account of his fear of death – through work. Paradoxically, then, the slave could recover a kind of freedom through the exercise of his own labour, which in itself became a form of self-expression and a form of freedom. Work, in other words, could free the slave and replace recognition of another person as a basic need thereby supplying the slave with the condition of humanity that the master, because of his mastery, could never obtain.[5] Patterson's refutation of Hegel takes force from the fact that Hegel's argument depends upon a version of slave-owning societies that probably never existed. In *The Tempest*, which also predicates an imaginary society, dreamed up for the purposes of drama, precisely half of the initial inhabitants are slaves and half are slave-owners.[6] The play is a curious anticipation of Hegel in its revelation of slave and slave-owner achieving self-consciousness through the experiences of 'lordship and bondage.'

In his justification of slavery, Aristotle may well have been responding to the presence in fifth-century Athens of ideological resistance that the institution of slavery may have provoked – presumably among the slaves themselves (slave revolts were known to have occurred) and among his non-slave-owning fellow citizens. Slavery on Prospero's island is unusual in that it is not institutionalized; that is, one of the essential elements of slavery is missing. According to Barry Hindess and Paul Q. Hirst, 'slavery is a legal or customary institution, which necessarily implies its subordination as a partial form to a larger structure of socio-political relations. Slavery is – as colonisation is not – a legal form of property which gives to an owner certain rights over the person of a human subject. But this form and these rights only exist *within* a distinct form of state or community.'[7] In these terms, Prospero has imported the ideology of the ownership of a human subject to the island he calls his, but not the institutional structures by which it is controlled. The slave, Hindess and Hirst continue, 'is neither a subject nor a subordinate, he is a form of property; the master is ... his *owner.'*[8] Along with Prospero's notion of owning human subjects, have come to the island what A.E. Voss lists as the essential coordinates of slavery: 'power, property, deracination, non-personhood, dependent labour, physical suffering and psychological damage, prejudice.'[9] Deracination of the human subject and non-personhood are two features of slavery that distinguish it from colonialism, whose concomitant missionary project implies the (inferior, but real) 'personhood' or humanity of its subject people. Although colonization often, perhaps usually, implied slavery – its centuries-older sibling – the connection is not automatic. Yet on Prospero's island we note the presence of forms of slavery that are differentiated by the unequal treatment of Caliban and Ariel and by the contrasting origins of their enslavement. Ariel is enslaved by Prospero from the moment he is released from his bondage in the cloven pine. Caliban, on the other hand, moves from a position of servitude to a benign master, where obedience was enforced by cooperation and the gift of a degree of freedom – a typical form of colonial dependence several degrees removed from slavery – to one of absolute slavery enforced, as slavery always is, by violence.

Though it is not unknown for slaves to appear to enjoy their slavery, it is always hard to credit that appearance as a true reflection of feeling in an institutional system where the use of violence is a normal means of instilling cooperation and obedience or compliance. The very means by which the institution is sustained is evidence of the constant potential resistance that slavery implies, almost by definition. If slaves have to be bludgeoned, raped, and brutalized into submission, and kept submissive by the constant fact and threat of more and greater violence, it follows that their resistance is constantly presumed to be imminent. Their powerlessness and their masters' power over them require persistent reinforcement as facts of life. The slave, who lives only at the behest and by the permission of his masters, lives on the edge of death. His life belongs to another, who can take it away at will. To remain alive requires the presence of a vital irony: the slave must be made to want to live despite the misery of his state. The master must make the slave believe that actual death is worse than the tortured existence he currently enjoys. Thus, while the master recognizes the presence of discontent and potential resistance in his slave, he needs to foster that resistance sufficiently to allow the illusion of freedom in the slave, while he needs to suppress it sufficiently to render it unthreatening to himself. Patterson is convincing on this feature of the practice of slave-owning. He writes that the slave-owner, by 'holding out the promise of redemption ... provides himself with a motivating force more powerful than any whip. Slavery in this way was a self-correcting institution: what it denied the slave it utilized as the major means of motivating him.'[10] Thus, the appearance of compliance in the slave is produced out of a deliberately created hope for freedom, which can be offered and withdrawn by the master as a condition of obedience and subservience. The psychological damage to the slave may be imagined; but, more relevantly, the effects of this kind of mental torture upon the slave are intended to demoralize and render him increasingly dependent upon the power of his master. Ariel is this kind of slave-victim.

Caliban is the opposite: he is an example of a slave who hates and who, through his hatred, lends validity to the Hegelian argument. To Hegel the phenomenon of the subordination of one self to another, enforced by all forms of servitude, including, most egregiously, the servitude of slavery, is a condition of the consciousness of self.[11] In Ariel the consciousness of self has been blunted by and subordinated to the prospect of freedom, while in Caliban, the thoughts of rebellion and the fact of his hatred keep that consciousness in sharp focus. Caliban's hatred fulfils the function that Hegel ascribes to work or labour in supplying the slave's awareness of himself: 'Thus precisely in labour where there seemed to be merely some outsider's mind and ideals involved, the bondsman [slave] becomes aware, through this rediscovery of himself by himself, of having and being a "mind of his own."'[12] Caliban's hatred is a kind of mediate discursive strategy that locates and identifies his social and emotional distance from his master. In a sense, his hatred keeps Caliban honest and self-aware and places Prospero at a safe – that is, uncontaminating – distance from himself. It helps Caliban to locate the 'other' and thus to define his self by its difference.

Prospero's hatred of Caliban, on the other hand, is much less self-aware than its counterpart, largely because it is suffused with the moral indignation by which it is justified and thus clouded, and also because it arises out of a fear of the hatred that oppression naturally induces. Prospero needs and uses Ariel to protect himself from the hatred, anger, and violence of Caliban. The word *monster* carried in the Renaissance the modern meaning of an unnatural creature, while it retained the idea of its Latin root, *monere* (to warn), thus suggesting a portent or menace. Caliban is, in the sense of the word by which he is constantly known, a living threat.

The fact that Prospero does not kill Caliban or Ariel is partly because they are entirely under his power and therefore offer no immediate danger to him. Being his slaves, by definition and despite the paternalistic sentimentalism with which literature has endued slave history, they are his enemies. Caliban is allowed to live because he is fearful of his master and, more, because he is useful to him. Prospero hates Caliban for apparently good reason. Ariel is a more ambiguous case, but his absolute subservience to and fear of Prospero are never in doubt.

Hatred is regarded as virtually synonymous with anger. But, while all anger is not informed with hatred, all hatred is informed with anger. Indeed, Ralph Berry opines that anger 'has long been banished

from the Deadly Sins. The anger of Prospero hints at a moral underpinning to his emotions. Who can admit to unrighteous anger? Since
no one is angry without cause, Prospero is making the case for himself
in the most vehement way. He is tapping one of the mysterious themes
of our time, the legitimization of anger.'[13]

II

Caliban has learned from his enslavement. His hatred of Prospero, visceral and direct though it is, is represented as a learned emotion. It is
viewed by the magician and his daughter as a perversion of normal
human emotional impulses, which have been forced into the forms
and structures of hatred by an irredeemable nature. It is directed out-
wardly towards his master as an almost liberating or empowering
form of self-expression. Though his body is entirely under the control –
even the remote control – of Prospero, his mind remains free to hate the
master who controls that body. Caliban's sole power under the circumstances of his slave condition is his power to hate and his desire to kill
his master. As a result, although he is Prospero's slave physically, he is
never his emotional slave. Successful enslavement of another human
being, Patterson argues, is the fusion of the slave's identity with that of
his master; the violent loss of any social sense of belonging to a community or society outside that which lies under the control and aegis of
his master.[14] Slavery itself, Patterson suggests, is a relationship of
power and domination originating in and sustained by violence. The
slave's 'social death' is a substitution for a commuted physical death
from war, execution, starvation or exposure. A major aspect of this
social death is 'natal alienation' from ancestors, relatives, and community in general.[15] Caliban's anger keeps alive in him the desire to resist,
to fight, and to kill Prospero: he refuses to accept his social death by
insisting that Prospero has stolen his birthright and by attempting to
recover it. His memory keeps alive an instinct for familial identity. The
passion that prompts him to clamour for his 'justice' gives him the
desire for freedom that has generated the numerous identifications of
Caliban with oppressed peoples of the world.[16]

Ariel has submitted unequivocally to Prospero's rule and in this
sense is the more successful slave, willing even to participate in the torture of his fellow slave in obedience to his master. Ariel has no known
natal origin, and he refers to no ancestors or relatives to whom he feels
tied. In his yearning for freedom he reveals no desire for community.

While it may reasonably be argued that Ariel is defined by the text as a spirit, not as a human being, it must also be recognized that Ariel has a strange but surely real corporeal identity, which makes judging him in anthropomorphic terms inevitable. His corporeality is what enabled Sycorax, after all, to impose a horrific physical imprisonment upon him and what enabled Prospero to free him and earn his lengthy servitude. His social death and natal alienation are complete. Patterson notes that one of the most subtle and brutal features of slavery is the master's response to the slave's yearning for dignity, itself part of his wider yearning for disalienation and relief from the master's all-embracing power. In almost every case the master exploits this very yearning for his own benefit. Prospero's apparently affectionate or benign treatment of Ariel is among the means he uses to motivate his sprite-slave to virtuoso levels of performance.

III

Earl Miner's description of the antithesis represented by Caliban-Ariel is typical of much writing on the play: 'There are other creatures on the island, one of them the good spirit Ariel, who is so far a creature of the element of air that he has no human feelings, and another is Caliban, who is so much a creature of the earth that his passions are monstrous.'[17] Reading these two characters as non-human is an established practice, which tends to remove from the reader the responsibility of moral judgment and from the characters the responsibility of and connection to motive. There are few feelings more intense than the desire for freedom, a feeling that motivates Ariel almost entirely through his narrow emotional range. Unlike Caliban, however, he has been educated to understand his freedom only in terms of a gift. Rebellion is not part of his thinking. The distinction is crucial; for the freedom that Ariel imagines has become compromised by being merely the other side of slavery. Ariel's freedom in imagination and in fact at the end of the play ties him forever to the magician who gives it to him. Patterson makes the point that manumission as an intrinsic part of the process of slavery reinforced the master-slave relationship. Caliban's freedom is the purer for having, even in the end, been associated in his mind with anger and hatred and resistance. Caliban's submission to Prospero is always costly to himself, yet he always attempts not to submit. While Ariel's submission is complete in both body and mind, Caliban submits only physically to his tormentor. Ariel has learned to believe that he possesses an essential self and that this self is defined by servitude and enslavement. While Ariel is manifestly discontented, he has learned how to flatter his master, as Caliban has not. Prospero has promised him freedom on condition that he behave well and remain faithful, and this promise supplies Ariel with the motive to please his master.

IV

The histories of Caliban and Ariel, while somewhat vague and partially drawn, supply some indications of their relation to their slave status. The word 'slave' is used eight times in *The Tempest*. Seven occur in act 1, scene 2, and all but one refer to Caliban abusively. The first use of the word in the play, however, is a reference to Ariel by Prospero, who says,

> This blue-eyed hag was hither brought with child,
> And here was left by th'sailors. Thou, my slave,
> As thou report'st thyself, was then her servant.   (1, 2, 269–71)

While Ariel has called Prospero 'master,' in our hearing he has not referred to himself as a slave, although he certainly doesn't demur when so described by Prospero. Most curious about Prospero's words, however, is the phrase, 'As thou report'st thyself.' Why does Prospero hang the responsibility for Ariel's identity on Ariel himself? By asserting that Ariel reported himself a slave in some pre-play moments, Prospero is tacitly acknowledging the moral ambiguity of his position as one who has enslaved another. For, according to Prospero, as Caliban has brought his enslavement upon himself, Ariel's slavehood has been purchased by his release from a horrible bondage. By making Ariel the namer of his own state, Prospero seems to be trying to absolve himself from a dilemma. Ariel is, after all, an entirely obedient, occasionally craven servant, who seems to receive no wages for his Herculean labours and who longs for the day when Prospero will release him. Yet at no time during the play does he report himself Prospero's slave, even though there is no ambiguity about his status; indeed, he even seems to take occasional pride in his accomplishments in his service. In the meantime it is Prospero's pleasure to remind Ariel of his debt to himself for releasing him from the cloven pine in which he had been imprisoned by Sycorax. Because Ariel has lost or suppressed his anger and hatred, he has also been robbed of the capacity for rebellion against his master/owner. It is he who, in a sense, has defined himself as a slave by reporting his previous servitude in relation to Sycorax and has thus taken upon himself one of Shakespeare's most degrading epithets. He has been shown his place and, if Prospero is to be believed in this regard, has virtually embraced it. For it is clearly by loyal and unquestioning slavery to the will and whim of his master that Ariel will recover his freedom. Caliban's integrity remains intact at the end, while Ariel's is compromised by unwilled compliance and cooperation with his tyrant. Ironically, the outcome of enslavement is the same for both. Having served the purposes of the magician/slave-owner, both receive manumission.

The word 'slave,' though sometimes capable of a neutral usage in Shakespeare, is overwhelmingly a term of abuse and is quite comfortably coupled with other abusive terms of which I here supply a random sampling: 'drunken' (*Comedy of Errors*), 'mindless' (*Winter's Tale*), 'cold-blooded' (*King John*), 'rascally' (*2 Henry IV*), 'devilish' (*Richard III*), 'unhallowed' (*Titus Andronicus*). In *The Tempest*, the adjectives that precede 'slave' and are applied to Caliban conform to the pattern: they are 'poisonous' (1, 2, 319), 'lying' (1, 2, 344), and 'Abhorred' (1, 2, 350). This fact is in itself of interest. Having created an economic situation in which dependence on slavery forms a substantial part and having then perpetuated the situation by the absolute suppression of the enslaved individual or group in physical, emotional, and psychological terms, slave-owners like Prospero turn the victims of their suppression into the *culpable* villains of their invectives. Thus, in the cultural lexis of the English world from which Shakespeare's slave-owners derive, the term 'slave' is used of a person who is cowardly enough to prefer a life of slavery to an honourable death (thus, incidentally, anticipating and confirming Hegel's thesis on the origins of society); when, in Shakespeare, the word does not refer to a condition of virtual imprisonment and servitude, it is a term of abuse.

What occurs, then, is a situation that requires and comes to rely upon the subservience of this underclass of human beings who are defined as lacking the true accoutrements of humanity. Simultaneously, slaves are then constructed as the appropriate victims of abuse because they have been compelled, under pain of death, to accept the position of slavery that the economic system into which they have been absorbed requires of them and upon which, often enough, that economy has come to rely.

V

Caliban's resistance to slavery takes the form of a constant rage against the authority that oppresses him. The history of his enslavement has a pragmatic as well as a moral slant, and its mystery exists largely because of the complicating problem of acquired language. Caliban has no choice but to accept Prospero and Miranda's constructions of events, because they control the all-powerful tool of interpretation. Because they taught him language they are the arbiters of the translation of events into history. Caliban simply lacks the words to interpret what happened in any other way. Caliban's gleeful acknowledgment that he almost raped Miranda brings him into a vicious agreement with Prospero about their common history on the island:

> O ho, O ho! Would't had been done!
> Thou didst prevent me – I had peopled else
> This isle with Calibans.   (1, 2, 351–3)

This admission, couched in the language of the oppressor culture, nevertheless has the side effect of contributing to the increasingly voluble defence of slavery, which, Margo Hendricks and Patricia Parker note, became ever more racialized.[18] Caliban's uncertain – and certainly unEuropean origins – fuel that defence. Paul Brown notes that 'Prospero's narrative demands of its subjects that they should accede to *his* version of the past,' even though that narrative 'reveals internal contradictions which strain its ostensible project and ... produces the possibility of sites of resistance in the other precisely at the moment when it seeks to impose its captivating power.'[19] One such 'internal contradiction' is produced by the apparent absence of a permissible challenge to the version of the truth of 'the right Duke of Milan.'

The history of the relationship among these three island inhabitants is perhaps less clear than it usually is made to seem. Caliban states that when Prospero and Miranda first came to the island they stroked him and taught him to name things. In return for this kind treatment, he loved them and taught them to understand the island.

> Cursed be I that I did so! All the charms
> Of Sycorax, toads, beetles, bats light on you!
> For I am all the subjects that you have,
> Which first was mine own king, and here you sty me

In this hard rock, whiles you do keep from me
The rest o'th'island.   (1, 2, 341–6)

The apparent straightforwardness of this account is challenged by
Prospero's angry response – 'Thou most lying slave' (1, 2, 345) – but it
is not precisely clear which aspect or part of Caliban's version is being
described as a lie. A clue to Prospero's motive, however, may reside in
the remainder of his speech, which invokes the charged image of the
violation of a daughter:

> Thou most lying slave,
> Whom stripes may move, not kindness, I have used thee –
> Filth as thou art – with humane care, and lodged thee
> In mine own cell, till thou didst seek to violate
> The honour of my child.   (1, 2, 346–50)

The options available for the punishment of this alleged virgin-violator
are multifarious and copiously precedented. Prospero could have
killed Caliban, or sexually mutilated him, or imprisoned him in a cloven pine. Instead, however, Prospero decided to make practical use of
him: simply, he enslaved him and, as we vividly see here and in his
next speech, a few lines below, taunts him with his slave status:
'Abhorred slave, / Which any print of goodness will not take' (1, 2,
353–4). Earlier, he has outlined Caliban's role:

> He does make our fire,
> Fetch in our wood, and serves in offices
> That profit us.   (1, 2, 313–15)

Who fetched fuel, hewed wood, or drew water before the enslavement
of Caliban is not explained. Now that Caliban has disqualified himself
as a friend and proved his fitness only for slavery, however, Prospero
has given himself both the moral and the practical edge. Not only must
Caliban now work off his debt to Prospero's society, but he must do so
willingly or suffer serious penalties. He must strive, in truth, to be like
Ariel:

> Shrug'st thou, malice?
> If thou neglect'st, or dost unwillingly
> What I command, I'll rack thee with old cramps,

Fill all thy bones with aches, make thee roar,
That beasts shall tremble at thy din.   (1, 2, 369–73)

It is this 'malice,' variously translatable as one motivated by rage,
rebelliousness, hatred, or resistance, that marks Prospero's failure to
transform Caliban into a docile slave. But perhaps the most mystifying
element of the speech is Prospero's apparent desire to transform Caliban into a slave who performs his master's tasks willingly. The example of Ariel indicates that the mere appearance of willingness would
satisfy the master; the question that remains is which desire in Prospero would be satisfied by this appearance of willing servitude. The
relationship of Prospero to Ariel indicates that his desire to understand
himself as a kind master would be fulfilled by having a compliant and
grateful slave. While Caliban is not precisely a 'wild man,' he possesses, for Prospero, some of the dangers that the wild man threatens
to civilization: these dangers cease to seem threatening when they have
been transformed into gratitude and 'willingness.'

Caliban threatens Prospero's lineage by what Hayden White calls
'species corruption,' a form of miscegenation that has been constructed by dominant cultures as a degradation of God's plan and
explains, in part, the universal demonization of the slave's group of
origin: 'Since at the Creation God fashioned the world and placed in it
the various species, each perfect of its kind, the ideal natural order
would therefore be characterized by a perfect species purity. Natural
disorder, by contrast, has its extreme form in species corruption, the
mixing of kinds ... the joining together of what God in his wisdom
had, at the beginning, decreed should remain asunder. The mixing of
the kinds is, therefore, much worse than any struggle, even to the
death, between or among them.'[20] Because he has been identified as a
savage, Caliban is historically a valid subject of colonization. Normally, colonization was initiated because the sheer numbers of native
inhabitants represented a threat to the adventuring colonizers as well
as, for the more far-sighted, an illimitable source of cheap labour.[21]
The 'primitivity' of the native peoples – one important component of
which was their technological and military inferiority – made them
subjugable. Enslavement of such peoples was merely an extension of
the colonialist project when conditions indicated their unwillingness
to comply with the subordination being forced upon them by invaders. This process of moving from a state of dependence and subordi-

nation to one of absolute slavery describes precisely the history of Caliban's relations with Prospero. Caliban's enslavement through what the invaders – Prospero and Miranda – in their official history call kindness has apparently failed, as such enslavements must, whereas suppression has succeeded at least in controlling his access to the means of rebellion. Crucially, it has not succeeded in controlling his urge to rebel. Ariel, whose magical powers have been recognized as usable by Prospero, oddly enough seems never to have been subjected to domestication in the way that Caliban was before his sexual crime.

Caliban's curse affirms more than anything else that he is bowed but undefeated:

You taught me language, and my profit on't
Is I know how to curse. The red plague rid you
For learning me your language.   (1, 2, 365–7)

The words are spat at Prospero. Cursing is Caliban's emotional salvation; it seems to contain and intensify the wrath by which he is driven. Through cursing, Caliban is able to express his resistance to Prospero – he has no other means. The second sentence, however, carries with it the heavy freight of bondage. Caliban curses Prospero for teaching him *his* language. In learning Prospero's language, Caliban has become enslaved to Prospero. In being compelled to communicate with Prospero and Miranda in their language, Caliban tacitly acknowledges his dependence on them. He recognizes a greater previous freedom in not having known their language. This is part of the lot of the slave: being forced to absorb the language and, concomitantly, the values and cultural norms of the master. Choice has been removed. Caliban recognizes that they have outsmarted him by using his own compliance in learning the language of his masters.

We do not know what language Caliban spoke before the advent of Prospero and Miranda, but it seems possible, if not likely, that there was a language for he was able to communicate with his mother, who was able to communicate with Ariel. As well, if communication through sound is language; and if the capacity to learn a language is evidence of the prior knowledge of language, then Caliban *had* language before the arrival of the Europeans on his island. And yet, to Miranda, the noise that Caliban made was not language:

> I pitied thee,
> Took pains to make thee speak, taught thee each hour
> One thing or other. When thou didst not, savage,
> Know thine own meaning, but wouldst gabble like
> A thing most brutish, I endowed thy purposes
> With words that made them known.   (1, 2, 355–60)

Any perception of the social arrogance of the position from which the speech emanates is a decidedly modern one, having to do with modern perceptions of colonialism and imperialism and the discourses that have sustained their political practice for centuries. More simply, European civilizations have historically justified the rape and plunder of non-European societies by the stated missions of Christianizing them and the heuristic project of providing them with some of the 'gifts' of more advanced civilization. It is interesting, however, that Caliban's response is a bitter agreement with the sense of what Miranda is saying and concomitantly a marker of the success of the discursive didacticism of Prospero and Miranda. Of course, it is only now, through the language he has been taught, that he can think of language at all, since he regards it not as a means of perception but as a means of communication. Was his 'gabble' language or mere noise? Was he capable of perception without language before the arrival of Prospero and Miranda? It does seem that the only language he now knows is *their* language. And he is utterly imprisoned within it.

The crucial absence of an article or a pronoun before Caliban's 'language' (362) is a powerful reminder of the extent to which he is trapped into understanding in terms defined by his owners, who possess him and possess his speech. Caliban does not accuse Prospero and Miranda of teaching him *their* language or *a* language, but language itself. Yet surely the text suggests that he knew language before they arrived; clearly, he possessed memory, by which he was able to distinguish between the sweet and the bitter parts of the island, 'the fresh springs, brine pits, barren place and fertile' (338). The sun was to him 'the bigger light,' the moon 'the less' (335). It is curious, though, that with his remarkable mastery of English, Caliban does not here use the words 'moon' and 'sun,' a lack attributable, possibly, to the dramatist's wish to represent his basic primitivity. Yet there is also something atavistic about these ways of naming sun and moon, as if they refer to a more primitive, older, and un-European way of speaking. Later in the play he refers to the sun in the curse, 'All the infections that the sun sucks up' (2, 2, 1). The enslavement of Caliban is reified by his enslavement to the language of his masters.

VI

The debasement of the slave takes a number of conventional but interesting forms. Prospero seems to have a stake in demonstrating Caliban's slave-worthiness. He constantly adverts to the justice of Caliban's low social position on the island by reference to his unfitness for human company. Caliban's antecedents, for example, form part of the structure of invective by which the monster is devalued. He is, for example, 'Hag-seed' (1, 2, 364). And Prospero first greets him with a related aspersion – 'got by the devil himself / Upon thy wicked dam' (318–19). He belongs, like most slaves in history, to a defeated tribe, race, nation, or people whose defeat is a cruelly syllogistic index of its inferiority. Indeed, the world of *The Tempest* goes farther than many enslaving societies have done by insisting that Caliban belongs to a different species from his enslavers. This species distinction, which historically has been the means of describing mere racial difference, has been one of the most powerful weapons of the oppressive group's demonstration of its superiority. By virtue of visible racial difference, the dominant group has been able to explain oppression as earned and the inferiority of the enslaved or oppressed group as just, often by reference to a divine plan that visibly and historically has valorized difference in terms of superiority and inferiority.

The evidence of that inferiority suffuses the slave's entire existence. Often (but not always) physically or racially different from their masters, the slaves' difference is translated into a physical or racial inferiority by the master group, who, as masters, determine and construct values such as superior and inferior. The slave's normally presumed intellectual inferiority is a product of his having to learn and hence to acknowledge the discursive power of the slave-holder. The thingness of the slave, his innate or definitional capacity to be bought, sold, or traded, enforced in both the slave and the master class the conviction of the slave's inferiority. The absolutism of Prospero's rule supplies a literary example of a situation that, according to Hindess and Hirst, never exists in reality – pure chattel slavery: 'In Rome and elsewhere,' they assert, '*pure* chattel slavery never existed in fact, for the law recognised the elements of personality in the slave and corresponding limitations on his master's rights ... These meliorations of the slave's legal condition on the part of enlightened Roman jurists, or, later in the Anglo-Saxon Americas ... reveal ... the nature of the slave's legal status and the social position following from it.'[22] Caliban, however, as an isolated subject whose subjection is sustained by magic, is a fantasy slave: he has no legal rights or sanctioned expectations. He has been taught and has learned to accept his own inferiority to his masters. He never sees himself as other than a slave, one born to serve the race of Prospero. Thus, when he meets Stefano and Trinculo, he sees them not as liberators but as substitute masters who will treat him kindly:

> 'Ban, 'Ban, Ca–Caliban
> Has a new master: get a new man!   (2, 2, 184–5)

VII

Caliban's body, like the bodies of all slaves, is the site upon which his slave status is most vividly proved. It is the violence done to his body that is the source of Caliban's most bitter and excruciating rages. His physical enslavement is the root of his rebelliousness. It is not political freedom that he seeks, or precisely liberation from servitude, but simply freedom from pain. Prospero is Caliban's torturer. The cramps and stitches and pinches and bone-aches and stripes are a Jacobean equivalent of electrical shocks and straws-under-the-fingernails treatment of the prisoner that Caliban truly is. And the fear of madness that Prospero has instilled into Caliban is a kind of psychological torture with all too many horrible analogues in the modern world:

> His spirits hear me,
> And yet I needs must curse. But they'll not pinch,
> Fright me with urchin shows, pitch me i'th'mire,
> Nor lead me like a firebrand in the dark
> Out of my way, unless he bid 'em; but
> For every trifle are they set upon me,
> Sometime like apes that mow and chatter at me,
> And after bite me; then like hedgehogs, which
> Lie tumbling in my barefoot way, and mount
> Their pricks at my foot fall; sometime am I

All wound with adders, who with cloven tongues
Do hiss me into madness.   (2, 2, 3–14)

The anguish and fear of madness and the loathing contained in the speech are partially compensated for in the mind of that reader who is sympathetic to Caliban by the spontaneous, instinctual impulse to reject tyranny contained in the single phrase, 'And yet I needs must curse.' That Caliban's desire to resist is so deeply ingrained in him that the curses erupt almost spontaneously is the only cheering aspect of this dark misery that defines his life. We cannot simply extend historical imagination backwards, as perhaps Shakespeare's audiences did, and see in this cruelty a just punishment for attempted rape. Four centuries of theory and practice of penology and jurisprudence have taught us that such treatment is immoral and violent and unjust, and we cannot merely cancel it at will. Skura, reflecting on the political element in Prospero's rage against Caliban, points to the 'conjunction of psychological as well as political passion' motivating that rage. She notes that while a colonial politics informs the discourse by which Prospero rules, he still needs, at the moment he erupts into anger (as he has just bestowed Miranda on Ferdinand), 'to repress his desire for power and for revenge at home, as well as any sexual desire he feels towards Miranda. Both desires are easily projected onto the fishily phallic Caliban, a walking version of Prospero's own "thing" of darkness.'[23] Prospero's fear of Caliban and the rage by which it is expressed can be understood in part as this fear of his own illicit desire to which Skura alludes.

The complicating factor of this slave narrative is that Caliban is *not* the Spartacus of myth and history. Nor is he, to use a more familiar example, Uncle Tom. Indeed, his story is a challenging counterexample to that of Stowe's hero. Where the beloved Uncle Tom's whole personality is suffused with spiritual and physical beauty and Christian muscularity, Caliban is the slave it has been easy and usual to hate. He is angry, nasty, ugly, and ungrateful. He has turned away – if Miranda is to be believed – love and affectionate treatment and repaid it with opportunism and violence.

Caliban, for all his physical and political bondage to his master, remains, in the end, outside the category of what Patterson calls 'the ultimate slave.' His anger, destructive and violent though it be, sets him apart from the world that has attempted to contain him, as it has successfully contained his counterpart, Ariel. The ultimate slave,

Patterson contends, 'is best represented in the anomalous person of the eunuch.'[24] In Ariel, we find that ultimate slave whose spirituality is, in the harshly real terms of much of the play, a kind of synonym for this kind of sexual incapacity. Patterson refers to the position of utter subservience and remarkable power enjoyed by Byzantine slaves and those of ancient China, between whom and their masters there was a frequent inversion of the power relationship. Part of the reason for the power of the eunuchs and their closeness to their masters, he argues, concerned their 'genealogical isolation, in other words their incapacity to reproduce themselves.'[25] Eunuch slaves were subject to contempt in all societies but, partly because of their social unassimilability, occasionally they were able to garner power and influence with rulers simply *because* they were eunuchs.

We note Caliban's gleefully expressed wish for an island peopled with Calibans. The fantasy, represented and given voice as a vicious threat to Prospero and as an index of Caliban's desire for power, is also strongly expressive of Caliban's desire for community, for assimilation in a group or community other than the one in which he is enslaved. It is a desire given form in his sudden allegiance to Stephano and Trinculo. It is, additionally, a wild and wrathful expression of how little his spirit is tamed, how reluctant a slave he is, and how unsuccessfully he has been reduced to slavery: the fires of rebellion still burn in him. The eunuch – and his analogue, Ariel – being incapable of reproduction, cannot realistically contemplate being reassimilated into the community from which he has been wrenched. His social function has been radically curtailed; his isolation has been entrenched by the mutilation of his body. Ariel, who labours so arduously on behalf of Prospero and who willingly, even gratuitously, betrays Caliban, his fellow slave, has no hankering for community. He is remarkably like those isolated characters in Shakespeare whose lack of direct connection to a community seem to be the source of a melancholy yearning for freedom without community. He is also depressingly like the eunuchs described in Patterson's history, whose cruel social marginalization made it safe for their cynical owners to entrust them with unusual powers. Stephen Orgel describes Ariel's 'Where the bee sucks' (5, 1, 88) song as a 'proleptic celebration of freedom.'[26] It is, indeed, a version of freedom, but it is also an image of a solitary, non-communal existence.

Ariel's ethereality, together with the cooing affection his virtuosity occasionally elicits from Prospero, provides his readers and audiences with a notion of him that supports descriptions of him like that of Earl Miner (quoted above). Being of the air, not of the earth, he seems to be endued with bodilessness, spirituality, and immitigable delicacy. The magic he practises is exquisite. The physical pain and suffering he causes others are represented as largely earned, and in any case inflicted at the behest of his master. The agonies and sufferings felt by Stephano, Trinculo, and Caliban are neutralized by comedy and farce. The suffering that Prospero inflicts on the other survivors of the storm is cathartic and morally improving. But Ariel is a slave, a thing of use, and as such his will and desire have no currency except as a cruelly used incentive to perform. Prospero, the slavemaster, determines what Ariel will do. Ariel's task is to do the best he can; his artistry must be his only satisfaction, although Ariel, like Hegel's bondsman, seems to discover in his labour a form of self-expression and, in this narrow sense, of freedom. Sadly, however, there is only one critic or arbiter whose evaluation of Ariel's artistry matters: that is, of course, Prospero. Ariel himself is a magician, whose practice is strictly circumscribed by the pleasure he gives to the man who owns him and the increased capacity for freedom that that pleasure may – or may not – supply. He is a reluctant, forced prostitute of his great gifts.

The idea of the violation of Miranda is harsh and ugly, and Caliban's part in such action is wicked and horrible. But rape and physical violation are, in different ways, political acts. They are almost always an indirect means of hurting someone other than the actual victim. The rape of Miranda was also, surely, a direct attack on the tyranny of her father. Countless acts of rape through history have very clearly been deliberate attacks on the men related to the women victims of those rapes. Prospero's response to the attempted rape of his daughter, a reponse that comprehended fear, hatred, and increased repression and violence against the would-be perpetrator, indicates the extent to which Prospero would have felt himself damaged and hurt by it. And the rage of Caliban against Prospero could have found no more effective expression than in the rape of his enslaver's daughter. The violent enslavement of Caliban is one effect of the would-be rape. But the enslavement of Ariel, perhaps even more encompassing, possesses no such justification. It is an enslavement that is brought about by something simpler: the fact that slavery was possible and precedented. It is not revenge, after all, that motivates Prospero to enslave, use, and control Ariel; it is a perceived need for a slave. Prospero's need for a socially destroyed, enslaved creature to carry out his program of punishment and public forgiveness outweighs the necessary obliteration of that creature's own social or individual freedom only because he has the power to make it happen.

CHAPTER FOUR

The Scapegoat Mechanism:
Shylock and Caliban

I

Of *The Merchant of Venice* and *Othello,* Michael Bristol remarks: 'The difficult pleasure of reading the great stories contained in these plays comes from the way they express the collective bad conscience of our civilization.'[1] An honest and accurate reading of *Merchant* must acknowledge in Portia's triumph over Shylock the affirmation of a community value that takes satisfaction in the humiliation and exclusion of the Jew. Similarly, *Othello* affirms a community value that takes comfort from the exclusion and destruction of the black alien. Despite the prevalence of liberal readings of the play, Bristol asserts that an honest reading or production of *Othello* would be just as intolerable as one of *Merchant,* in view of its dependence on a background of racial hatred and violence. We tend, perhaps guiltily, to dismiss racist readings of the play as misguided or so ideologically transparent as to be facile. But a racist agenda is present in the narrative: it is that of an African whose Africanness, when tried to its limits, expresses itself in a savage act of violence, whose source is in the non-European origins of the perpetrator as they become embroiled in the European culture to which he has been grafted. Othello's presence in life and in death compromises the community's self-regard, thus making his expulsion a social necessity. The racial rage focused on Othello, however, is even more blatant and less ambiguous than that directed at Caliban. Though Caliban is no African, he most certainly is a physical specimen who is regarded as monstrously different from the European invaders of his island. Being of a unique race, Caliban is uniquely positioned to put to the proof the European practice of marginalizing its outsiders through whom European culture reifies and revalidates the superiority of its own cultural values.

In primitive and ancient practice, the scapegoat typically comes from outside the community, often as a prisoner of war. His or her sacrifice and death, then, does no lasting damage to social ties within the community because he is essentially external to it; indeed his sacrifice is a mechanism for strengthening those ties. Shylock and Caliban (and, of course, Othello), while positioned as external to the social centre, are nevertheless functioning members of the societies represented in the plays; their alien and marginal status is therefore ambiguous and uncertain. The ancient practice of sacrificing the scapegoat is not, René Girard has argued, the product of mere blind superstition; it displaces social malady and anxiety upon the scapegoat in order to symbolically drive these ills away from the group, essentially redirecting them onto the selected victim: 'This unique mechanism structures all cultural values even as it conceals itself behind them.'[2] The effect, however, of constructing a marginal but visible and present segment of the society as its scapegoat is different from, but indebted to, the traditional practice in which the scapegoat is sacrificed and killed. In the societies represented in *The Merchant of Venice* and *The Tempest*, the scapegoat, a hated Jew on the one hand and a loathed slave on the other, is a useful means by which the oppressing culture is able to reassert its value structure. One effect of the scapegoat's being retained within and as a part of the community is the displacement of violent and potentially violent aggression within the dominant culture onto this scapegoat, this object, which, by its mythologized nature, is seen to deserve the aggression directed at it. Shylock and Caliban, both physically set apart from the mainstream, are understood, at least by the social insiders, to deserve the violence that is visited upon them. What those insiders do not easily acknowledge, however, is the concomitant fear that the scapegoats evoke in them. The revulsion that Shylock and Caliban inspire in their oppressors is an index of that fear. A portion of alienating mystery belongs to each – they come from strange or unknown places (a mystery of origins), and they fit poorly into the places where they are now found (a mystery of species). This poor fit makes them awkward and visible, unpredictable, and somewhat physically repellent. Both are evidently driven by destructive and murderous rages that generate widespread nervousness and anxiety in others. The fear that they engender produces an increasing need to suppress and contain them; this need, in turn, produces more anger and more fear. The only way to control them is to break them; they are represented as being ultimately unassimilable into the community. The failure to 'fit in,' paradoxically, serves the community by channelling much of its aggressive energy towards the stranger.

Scapegoats are, by definition, demonized participants in the dominant culture. They help to define that culture by their unambiguously foreign and marginal – and sometimes only notional – presence within it. James Shapiro alludes to this definitional function of the scapegoat in his treatment of the Jew in early modern English society. He writes: 'I ... also believe that there is something called Englishness and something called Jewishness, though their meanings too have changed under the pressure of competing historical narratives. Finally I believe that Englishness would not be the same without the existence of Jewishness, even as it would not be the same without the existence of of Irishness, Scottishness, Welshness, Frenchness, or Spanishness.'[3]

II

The slave-owning society of the American Old South and Germany under the Nazis are extreme examples of social formations whose ideological distortions became accepted as normal by a majority of the members of the dominant culture under the pressure of changing social realities. Both societies, in a time long after Shakespeare's, institutionalized through laws and practices the inferior position of the minority cultures that existed within their confines. Institutionalization is the crucial point. Shakespeare wrote about individuals who were markedly different in culture and in physical appearance, or in what is sometimes called race. The effects of the subsequent treatment of difference in the two more modern cultures of the South and Nazi Germany is a direct outgrowth of some of the attitudes and issues touched upon by Shakespeare in several plays, including, for the purposes of this chapter, *The Merchant of Venice* and *The Tempest*. Shakespeare wrote about the evident incapacity and reluctance of the majority cultures to accept and absorb alien persons and their customs. The 'philosophies' of the dominant groups of these two plays seem quite simple. The aliens must adapt to the culture that has been imposed on them or to which they have been permitted access (as Jessica successfully does), or they will remain peripheral to it and suffer the consequences of marginal status. Marginality can, of course, be benign – but that is not the case in these two examples.

My point in raising the examples of the slave-owning southern U.S.

culture and Nazi Germany is simply personal. I cannot read Shakespeare's plays in which slavery and anti-Semitism are issues as though they are merely sociological or historical examples of discrimination belonging to another time and place, academic protocols notwithstanding. It is a fact that Africans, in the seventeenth and eighteenth centuries in particular, were murdered, tortured, and enslaved in huge and staggering numbers – estimates of Africans killed by slavers during the two centuries range from 20 to 80 million. Jews were murdered by the Nazis and Nazi collaborators by the millions. These are unforgettable realities to me and intrude violently into my reading of the various brutalizations of Shylock and Caliban. Even ambiguous, or to many readers of Shakespeare innocent, dramatic moments, such as the account of Antonio's spitting on and kicking Shylock in the Rialto, fill me with rage, because I know that a real-life Antonio could not get away with habitually spitting on and kicking an actual Venetian; nor, probably, would he want to. The vicious, violent punishments to which Prospero subjects Caliban and the verbal abuse of this 'slave' have the same effect on me. I take it personally and I am enraged at the inhumanity of the tormentors of these two definitely *not* innocent characters. I also believe that it is the force of the history and reality of anti-Semitism and the enslavement of weak people by strong people that cause my admittedly emotional and critically distorted – some might say critically useless – reaction. The lens of atrocity through which we see the kind of national and species hatred of these two old plays has been – for me – irrecoverably darkened by history. Hence this digression into a history that Shakespeare adumbrated but whose scale he would not have foreseen.

The importation of slaves to the South necessitated the development of social forms (including adjustments to the legal system) by which life could carry on in apparently normal fashion while the society adjusted to the reality of increased numbers of slaves in its midst. In the German society of the 1930s belief in the evil consequences of the presence of Jews, coupled with the economic, social, historical, and political pressures that converged during the decade, increased the persecution of Jews to the point where persecution and discrimination became legitimate. In both societies normality required a definition that included legitimizing the use of violence by members of the citizenry against targeted minority groups within the social network. The institution of slavery was sustained by violence or the threat of violence; the presence of Jews in pre-war Germany became subject to the condition that violence against them become legitimized and normalized by its practice. Ironically enough, both cases of subjugation were contingent on a quasi-democratic principle. A majority of members of the prevailing cultural and political systems needed to agree – or at least not disagree – on the basic rule that a minority could be oppressed and violently persecuted with impunity by ordinary members of the citizenry.[4] The members of the minority, in short, had little or no recourse in law for acts of violence against them.

These are only two extreme examples of the elasticity of social normality. History furnishes thousands of other moments and periods when societies and communities have extended their ethical and ideological boundaries to make acceptable those practices that, in hindsight, seem criminal and pathological. It is nevertheless true that in neither Germany nor the Old South was the social norm of subjugation agreed to and acted on by all members of the oppressing system. There were, of course, Germans who hated anti-Semitism and Southerners who hated slavery. In both societies, however, the power-holders saw the need to maintain stable political regimes that could accommodate the alien and subordinate presences of black slaves in the one instance and Jews in the other. While slaves and Jews remained subject to the majority, the reality of their presence meant that they needed to be recognized as living and labouring social entities within the systems that oppressed and mistreated them. Thus, in each case a social pattern developed that acknowledged the humanity of the members of the inferior group and compelled their participation in legal and social doctrines of reciprocal obligation. Doctrines of oppression and demonization of oppressed groups were tacit and reluctant but nevertheless paradoxically acknowledged the humanity of the vilified groups. The slaves were subject to a form of paternalism that, in recognizing their free will and natural ability (in order to be able legitimately to punish them when they transgressed the law), acknowledged their humanity. The Jews of Nazi Germany were victims of an equally ambivalent kind of stereotyping: instead of being regarded as a merely inferior human species, they were also seen as the incarnation of a malevolent and destructive free will that threatened the dominant culture. Their humanity lay in their perceived economic and political superiority to the mass and their capacity to control and destroy it. Thus, their extermination – unlike the slaves' subordination – was represented as the only effective means by which the dominant culture could maintain or restore its dominance.

A significant difference between the cultural representations of Jews and slaves in the two cultures reveals the workings of oppression in conditions where it becomes enshrined in law. Economic and political self-interest produced in each case the simplified cultural representations by which the oppression was maintained. Without those simplifications, in a society that, for example, might choose to humanize its ethnic minorities by attempting to understand, respect, and explain cultural difference, oppression becomes more difficult. Thus, slaves were represented to be, and generally accepted as, intellectually and morally inferior to white Southerners. Eugene Genovese gives the example of a slave-holder who excoriated one of his slaves for concealing from his master his ability to read and write. The master's sense of betrayal upon this discovery reveals the dismay caused by the slave's challenge to his preconceptions.[5] Clearly, treating human beings as workhorses requires that the notion of their humanity be subsumed by the notion of their innate fitness for hard labour.

German Jews, and subsequently all Jews, were represented by National Socialist ideology in a contrasting but equally self-serving way. Given their social, political, and economic prominence in Europe, it was impossible to convincingly represent Jews as intellectual inferiors. Thus, the representation of Jews was marked by their intellectual and moral danger to the majority. They had to be oppressed, in other words, because they were too clever. They had been carefully and deliberately shut out from full economic participation in European cultural, political, and intellectual life; their separateness was then used as evidence of their dangerousness. Being denied full participation, they were damned for not having fully participated and for having kept themselves out of the mainstream. Their intellectual danger lay in their ostensibly innate desire for power (an obvious product of projection but represented as an international Jewish conspiracy to dominate the world and oppress Gentiles) and the moral danger implicit in their lack of ties to the European, Christian communities from which they had historically been deliberately excluded. Lucy Dawidowicz has described the two irreconcilable constructions of the Jew in Nazi Germany, inherited from medieval anti-Semitic literature: 'One was the image of the Jew as vermin, to be rubbed out by the heel of the boot, to be exterminated. The other was the image of the Jew as the mythic omnipotent super-adversary, against whom war on the greatest scale had to be conducted. The Jew was, on the one hand a germ, a bacillus, to be killed without conscience. On the other, he was, in the phrase Hitler repeatedly used ... the "mortal enemy" (*Todfiend*) to be killed in self-defence."[6]

Each example is marked by an almost irreconcilable ambivalence, which exposes a social and psychological need in the dominant or majority culture. The convenience to each society of being able to represent the subordinated minority group as monstrous, inhuman, inferior, and thus morally deserving of subordinate status gave way to an equally urgent social and political necessity – the necessity of being subject to the law. In the case of slaves, this necessity was met, as Genovese has pointed out, by officially acknowledging their possession of free will and thus their responsibility to the laws of the land. Similarly, the Jews of Nazi Germany – and, indeed, of much of Europe for many hundreds of years – were officially endued with humanity as a partial means of making them subject to the law. This contradiction, which is able to contain the scapegoat both as an inhuman monster and as a sentient, moral human capable of rational crime, is the essential component of a culture whose viability depends upon the presence of the alien within its midst.

Shakespearean drama is usually contingent upon the odd or the unusual or the politically unacceptable threatening the predominance of the ordinary, the usual, or the politically conventional (i.e., the dominant practice). From this tension much dramatic action and excitement follow. Shylock and Caliban are only the most extreme cases of difference threatening the prevailing political practice represented in the plays. In fact, difference always threatens and is always, therefore, in danger of suppression. Shakespeare has his slaves and his German Jews (Shylock has, at least, a Frankfurt connection [3, 1, 84]) – and they, too, break the illusorily smooth surface of the normal, which his protagonists seem to yearn to recover or restore. His most visible slave is Caliban, the conditions of whose existence, as was argued in chapter 3, precisely define a life of enslavement. The play's action is predicated on a tussle between a nostalgic longing for a peaceable and unruffled existence and the reality of its impossibility. But the Jew and the slave are contingent. Onto them is displaced a host of social and personal anxieties. Thus, they have almost no inherent existence or identity but are, rather, the product of self-doubt and anxiety inevitably produced by the social formation. In both Shylock and Caliban we have an embodiment of the unacknowledged fears of the dominant culture, and hence the desire to extirpate them determines attitudes towards them. At the same time, they are necessary parts of those societies.

They are hated, in other words, but they are also needed. For the forces shaping culture require validation through the representation of what they are not. Thus, the desire to exterminate is not merely destructive; it is unconsciously self-destructive.

Every social and cultural formation requires its villains. They are hated, in part, because they are needed. The hatred of difference derives from a deep fear of the presence of difference within the threatened self of the one who hates. The imperfections and eccentricities that surround representations of the self are conveniently displaced upon the outsider. The qualities for which Shylock and Caliban are feared and hated are manifested, thinly spread, throughout the cultures from which they are deliberately shut out, so as to enable their detractors to discover these qualities in undiluted form, distilled into one single deformity. The physical differences of Shylock and Caliban from the mainstream must not be underestimated; for those distinctions, in considerable measure, make them both harmless and dangerous. On the one hand, the perception of ugliness and difference in these two characters is intimidating, because it alludes to the possibility and occasional reality of ugliness and deformity in the oppressing subject. On the other, it makes them harmless by marking them publicly and placing them beyond disguise. Knowing them and knowing where they are constitute half the battle of utterly suppressing and controlling them.[7]

III

While Elizabethan England harboured few Jews and few slaves, Jews and slaves nevertheless formed a real, if marginal, part of the social landscape. Lucien Wolf calculated the number of London Jews in the 1590s to have been slightly under one hundred and although their lives were necessarily rather covert and secretive, their presence was more generally known than they would have liked. James Shapiro points out that the records from the 1590s indicate that during that period Jews continued to visit and live in England; that the Portuguese Marrano circle in London alone during this decade numbered at least eighty or ninety.[8] A kind of tacit agreement seems to have been in effect to allow them to live in London as long as their presence remained publicly or officially unacknowledged.[9] There were legally owned African slaves as well in the England of the period; they were few in number but nevertheless were present and known to be so.

Black slaves had been kept in Britain, often as mere curiosities to be gazed and wondered at; as early as 1508 the captive 'ladye with the mekle lippis' was described by William Dunbar in 'Ane Black Moir.'[10] England's first involvement in actual slave trading, according to Kim F. Hall, occurred in the 1550s.[11] Evidence of slave-owning among Englishmen remains in those portraits of the period that include in their background representations of wealth and privilege the shadowy depictions of black slaves and servants; they are encoded into the paintings largely as further evidence of the wealth of the paintings' aristocratic subjects. Like the objects in the *vanitas* paintings of the period from which the subject seems to have been evicted, the black slave or servant in these family portraits is equally an object used to augment the impression of the prestige and wealth of the subject, '[an] additional earthly thing to be coveted, purchased – often at great price – and displayed as ornament.'[12] The Africans who lived in Britain in the age of Elizabeth caused the queen sufficient anxiety to license sea captain Caspar van Senden to transport blacks out of England, following a royal proclamation on the subject. They had been imported, Virginia Vaughan suggests, 'as part of the booty brought home from Spanish ships by Drake, Essex and other privateers. These Africans were almost certainly slaves, perhaps en route to Portuguese and Spanish colonies in the New World before they were seized by the British. In England they probably continued as slaves or very long-term servants.'[13]

In *The Merchant of Venice* Shakespeare is able to imagine the life of a society in which the Jewish scapegoat fashions – in a negative sense – the majority culture's perception of itself. Similarly, in *The Tempest*, he is able to imagine a world in which the slave presence validates the culture of the power-holder. Now it is true that in the whole society of 'Venice' there are only three Jews, while on Prospero's island, in the years before the tempest and during Prospero's occupation, there are only four characters, of whom two – that is, half – are slaves. In each of these plays, Shakespeare represents a profound social need of the dominant culture for 'inferior' human subjects to complete the circle of humanity. The physical otherness of those subjects in these two plays makes the search for social identity that much easier. In each play it is the presence of socially sanctioned violence against the offending 'outsider' that encapsulates the contradiction most completely and vividly.

No production of *The Merchant of Venice* that I have ever seen or heard of does not stress Shylock's physical difference and the oddness of his appearance even if, as is often the case, that difference is concentrated in his clothing – such as characteristic gaberdine (a feature commented on by Shylock himself), head covering, or even sidelocks – rather than his racial characteristics, such as his large 'Jewish' nose and red hair. This aspect of Shylock's character is as fundamental to the play as Caliban's physical difference is fundamental to *The Tempest*: it reflects a deep-seated and ancient English notion about the essential physical difference of Jews from Christians deriving, Shapiro argues, from a universal awareness of and anxious fascination with Jewish circumcision practices. The relative ease with which Shylock's daughter, Jessica, is able to cross the religious boundaries of the play reminds us of an additional and crucial difference between Shylock and the Venetians: his and all Jewish males' difference is inscribed on their bodies by circumcision, whereas Jewish women have no such physical mark differentiating them from Christian women. The Jewish man, thus stigmatized, is eternally divided from the Christian community.[14] The physical difference of these two characters from the majority or dominating culture is central to the expression of the contradiction and to the irreconcilable force that it represents to the power-holders themselves.

We are clearly in Hegelian territory here. The need of the Christian rulers of Venice and of Prospero on the island to express their sense of moral superiority to the objects of their vilification through the exercise of physical violence represents their dependence upon these 'others' in the way that Hegel claims the slave-holders at the beginning of history inevitably came to depend upon the slaves for evidence of their identities; thus, in an abstract and psychological sense only, the positions of dominance are reversed.[15]

How the dominance of the two dominant cultures is achieved is instructive. The island of *The Tempest* is occupied by Prospero and Miranda and ruled by Prospero through the use of what we probably recognize as physical force, symbolized and applied by Prospero's magical powers. Prospero and Miranda's initial 'kindness' to Caliban is entirely conditional upon Caliban's behaving in accordance with their notions of respect and gratitude. As soon as his behaviour displeases his tutors, he is punished. Thus, the dominance is enforced, first by the threat of physical punishment and then by its reality. The dominance of the Christian culture in Venice is similarly a virtually physical dominance, represented by the numerical, physical, and political superiority of the majority and, of course, the inherent displaced-ness of the Jews who have no homeland or geographical nation to which they belong. Colonial history and the history of slavery in the West differ from these two examples in a significant way: the colonizers were always a minority culture that imposed itself upon the native majority by physical violence. Slave cultures of the West imported helpless victims of raids and barter into cultures where the majority culture's dominance was already an established fact and was never under threat from the enslaved captives.

IV

In an early speech to Antonio, Shylock recalls Antonio's treatment of him 'in the Rialto' (1, 3, 101–32). The recollection includes his having been 'rated' and called names, and it intensifies with details of even worse abuse: he remembers having been spat upon and 'footed' or kicked like a dog. Antonio's response to this account of his treatment of Shylock is to confirm Shylock's memory of the verbal abuse and the spitting. The passage is very familiar; Shylock is responding to the request for a loan:

> You call me misbeliever, cut-throat dog,
> And spet upon my Jewish gabardine,
> And all for use of that which is mine own.
> Well then, it now appears you need my help:
> Go to then, you come to me, and you say,
> 'Shylock, we would have moneys,' you say so:
> You that did void your rheum upon my beard,
> And foot me as you spurn a stranger cur
> Over your threshold, moneys is your suit.
> What should I say to you? Should I not say
> 'Hath a dog money? Is it possible
> A cur can lend three thousand ducats?' or
> Shall I bend low, and in a bondman's key
> With bated breath and whisp'ring humbleness
> Say this:
> 'Fair sir, you spet on me on Wednesday last,
> You spurn'd me such a day, another time
> You call'd me dog: and for these courtesies
> I'll lend you thus much moneys'?   (1, 3, 106–24)

Antonio's reply confirms Shylock's version of their previous transactions:

> I am as like to call thee so again,
> To spet on thee again, to spurn thee too.   (125–6)

Let us make no mistake. Antonio agrees with Shylock – he *has* spat on
and spurned him. To 'foot,' 'spurn,' and have 'spet upon' are highly
charged symbolic acts of physical violence upon or against the body of
another. They express something other or larger than a desire to harm
or injure or even to subdue the subject. Simply, in this context they
express the recognition of the subject's subordinate status and seem
designed to confirm and reinforce it, rather than to determine it. Spitting and spurning (kicking) imply contempt, certainly, but they also
imply the lack of fear of reprisal. Shylock does not complain that
Antonio has struck him with his hands or fists; the form of Antonio's
violence is suggestive in itself. It is easy enough to imagine Antonio
spitting on Shylock – he would have faced him and spat upon him. But
how were the two men physically positioned when Antonio kicked
Shylock? It seems unlikely that Shylock would have been standing and
facing Antonio when he was kicked; this conjures up an image of being
kicked in the knee or groin, possibilities that seem unlikely. So, was
Shylock sitting on the ground like a beggar when he was 'footed' by
Antonio? These seem to me the only plausible ways in which one man
kicks another without any fear of reprisal. The kicking can be a simple
gesture of contempt, not necessarily a desire to injure. Its public nature
provides a way for the kicker to announce something about himself to
those around him. Did Antonio kick and spit upon Shylock when they
were alone on the street, or was it always a public act? Of course, there
is no answer to the question, but it raises the issue of Antonio's deeper
motives for his treatment of his enemy.

   It is not hard, therefore, to understand why Shylock hates Antonio.
The violence of Antonio's hatred, reified by physical acts of aggression
performed upon Shylock's person, act, almost paradoxically, to estab-
lish a relationship of physical intimacy between the two men. Shylock's speech constructs an Antonio who needs to express his feelings
for Shylock in a physically aggressive manner. This seems a reasonable
reading of the actions to which Shylock refers. Yet no one would call
Antonio a violent man (indeed, he used to be regarded as one of
Shakespeare's legion of 'Christ figures'). At the beginning of the play,

safe among his peers, he is sad and depressed, strangely pacific and accepting. His initial melancholy among his little group of friends and his instantaneous generosity to Bassanio leave us entirely unprepared for Shylock's characterization of him as a nasty, violent bully. Shylock's speech reveals an Antonio whom we have not seen, a man who seems unable to restrain himself from publicly assaulting another man with whom so far he has had no serious contact. Antonio seems to have been impelled by some dark forces in himself to attack a man whose simple presence evokes feelings of rage and violence in him. He himself, rather simplistically, understands this impulse to violence as moral disapproval. Furthermore, the form of the past tense that Shylock employs in his description of his treatment by Antonio makes it clear that these assaults and the abuse of Shylock by Antonio have been carried on for some time. They have occurred frequently and over a sufficiently long period of time to justify Shylock's phrase 'many a time and oft.'

It is interesting that Shylock's perception of his own relationship to Antonio is different from Antonio's perception of his relationship to Shylock. There is no mistaking the seething hatred of the Jew for the Christian. This goes far beyond his simple declaration that he 'hates him for that he is a Christian.' It is a hatred that begins and ends in violence. In contrast to Shylock, Antonio seems almost innocent; he is indifferent to and oblivious of the effect of his treatment on Shylock. He sends Bassanio to the moneylenders without any awareness of the need for caution:

> therefore go forth
> Try what my credit can in Venice do.   (1, 1, 179–80)

He wanders into Shylock's place of business in a mood of evidently casual and incautious ease. Yet this is the same man whom he has publicly kicked and berated. It is very much as though Antonio does not hear Shylock, does not listen to the modulations of hatred, rage, and sarcasm in the simmering 'Signior Antonio' speech. Shylock remembers Antonio's violence. It is this that determines his behaviour once he has Antonio upon the hip.

Antonio's brutality towards Shylock establishes a fundamental physicality in the relationship between the two men: as Antonio has seen fit to enact his aggression on the body of his enemy, Shylock, so Shylock follows this lead (and betters the instruction) when the tables are turned. However, initially Antonio seems curiously indifferent to Shylock and shows no hatred for him. Physical violence can produce what Haniff Kureishi describes as 'a reluctant intimacy.'[16] Shylock's response to the cruelty is expressed in his own desire to return the blows with interest. He reveals a desire to kill Antonio – to cut open his chest and cut out his heart. And he sharpens a knife for the exact purpose.

The craving for dissection, for opening up Antonio's breast and cutting out his heart is a curious example of violent desire. Michael Neill has written about the ways in which the stage borrowed elements of the design and language of the science of anatomy.[17] Shylock's pleasure in the details of the operation seems, not coincidentally, to develop out of an awareness of living and dead bodies. Initially, he says in feigned innocence,

> Let the forfeit
> Be nominated for an equal pound
> Of your fair flesh, to be cut off and taken
> In what part of your body pleaseth me.   (1, 3, 144–7)

When his time comes, however, Shylock is clear. He seems intent on performing a dissection on Antonio's living body, refusing him even the courtesies of a surgeon, 'To stop his wounds, lest he do bleed to death' (4, 1, 254), as Portia urges, although, of course Shylock's intention to kill Antonio is perfectly obvious. The clinical details surrounding the no longer abstract pound of flesh, including the knife for cutting it out and the scales for weighing it – always foregrounded in production – turn the imagined murder of Antonio into a form of deliberate, specific, and deadly surgery. The imagination of the reader/spectator is compelled into alignment with that of Shylock. There seems to be no way out of this enforced and reluctant sympathy between the villain's imagination and that of his audience. The knife and the scales are silent but eloquent props and compel us to think of their functionality and the uses to which Shylock intends to put them. The act of imagining Shylock plunging the knife into Antonio's breast and then cutting the heart out of that breast is made irresistible by the presence of the props. And the pleasure Shylock takes in anticipation of the act is part of the pornography of the scene, which produces a contest within our minds between fascination and revulsion, a contest that fascination wins. Part of that fascination resides in the way that the relationship of antipathy between the two men will find some kind of fulfilment in the physical closeness of a murderous embrace that the act of excision will demand.

This moment, seconds before the denouement, is the real climax of the drama. The undoing of Shylock has the effect of a let-down, a deflation of the momentum that has been building as Shylock reaches for his knife. This moment and its aftermath are charged with a special kind of symbolism. Into the image of Shylock, poised and ready to plunge his knife into Antonio's breast, is concentrated the nexus of human fears of the scapegoat. This is what separation from the mainstream, what othering, is truly about: the distillation of social and psychological fear into the available person or group whose existence and whose living *presence* confirms the possibility of the individual subject's being separate from his worst and most feared primal self. The Jew, a convenient symbol of Western history, carried down the ages as an emblem of another self, a human who is like and unlike the world that repudiates him, is as dangerous as our fears and, as his undoing shows, simultaneously as vulnerable as our weakest selves.

Denying Shylock the fulfilment of his deepest desires upon grounds manufactured by Portia, while it advances the play, almost visibly diminishes the force, character, existence, and identity of Shylock. In Harriett Hawkins's words, in the context of another play, 'At the very same time that it shelters the characters from the ultimate consequences of their own decisions and desires, it denies them the dramatic magnificence which comes only from facing such consequences. And it deprives the audience itself of an ultimate dramatic confrontation with the terrible facts of life, with the crushing dilemmas, the human vice, the human pathology which all lurk in the wings.'[18] Yet such an action would rob the Shylock symbol of its power to return social forms to the representation of orderly reality or social normality upon which the play's politics insists and upon which the protocols of comedy within which the play is operating depend. Thus, while the murder of Antonio would have brought some psychological resolution, it is necessarily prevented in favour of a more urgent interest: that is, the restatement, in the discourse of the play's own narrative, of a truism about the social and personal subject's need to distinguish between good and evil. No resolution is offered concerning the essential inequality of the two antagonists.

Thus, two forms of violence, deriving their energy from opposing notions of justice, come into contention in the play. Antonio has kicked

Shylock, frequently, in public. Shylock then stands poised for revenge, thirsting for the opportunity to stab Antonio in the bosom and cut out his heart with a knife specially sharpened for the task; his motives for his violent rage against Antonio are as mysterious, multifarious, and complex as those of Iago. And where is the law in all this? As it turns out, the law is all for Antonio. Shylock, the stranger, stands condemned for the attempted murder of a *citizen* of the state. He is explicitly 'an alien' (4, 1, 345), as Portia reminds him, and hence is not entitled to the kind of legal protection that has given Antonio the impunity with which in his glory days he was able to persecute Shylock. Antonio's salvation by the law is one more of the social and political realities designed to reaffirm the rectitude of the conservative normality that promises order. It is surely interesting that while Antonio is protected from Shylock's violence by the law, Shylock seems to have had no legal protection from Antonio's freely acknowledged assaults. This anomaly stresses one of the key differences in status of the two men as subjects of the state. When it comes to money, the thing that sustains and fortifies the state, however, then the law stands in equal relation to each man. Shylock wants the law to defend his commercial agreement with Antonio, and, curiously enough, Antonio acknowledges his right to that protection. Thus, Shylock has some rights in Venice that are predicated upon one thing – the fact that he is rich. As a wealthy man, Shylock has a significant role in the Venetian political process. He helps to keep it moving and serves the acquisitive force by which the economy is sustained. He is correct in his perception that to deny him the law in regard to the use of his money is to undermine the entire economic structure of Venice – a point noted by the duke himself. Shylock may as well be talking for all Venetian gentry when he complains,

> You take my house, when you do take the prop
> That doth sustain my house: you take my life
> When you do take the means whereby I live.   (4, 1, 371–3)

V

Here we have a crucial point of distinction between Shylock, the man of business of Venice, and Caliban, the illiterate, native slave of an invaded island. Caliban, like most slaves, has nothing to link him to the apparatus of authority except his expendable labour. He stands outside the system. Caliban has nothing, while both Prospero and Shylock have wealth and power. Shylock's wealth links him directly to the machine that drives the state: for him, as a Jew, that link is tenuous and entirely contingent on his possession of wealth, which, in turn, determines his function within the system.

Let us take account of Caliban's poverty: it obtains in a world where others have more. Caliban has lived with Miranda and Prospero, who have carried some of the accoutrements of Western civilization with them into exile. Frank Kermode addresses this matter: 'He might even be costumed as a conventional salvage man. Malone says that Caliban's dress, "which doubtless was originally prescribed by the poet himself and has been continued, I believe, since his time, is a large bear skin, or the skin of some other animal; and he is usually represented with long shaggy hair" [*Variorum*, XV. 13].'[19] Many productions of the play that I have seen have attempted quite clearly to imply that Caliban is naked, as a way, presumably, of stressing his closeness to nature. Where Prospero has a 'cell,' Caliban seems to sleep where he lies down or in a 'sty ... In this hard rock' (1, 2, 345–6). Wherever he does sleep, he seems to live nowhere that is safe from Prospero's omniscience and, even as he attempts to sleep, is subject to invasion and punishment from Prospero's messengers.

Caliban occupies the roles open to slaves in their relation to their masters. By Miranda's account, he once was the epitome of the 'good' slave: obedient, cooperative, educable – all under the tender care of a master who has valued him. We do not know how Caliban served Prospero and Miranda at that time except that he introduced them, trustingly, to the secrets of his island. The trust was broken, of course, when Caliban tried to rape or seduce Miranda.[20] Secondly, for most of the play Caliban is the grudging, unloving, untrusted, and untrustworthy slave. He hates his master, and his master hates and mistrusts him and uses his powers to control him. This he does by instilling in the primitive slave a continuous fear of violent punishment and possibly death. His master has proved his ability to discipline him even when Caliban thinks he is safe. He can reach and hurt him while he is sleeping or far away. Caliban's punishment for being Prospero's slave is to be denied everything. He has no possessions, no safety, and no secrets. He is spied upon by the island's other slave, Ariel, and is, body and soul, the possession of his master.

> tonight thou shalt have cramps,
> Side-stitches that shall pen thy breath up; urchins

Shall, for that vast of night that they may work,
All exercise on thee; thou shalt be pinch'd
As thick as honeycomb, each pinch more stinging
Than bees that made 'em.   (1, 2, 327–32)

His food is the natural produce of the isle, though he once tasted Prospero's delicious drink of 'Water with berries in't' (1, 2, 336), when he
was in favour. The simple facts of the situation on the isle invite comparison with the history of colonization, where a primitive native population, whose technologies of defence and aggression are no match
for those of the Western invader, is made subject to that invader and
enslaved. That phase of eighteenth-century colonialism in which the
colonizers attempted to 'civilize' the natives, usually by passing on
Christianity to them, seems to have been a failure on this island, and it
stands as a painful memory for the civilizers, who typically are surprised to have met ingratitude of the kind Prospero and Miranda find
in Caliban.[21]

He has also become a rebellious slave, waiting for an opportunity to
rid himself of his hated oppressor. This is the Caliban with whom
oppressed races in the nineteenth and twentieth centuries have been
willing to identify because of his narrative of resistance to oppression
and injustice;[22] it turns the oppressor's rage and violence against him,
satisfying a desire for justice and revenge. Caliban's darkness is the
substantial factor that sets him apart from his masters. Even the most
exploited English working man (equivalent, perhaps, to Stephano and
Trinculo) in the original audiences would have recognized a kind of
superiority to the dark slave of this drama. Expressions of fellow
feeling with Caliban in other literatures and societies did not begin to
permeate the cultural consciousness until about two centuries after
Caliban's first appearance on the stage, notwithstanding the fact that
the occasional African or 'Indian' slave had already begun to enter the
English awareness, albeit chiefly as a kind of curiosity with different
and only arguably human characteristics.[23] Hall notes that the text
itself locates Caliban 'on one side of a binarism in Prospero's final pronouncement on Caliban, "this thing of darkness I / Acknowledge
mine" (5, 1, 275–6), and in clearly marking him as a slave who is associated with darkness and dirt.'[24] It is significant that, when he is first discovered by Stefano and Trinculo, his appearance prompts a discussion
about whether or not he is even human. Such dehumanizing representations, even when they are only theoretical, are the ancient and his-

toric bases for the validation of ideologies of ethnic superiority of one race or people over another and have served to justify many discriminatory laws and customs.

The Tempest expresses this ideology on a basic level. The white / non-white contest is fought in a primordial landscape in which emotions are raw and uninhibited by predictable social conventions. Prospero's notorious anger simmers in all his dealings with Caliban, and his willingness to inflict physical pain on the slave is unimpeded by a single moment of compassion; his frank concern with his daughter's sexuality is expressed without restraint. All of this is sustained, furthermore, by the way in which the magician is 'completely authorized by the play.'[25] Caliban's marginality to the authorized culture of the play and its contextual parameters is actually and symbolically concentrated in his physical appearance. Difference, in this world, is ugly. Prospero observes:

> And as with age his body uglier grows,
> So his mind cankers. I will plague them all,
> Even to roaring. (4, 1, 191–3)

The consequence of this perceived ugliness (all ugliness and all beauty are, of course, only perceived) is of great significance to the play. It renders Caliban unassimilable. The history of racism reminds us that the physical difference of slaves from their masters, a difference that resides chiefly in their blackness, was usually translatable as irredeemable ugliness and referred to as a kind of eternal curse. This physical difference made their continued suppression easy on the consciences of their oppressors. The blackness of the slave, and the association of blackness in white culture with sin and moral degeneracy, has helped over the ages to justify a plethora of white crimes, including the belief, fostered over the centuries, that slavery was the black man's 'normal condition.'[26] There may even be social value to the dominant culture in constructing slavery as normal; for it has the unusual result of maintaining a scapegoat within the culture itself.

VI

The story of Jessica illustrates the crucial difference between the plight of Caliban and that of Shylock. Jessica's apostasy demonstrates that the Jew has a point of entry into the social formation and, thus, a point of escape from his marginalized status. The chief basis of this difference is physical, but it is also true that Jessica's willingness to adopt the manners and customs of her father's enemies, the Venetians, also confirms their belief in the superiority of their way to Jewishness and allows the young Jewish woman to be assimilated into their midst. Caliban's colour and non-European physical characteristics mark him as irretrievably beyond the possibility of being absorbed into the society: his marginality is as definitive as his physical difference. But the Jew can disappear into the mainstream culture by marriage and, possibly, by conversion (an act that would imply superficial but necessary dress and appearance changes like doffing the 'gabardine' and other accoutrements of religion). Caliban's potential use of sex and violence is represented as an evil attempt to transgress divinely ordered racial boundaries, while Lorenzo's elopement with Jessica is represented as her perfectly feasible absorption into a Christian culture, leading, presumably, to the eventual disappearance without a trace of all vestiges of her religious origins. In contrast to this is the intentionally disturbing image of the tribe of Calibans threatened by the 'monster' (1, 2, 352–3) – what Prospero authoritatively describes as a 'brutish,' 'vile race' (359–60). In *The Merchant of Venice*, the barrier to the Jew's salvation is his religion and his historic affiliation to a set of religious and economic practices that set him outside the pale. He is, however – with some changes on his part – capable of redemption from this history. The same opportunity is not available to Caliban, whose marginality is permanently fixed by what is called 'racial difference.'

Caliban experiences a kind of primal colonial nightmare from which he finally is allowed to awaken. Not merely is his island invaded and taken over by alien Europeans; not only is he forced into subjection in his own home; not only is he turned into a social outcast and undesirable by the thief of his independence; but early in the play, early in the story of his experience of slavery and oppression, the invasion of his home takes on the proportions of a flood. In short order he is turned into an alien on his own island as the invaders arrive in their numbers and entirely overwhelm him. Normality on the island is inverted: European values are not simply imported into this outpost of the world; they become the norm, the basis of the judgments all the inhabitants of the island must face in working out their destinies. In addition to having to submit to Prospero's iron-fisted rule of the island, Caliban is suddenly faced with a host of Prospero-like creatures from another world who regard *him* as the oddity and whose authority he sees no alternative but to accept.

Shylock seems to have drifted into Venice by whatever wind or historical necessity has blown him there. Caliban, on the other hand, finds his private dwelling place suddenly populated by a race of strangers who wish him no good and who, curiously enough, regard *him* as the stranger. Like many a colonized native before and since the advent of Caliban into the European consciousness, he can do nothing about it. Following his own way of life is impossible. He himself, his very body, is colonized and transformed into the property of those who decide they own him and have the right to control him. Their means of controlling his body are violent and fierce.[27] He is punished for his evil thoughts as well as his deeds; he is violently tortured at night, even as he tries to sleep. He attempts to enact a savage revenge against his oppressor, whose technological superiority makes his rebellion hopeless of success. He is sustained as a figure of outrage by his lust for revenge. Shylock, too, is motivated by thoughts of revenge. His cause is represented as flawed, at best, and his motivating passion is confined within the boundaries of a legal system larger than himself and as powerful, proportionately, as the magic of Prospero.

PART II

CHAPTER FIVE

The Self-Representations of *Othello*

I

The various human dramas contained in *Othello* depend in large measure upon the exercise of memory. Personal memory is not separable from the artificial memory whose construction and architecture have been so impressively analysed and historicized by Frances Yates in *The Art of Memory*. Individual memory includes everything not forgotten, from, at the one extreme, highly formulaic and deliberately constructed cultural information to, at the other, the spontaneously, sometimes imperfectly recalled detail of the past, including that invented past that has become personalized and absorbed into the amalgam of private history. While the nineteenth-century – essentially Burkhardtian – notion of the autonomous individual is no longer a credible or acceptable way of conceptualizing early modern dramatic characters,[1] it is nevertheless the case that by enduing his characters with apparently individualized, unique memories, Shakespeare manages to give the impression that they possess an autonomous interior life and that they are constituted as subjects in the same way we are constituted. This is not to argue that the interior self exists somehow independent of its social context. Indeed, one of the bases of memory, one of its cornerstones, is its concrete and real connection with that very exterior social context. Katharine Eisaman Maus has effectively argued for a 'symbiotically related or mutually constitutive' relationship between the inward and the external selves.[2]

One of the chief modes by which subjectivity is constructed is the representation of memory. Subjectivity is not, says Maus, a unified or coherent concept, but is, rather, 'a loose and varied collection of assumptions, intuitions, and practices that do not all logically entail one another and need not appear together at the same cultural moment.'[3] I would suggest, further, that memory is one of the subject's chief repositories of the 'assumptions, intuitions and practices,' one of the chief means of access to the forms and modes by which subjectivity is constituted. Few elements of the dramatic makeup compel identification with the constructed dramatic character more intensely than the representation of memory. For memory is obviously the conduit to the past – to the impression, that is, that the narrative being enacted is occurring in a continuum of time. It is this location of the drama in the temporal that powerfully sustains the illusion of identification.

Memory takes different forms in the plays and produces different dramatic effects. All the things that happen, from the deliberately planned event to the merely fortuitous, are directly relatable to something already known and experienced. The characters of *Othello* habitually look backwards to prior knowledge as they strive to organize the present into forms that make the future predictable and hence secure. This may seem like normal behaviour in life, but in Shakespeare it forms part of the artistic contrivance of the text. We may consider, for example, that in the dialogue of *Macbeth* there are only about a dozen references in total to the personal experiences of the characters before the play began: this pre-play personal past of *Macbeth* thus is narrow and attenuated, possibly as a means of stimulating the panic by which that play seems to be driven. By contrast, *Othello* possesses about fifty-four such references and thus produces a quite different effect: the past is palpably in evidence in this play. An almost compulsive habit of referring or alluding to the pre-play experiences is a visible mechanism of the practice of self-fashioning that *Othello*'s characters indulge in. Of the many discourses that constitute self-fashioning, memory and the ideological influences to which it is automatically and axiomatically subject seem in *Othello* to constitute a dominant force. The modalities of memory in the play are presented in a variety of ways. For example, in his senate speech, Othello talks about how he has talked about his memories of his difficult and dangerous past; he tells the senate of having told his story and of having often retold it. These seem to be cherished, socially contextualized memories, which have assisted him in fashioning one of the personae that sustain him as a stranger in Venice and that helped him to win Desdemona's love. Shakespeare shows Othello in the act of producing a self in a public forum through the agency of memory. Here, according to Greenblatt, he is reconstituting his nobility for others and himself and re-establishing his subject position in relation to Venice, in an act of 'narrative self-fashioning.'[4] Words are the means by which these memories acquire form and focus. Later in the play, when Othello erupts with the apparently random ejaculation, 'Goats and monkeys!' another mode of remembering is represented. The words come from another part of the memory: the animals are remembered in a way that lends force to his feelings of sexual and social torment, and the way they seem to be 'meant' by Othello in this tortured phrase indicates an unfamiliar context for the suddenly surfacing image. The images of goats and monkeys arise unrehearsed, unbidden, unwanted, perhaps, but it is certain that they emerge from a kind of grab bag of memories all of which are undoubtedly subject to cultural formations and illustrate the often overwhelming force of social and ideological forms in the production of the individual subject.[5] It has been speculated that these two beasts are notoriously and proverbially known for their voracious sexuality; and the context of the ejaculation supports the idea that socio-sexual anguish lies behind the phrase, the very pain of the speaker being contained in the uncontrolled mode of speech as it informs the bestial image. It is a fact, too, that the referents must have for each speaker a common source and touchstone in memory. Language itself is possible and employable only through the reality and fact of memory. And language, Paul Smith reminds us, is one of the forces that dominate the subject, together with other forces such as social formations and political apparatuses.[6] Language, and the memory by which it is activated and enabled, helps to determine the subject.

II

The very first lines of the play refer to a pre-play event. Roderigo reproaches Iago for taking money from him and recompensing him only with silence or, at best, withheld words. His complaint refers to the absence of spoken language, the lack of information about Desdemona already known to Iago:

> Tush! Never tell me? I take it much unkindly
> That thou, Iago, who has had my purse
> As if the strings were thine, shouldst know of this.   (1, 1, 1–3)

Roderigo's sour complaint is based entirely upon remembered love (of Desdemona), remembered largesse (towards Iago), and remembered dependence (upon Iago's promises); it indicates a self whose autonomy is threatened, a self fashioned by circumstances rather than will or desire, by dependence rather than autonomy. Only when he gets to speak his last words does Roderigo show recognition of the sad and desperate thing his life has become – he seems to see that his faith in Iago's words has destroyed his life. His dying words are helpless but utterly clear and reconfigure the pathetic conspirator and would-be murderer by an astringent wrath that is full of bitter truth. In the dramatically appropriate clamour and turbulence, Roderigo bursts out: 'O damned Iago! O inhuman dog!' (5, 1, 62). Damnation and inhumanity are powerful forms of invective, the former adumbrating Othello's self-lacerating image of his own future in eternity, when he must confront the reality of Desdemona's look. It is, of course, only by the exercise of memory that Roderigo is allowed to see this truth, and it is only by the exercise of memory that Othello will be damned as he recalls 'this look of thine' (5, 2, 74) that will hurl him to his own damnation.

III

Iago's performance in the play, as early as the first scene, reminds us that the past, always ultimately inaccessible, is inevitably invented. The motive for such invention and the ideological circumstance surrounding it are of paramount importance. His words recapitulate parts of his own and other peoples' lives, which are sometimes close to and sometimes far from the facts. And sometimes we have no way of judging their relative proximity. The importance of our judgment of the veracity of his history is not obvious until later in the play, when we literally see him inventing history out of incidents we ourselves have observed. This dramatic experience, whose full flavour and force belongs to Iago and the audience/reader exclusively, is that of his own account of the brawl – which we have just witnessed – involving Cassio and Montano. Iago's brilliant and creative invention throws into doubt everything else he has said, and later says. We find, in other words, that Iago is an accomplished liar, a discovery that poses large problems of (retrospective) interpretation. What we make of the story of Cassio's advancement and Iago's own rejection in scene 1 –

> Three great ones of the city,
> In personal suit to make me his lieutenant,
> Off-capped to him   (1, 1, 8–10)

– depends upon when we read or hear it. At first reading it seems reasonable. On the other hand, once Iago has become better known to us, even this story acquires the taint of his lying nature, and a retrospective reading throws the account into question.

Scene 1 is full of references to the recent personal histories of its characters. In lines 24–9 Iago, still complaining about being passed over for Cassio, reminds his audience and himself that Othello had actually seen him fighting at Rhodes and Cyprus and still – unaccountably! – nominated Cassio over himself. He relieves his aggrieved heart by telling Brabantio of more recent events just prior to this opening scene, telling the father that his daughter has fled her father's house and 'now, now, very now' (85) is being tupped by 'an old black ram' (86). Producing misery in others seems to assuage his own.

To this point we have seen two kinds of memory put into play. There is the justificatory memory of an injustice being nursed, almost contained, in an alcove of memory, available to be trotted out to meet the occasion when explanation of motive is called for. Iago, for example, hates Othello within a rational and complete context of situation, circumstance, cause, and effect. There is also the memory that functions more like knowledge of incontrovertible and fixed truth – the memory that seems like knowledge of scientific immutable fact: Iago knows for a fact that Desdemona has run from her father's protection into that of her new husband. No interpretation is relevant: Desdemona has demonstrably left her father's house. In this latter case, therefore, memory is concomitant with a version of the real – the signifier and the signified are indistinguishable or fused. Iago uses his private knowledge of the elopement to stir up trouble and to initiate a process of panic in Venice – or, more accurately, in that part of Venice where trouble will inevitably ensue. There is, then, the presence of memory as narrative – his story of the elopement – and memory as known, unarguable fact: Desdemona has run away from Brabantio; that is, the force of living memory that motivates and animates behaviour, belief, and ideology by its continuous presence.

Living memory gives temporary confidence to Brabantio. Recognizing Roderigo to be among his tormenters in the dark night, he splutters:

> The worser welcome!
> I have charged thee not to haunt about my doors.
> In honest plainness thou hast heard me say
> My daughter is not for thee.   (94–7)

It is hard not to derive a drop of pleasure from his pain when, believing that his daughter has found a worse husband than even the odious Roderigo, Brabantio returns from Desdemona's empty bedroom to groan, 'O that you had had her!' (176). This is one of the truly naked expressions of racial prejudice in the play, this repulsive self-pitying moan as the father reveals his preference for a loathed and loathsome white man over a known and admired black one. He has, he confesses, dreamt something of this kind, has anticipated this dreaded outcome, which he calls an accident:

> This accident is not unlike my dream.
> Belief of it oppresses me already.   (139–40)

There is no morality of racial tolerance that will efface the pain of the father who has lost his daughter to a man he cannot desire as her husband and whose dreams taunted him with the preordainment of their marriage. The motive for his hatred of Othello is base; his subsequent death of grief demonstrates its depth, the sheer hold her betrayal has on him. But it is from his past, from some inexplicable and unexplained notion, that he has come to believe in Othello's wrongness for his child. To what extent ancient racial theories or a visceral fear of Othello's racial difference determine his idea of the evil of this match is left vague. Somewhere in his memory, in the complex caverns and labyrinths of his past conscious and unconscious existence, lies a lesson about the danger of the black man. That this fear remains unanalysed and left to suggestion and implication has made the play fodder for racial theorists who have used it to demonstrate the moral and social danger of miscegenation. The basis of Brabantio's aversion to the match lies in simple prejudice – as his awkward preference for Roderigo as son-in-law shows; but prejudice can exist only through the memory of the ideology of prejudice.

Numerous theories have been propounded about the black man as sexual threat to white civilization, and many studies of *Othello* are contingent on this belief. The play itself, however, notwithstanding the conviction such studies carry today, is silent on the subject of Othello's sexuality. That he has slept with Desdemona is evidentially demonstrable (see p. 98, below). But that his blackness marks him in some way as an especially menacing sexual presence in Venice is a notion that has been applied to the drama by subsequent rather than precedent history. Shakespeare is not noticeably shy about adverting directly to sexual prowess or the lack of it in his male characters; neither is he reticent in supplying the white men of *Othello* with epithets that insult Othello's physical nature. There is some sneering about his lips and his age and much comment on his colour; these characteristics are seen as ugly, even by his wife. But on his sexual prowess – or that of black men in general – there is not a single remark, despite the information historians and critics have presented to generations of readers about the current mythologies on the subject. Iago enjoys instilling a kind of sexual fear into Brabantio, but it relates more to the possibility of biracial offspring ('you'll have coursers for cousins, and gennets for germans' [1, 1, 112]) than to any awesome sexuality of the Moor. He does, indeed, refer to the lovemaking of Othello and Desdemona in racial terms, but not in such a way as to suggest that Moorish sexual practice or prowess is more fearsomely sexual than Venetian.

Sexuality is, of course, a partial by-product of memory itself; it is a contingent aesthetic value with strong underpinnings in human narrative consciousness and cultural memory. Cassio seems to have sexual qualities that appeal to women: the obviously sexual woman, Bianca, for example, is passionately in love with him. To the sexually unhappy Iago, Cassio has 'a smooth dispose ... fram'd to make women false' (1, 3, 396–7). Lodovico, too, sets the women's hearts fluttering. Emilia knows a lady in Venice who 'would have walked barefoot to Palestine for a touch of his nether lip' (4, 3, 39). Othello is not in this company. If there were known or believed to be a sexual attribute that marked Othello as extraordinary (especially, surely, the vaunted African penis which historically has struck such fear into white male culture), the uninhibited satirist Iago would undoubtedly have made a comic defect of it, either to cheer himself up or to entertain the gullible Roderigo. But this does not happen. In short, the memories of experience and the storehouse of known and remembered facts supply no evidence that Othello's blackness is a sign of his sexual power. Iago believes that Othello has slept with Emilia, but he does not attribute Othello's success with her to any of Othello's singular attractions; rather, he blames her female weakness and susceptibility and surely, without saying so directly, he feels his own sexual inadequacy when he compares himself with other men, especially Othello and Cassio. Following the example of Harold Bloom, who recognizes an ugly intention behind *The Merchant of Venice*, Bristol writes challengingly, 'I intend to make a similar argument for *Othello*. I read the structure of the play as a comedy of abjection that depends on a background of racial hatred and violence.

An honest production of *Othello* would be just as intolerable as an honest production of *The Merchant of Venice*. In fact ... many readers and spectators of *Othello* have indeed refused to tolerate what is expressed so brutally in this play.[7]

IV

The first appearance of Iago and Othello together is eloquent with reference to memories of their shared past. Today we have become desensitized by the frequency of references to slaughter and warfare and violence; we are thus, perhaps, too little moved by Iago's casual observation that 'in the trade of war' he has slain men (1, 2, 1). The male code of valour and glory through the exercise of violence leads to the attitude of casualness with which transforming experience is absorbed into the everyday. Othello is moved to recall, far less comfortably than Iago and with a transparently self-conscious asseveration of his own worth, that he has done services for the Signiory. Furthermore – and as a kind of enlistment of authority that will demonstrate that worth – he adds a few remarks on the value of his birth and blood: 'I fetch my life and being / From men of royal siege' (1, 2, 21–2). Already, in other words, Othello is on the defensive. Already, though he insists that he has done no wrong, he seems to recognize a need to explain and defend his recent, pre-play action of marrying the willing Desdemona.

The pasts of Iago and Othello have equipped them differently for the present and future: Iago is able to seem relaxed and easy, his position secure. Othello anticipates trouble and prepares for defensive reaction. In the teeth of terrible accusations by a senior Venetian senator, it is a reality that the Turkish fleet bearing down on Cyprus protects him from the law far more effectively than his legal right to marry Desdemona. The Duke of Venice needs him. The immediate past is bearing heavily down on the present; the Turks are approaching the stronghold of Cyprus and threatening Venetian domination. The nation is under siege and Othello is generously supplied with the instruments of defence and aggression. There is evidence of panic in the senate, with conflicting information flying about and exaggerating the danger to the state:

> *Duke.* There's no composition in this news
>   That gives them credit.
> *First Sen.* Indeed they are disproportioned.
>   My letters say a hundred and seven galleys.

Duke. And mine a hundred and forty
Second Sen. And mine two hundred ...
                                    – yet they do confirm
A Turkish fleet, and bearing up to Cyprus.   (1, 3, 1–9)

Thus, the stage is set for Othello's famous explanations of his recent activities.

V

While Iago can talk breezily about killing men in the trade of war, Othello seems to have a grasp of the trade of warfare and its concomitant – killing men – as something more; he likes his work and believes in it. More than a job, it is a calling. He looks back on his life of soldiering and is pleased with what he sees. The 'dearest action' (1, 3, 90) of his life has been the very thing that Iago can so dismiss. Othello doesn't love himself so much as he loves the idea of himself becoming the thing he wishes to seem to others. His energies have been, he asserts, those of a hero, not of a mortal and ordinary man. The language he speaks is a borrowed one – not merely literally borrowed, but literarily borrowed. His is the idiom of the classical warrior, a professional language of command. The idea of himself projected in this senate scene is something he seems to assemble – before our very eyes – as a kind of composite of carefully selected images derived from the past – a memory that possesses an architectural structure contrived through much practice. His is, it would seem, a 'self' fashioned as much from the mythology of heroism as from the personal memories to which it ostensibly alludes. A self-conscious greatness pervades, informs, and suffuses the construct.[8] Naturally, it begs questions: the processes of autobiography and fiction are similarly selective and reductive. What is untold in this glorious recreation of the known past floods the later scenes, as we observe disaster and chaos re-form that past, when the heroic collapses before the cruel, the brave before the cowardly, the decent before the vile, the fine before the crude. It appears when the heroic self has died and the brutish has surfaced.

Hence the appealing story of a uniquely tested hero:

The story of my life
From year to year, the battles, sieges, fortune
That I passed.   (1, 3, 129–31)

It is not an exaggeration to speak of the theatre of Othello's memory, which does indeed contain the dramatically terrible – images of slain soldiers lying on the battlefield, the dew rusting their once-bright swords; the reality of slavery; the experience of being taken into captivity; the knowledge of a world that contains horrors like men whose heads grow beneath their shoulders. These details, all remembered, constitute the formative memory of deformation, of the unnatural and the unspeakable. Subsequent events produce the discovery that they have brutalized Othello's self-inventions quite as surely as they have glamorized it. Maus makes the relevant point that Othello does not so much tell his story to the Venetian court as he recounts having told it to Desdemona, 'and that telling is itself a repetition of a narrative previously offered to Brabantio.'[9] That is, the attractions for Othello of the confessional narrative Greenblatt has convincingly identified in his discursive practices are clearly unspontaneous and, even by his own admission, rehearsed, notwithstanding their undoubted sincerity: 'his identity depends upon a constant performance ... of his "story," a loss of his own origins, an embrace and perpetual reiteration of the norms of another culture.'[10] Othello's rehearsals of his past have a quality of fragility, as though the reiterations help to keep him within the present, and the performance of the past through frequent memorial reconstruction wards off the dangers it seems inherently to possess. The re-presentation of the past is one of the most eloquent indices to the fragility of Othello's sense of present existence.

VI

Desdemona's response to her anguished father presents a model of another kind. She, too, produces a version of herself. The place, time, and occasion demand an explanation from her as they have from her husband. But her words seem to come from a self that is solidly planted in the past; she can make the separation between then and now, past and present, with the kind of confidence and certainty that Othello notoriously lacks. Indeed, she does so when she virtually resigns her 'daughterhood' with the line, 'I am hitherto your daughter. But here's my husband' (1, 3, 184). While the distinction is consistent with orthodox Elizabethan views of father/daughter relationships, it is nevertheless the neatness of the division between past and present that indicates the invisible line of the present. 'Was' is softened into 'am hitherto' – that is, until this moment. The past and the history shaped from it have produced a sense of obligation in Desdemona. Her father, in fulfilling his obligations to her, has provided life and education which, in turn, have taught her to respect her father. More interesting, of course, is her implication that the life and education provided by her father have taught her the *limits* or boundaries of respect, obligation, and duty. The chief limit is also clearly and temporally defined as the moment when the husband becomes husband. Past and present existence, in short, so important for Desdemona's sense of self, are rationally perceptible constructs, the one leading into but different from the other.

Desdemona's speech reveals a self founded on the bedrock of reason and faith in the sequential logic of cause and effect. It seems a somewhat heartless speech, but perhaps a frequently spoken and heard one in ordinary domestic life, and it is certainly in line with Elizabethan commonplaces of remembered lessons leading to rational filial conduct. Desdemona appears to possess a confident sense of moral right, of having both morality and history on her side; thus, her performance is also a way of ignoring or circumventing the damage to familial traditions that has been caused by her act. Shakespeare compounds the damage to familial hierarchies of respect by introducing into the equation the unpredictable element of racial difference. The hurt to Brabantio may, of course, be read as a consequence more of hurt pride than of wounded affections. The fact that furtive escape was necessary for Desdemona does indeed allude to a failure of trust between father and daughter and to a daughter's accurate estimation of her father's reaction to her marrying outside the familiar and socially validated pool of suitors.

Desdemona's speech is informed with standard language of duty and respect, of the awareness of the relationship not to men but to their roles – the father, the husband. She has switched, she says, the object of her duty by a right that has precedent in her father's own marriage to her mother. The silences of the speech are surely as eloquent as the words, and they advert, without language, to a relationship of the past right up to the present. The play interrogates the mythologized relation between love and duty. Brabantio's feeling for his daughter is realized in his approval of her, his pride in her beauty and modesty, his memory of the wealthy and curled darlings of her nation who courted her. Yet when Desdemona asserts her right to marry whom she wishes without parental approval, the play is curiously neutral, though it foregrounds that moment as a transformational one. When Desdemona appears to support Othello against her father, Brabantio addresses her as 'gentle mistress' (1, 3, 177) and reminds her of her duty to obey him (179). To her divided duty speech, he responds bitterly, 'God bu'y I ha' done ... I had rather to adopt a child than get it' (188–90). This speech is ominous, heavy with loss and disappointment, and it lends a tragic prefiguration to Desdemona's anticipation of the effects of separation from her love:

> If I be left behind,
> A moth of peace, and he go to war,
> The rites for why I love him are bereft me,
> And I a heavy interim shall support
> By his dear absence.   (1, 3, 255–9)

VII

Memory supplies each character with motives and impulses that can be ultimately transforming. Iago's behaviour is ruled by the memory of a piece of gossip, a rumour that holds him by the throat. It is a rumour that produces the nightmare image for him of his own wife and the Moor making the beast with two backs.

> And it is thought abroad, that 'twixt my sheets
> He's done my office. I know not if't be true.   (1, 3, 385–6)

Iago, the young man of twenty-eight, is tormented by the thought that his young wife has been unfaithful with his commander – he who woos with 'fantastical lies' (2, 1, 220). He is powerless to pursue the suspicion by legitimate means; to whom should he complain? All he can do is let the poisonous image gnaw at him and take solace from the prospect of vengeance that has tantalized him for a long while before the events of the play. The play is Iago's time for revenge, his hour come round at last. He has often bidden his wife to steal Desdemona's handkerchief, she reminds him (3, 3, 307), etching a disturbing image of an old grudge waiting to be settled. And, in truth, Iago eats his dish of revenge cold. Emilia's outburst late in the play points explicitly to the equivalence of Iago's and Othello's plights in love. Like Othello, Iago has been persuaded by a contemptible 'squire' of his wife's infidelity:

O, fie upon him! Some such squire he was,
That turn'd your wit the seamy side without,
And made you to suspect me with the Moor.   (4, 2, 147–9)

Getting even, 'wife for wife' (2, 1, 294), has become Iago's purpose in life: Othello's perceived infidelity – through adultery – to his own ensign must be avenged by the wronged husband. He does so by repeating the exercise and then enjoys it by adding some stunning aesthetic refinements that better the instruction.

VIII

It is useful to be reminded that Emilia is Desdemona's servant, not her friend. The handkerchief upon which Desdemona's rescue is made to seem to depend is the testing site of that relationship. It supplies the material evidence of Emilia's complicity in the destruction of Desdemona; its re-emergence as evidence of Iago's crimes and Emilia's role in acquiring it for him, link her to the crime. Her rage against Othello thus partakes of rage against herself. There is a chillingly direct link between this little dialogue:

Des. Where should I lose that handkerchief, Emilia?
Emil. I know not, madam;   (3, 4, 19–20)

and this exhange:

Othello.   I saw it in his hand,
   It was a handkerchief; an antique token
   My father gave my mother.
Emil. O God, O heavenly God!   (5, 2, 216–19)

Emilia is struck with the brutal, staggering realization that a word from her might have saved Desdemona's life.

The handkerchief does not merely emerge from the pasts of Othello and Desdemona, is not merely a sign of their bond; it is the symbol of their united commitment. It is not merely from the past, but is of it. As the play progresses, the handkerchief acquires a history that seems to recede farther and farther into the mists of time past. It becomes the measure of the verity and solidity of life before the play. Its mysteries have often been pondered, as have the stories of its creation as a magical token with a mysterious past. But perhaps more than anything in the play, it originates physically in the past, possessing the properties of history and history's capacity for invention, interpretation, and reinterpretation. To possess this handkerchief is to possess a physical link with exotic history; to let go of it is to submit to the dangers of a rudderless present where peril always resides.

IX

Des.   Prithee, tonight
Lay on my bed our wedding sheets; remember,
And call thy husband hither.   (4, 2, 106–8)

Like the strawberry handkerchief, Desdemona and Othello's wedding sheets possess hermeneutic power. It is the case that if Desdemona was making a special request for her wedding sheets, bidding Emilia not to forget them – her word 'remember' is an added emphasis – then obviously the wedding night had already passed. The wedding sheets are not presumed automatically to be on the bed in preparation for a first use and must, therefore, have been previously used so that Emilia could identify them *as* wedding sheets. Like the handkerchief, the wedding sheets are, for Desdemona especially, a token of the past that she seems to hope will carry her forlorn and angry husband back into a happier time, a recent past when love reigned. The visible means of entry into history and memory, recent and antique, is through the agency of flimsy cloth. The most memorable 'things' of this drama of warfare and violence are these seemingly innocent linen props carried from history into the arena of violence, mayhem, and murder.

X

Iago is the maker of tales and the author and forger of false memories. But he is not merely a dreadful liar – though he is that; he also is a master of manipulation through words and of words:

In sleep I heard him say, 'Sweet Desdemona,
Let us be wary, let us hide our loves;'
And then, sir, would he gripe and wring my hand,
Cry out, 'Sweet creature!' and then kiss me hard,

As if he pluck'd up kisses by the roots,
That grew upon my lips, then laid his leg
Over my thigh, and sigh'd, and kiss'd, and then
Cried, 'Cursed fate that gave thee to the Moor!'   (3, 3, 425–32)

This speech is story-telling by a master, and Othello's credulity is entirely understandable. The lie is realistic: the speech is richly and precisely detailed; it is replete with direct speech, cunningly metaphorical with its tangible image – 'As if he pluck'd up kisses by the roots' – and convincingly concrete.

A later scene forces the reader to question the way in which evidentiary and historical truths are made plausible and compels a suspicion of the nervous presence of the past as it is so variously manifested in this play. The passage above seems to be a pack of gratuitous lies. But in the drinking scene when Cassio is disgraced, although lies issue from Iago's mouth, they look suspiciously unlike lies and stand in a curiously and uncomfortably close relation to the truth as we have experienced and now see it. We watch Iago arrange the calamitous drunken brawl, and then we see him turn it into narrative in such a way as to throw into doubt the reliability of all narratives of the past, possibly even including those of Othello. The tale of the brawl as Iago relates it is true and false at the same time.

The details of Iago's narration are accurate (or, in some conventional way, 'true'), but they are selected and ordered in such a way as to hide the truth. He begins his story of the event with, 'Montano and myself being in speech' (2, 3, 216), leaving out what anyone who has watched the business would regard as crucial – how he persuaded Cassio to drink when he didn't want to – that is, omitting the real beginning; he leaves out, too, the fact that he already knew of Cassio's weakness for drink. The point, applicable by example to most of the histories of this play, is that the story of an event, which we here witness in advance of its transformation into narrative history, is simultaneously true and not true. Iago's remarkable competence – even omniscience – as his narrative manipulation shows, lies largely in his steady awareness of the connections of the past to the present and future. This awareness is revealed in his relation of the story of the brawl. Here, he narratively organizes a sense of the violence and chaos of the event we have just observed by bringing the action forward to the very moment in which it is being described. All the while, of course, the entire scene is orchestrated by the master director, Iago. He has demonstrated the sleight of hand necessary or even inevitable when the past is brought, by language, into the present – the process upon which all the major actors in the drama depend.

XI

There are two deceased mothers in *Othello*, that of Desdemona and that of Othello. They emerge, in passing, as the enablers of others' histories, histories that bear down with direct and dreadful force on those of the doomed lovers of this play. Othello's invocation of the memory or past example of his mother drags the remembered past into the present with the additional force of affectionate, even, in at least one case, passionate memory. He warns Desdemona:

> That handkerchief
> Did an Egyptian to my mother give.
> She was a charmer, and could almost read
> The thoughts of people; she told her, while she kept it
> 'Twould make her amiable, and subdue my father
> Entirely to her love; but if she lost it,
> Or made a gift of it, my father's eye
> Should hold her loathly, and his spirits should hunt
> After new fancies: she dying, gave it me,
> And bid me, when my fate would have me wive,
> To give it her.   (3, 4, 53–63)

The recollection shifts between present anger and passionate memory, between Othello's perplexed and confounded love of Desdemona and the love of his dying mother, who passes on a gift of love to the grieving son. Her words lend moving authenticity and feeling to the remembered scene; the past asserts itself in Othello's mind with the passionate force of new loss. The play and Othello's anger are suddenly tinged with sadness emanating from many directions at once. The handkerchief is not innocent, after all, but is the locus of pure meaning in Othello's life: it provides and proves truth, purpose, and the value of life for him; its presence and absence lend the substance of demonstrable, tangible reality to his freighted, fictional, and shadowy life. The force that here constructs subjectivity, the power that give shape and presence to the experience is mimesis: Othello locates his disappointment in a mimetic structure that depends upon his memory as means of shaping the reality of the present.

Desdemona's mother occupies a more ambiguous place in her daughter's memory. The new bride coolly uses her mother's example in marriage to counter her father's arguments about duty and obligation. Later, she recalls her mother as having had a maid, Barbary, whose plight was like her own – a mad lover whose turning away caused her death. Two simple tales of tragic, doomed love ending in death. Barbary's experience has become a closed and complete story, while Desdemona's story has not yet played itself out. Desdemona's mother, however, is remembered only as a means, as a conduit to Desdemona's memory of Barbary, her tragic predecessor and exemplar. In her two memories of her mother Desdemona reveals little feeling, unlike Othello, whose memory of his mother is charged with emotion. What this silence about her mother adverts to is unclear, but in the volatile and dangerous world Desdemona comes to inhabit, as her life draws towards its brutal and dreadful close, the silence becomes more resonant. Her absent mother seems to have been virtually forgotten; she is accorded no significant place or thought in the burgeoning disaster of the marriage for which she once was the model.

XII

The imagined past is inhabited by those pictures and fantasies that are transmogrified by forces of the imagination into perceptions of factual memory. So real can such images become that they can be the motive for acts of terrible violence, terrible deeds, terrible wrongs. Othello is obsessed by the image that has formed in his imagination of Cassio and Desdemona in the act. To him its reality has become a given, an objective fact as real and visible as night:

> 'Tis pitiful, but yet Iago knows
> That she with Cassio hath the act of shame
> A thousand times committed. Cassio confessed it;
> And she did gratify his amorous works
> With that recognizance and pledge of love,
> Which I first gave her. I saw it in his hand.
> It was a handkerchief, an antique token
> My father gave my mother.   (5, 2, 211–18)

'A thousand times,' he declares with tremulous certainty. His circumstances have become desperate and he speaks as one who remembers his injury, not as a man who is inventing or justifying his crime.

XIII

Memories old and new invade and possess Othello's mind in his last moments. A recent memory is his last – I kissed her ere I killed her; it is his vain attempt to present a palimpsest, to hide the murdering self behind the loving self, or, more plausibly, to separate the memories of good and evil from each other. But the connectedness of the one to the other, much like the connectedness of private and public, is too deep. A much older memory forms the coda of his life; the past bears down on him in a complete and devastating memory of violence and murder. Throughout the play, Othello is engaged in a vain quest: he strives to discover a defining quintessence of himself. But it is surely significant that, in his last moments, as he describes the self he has so painstakingly constructed through the conscious and deliberate construction of a public narrative of public service to the state, his speech should be charged with an image from his storehouse of memories of killing:

> in Aleppo once,
> Where a malignant and a turban'd Turk
> Beat a Venetian and traduc'd the state,
> I took by the throat the circumcised dog
> And smote him – thus.   (5, 2, 352–7)

The remembered past and the present are brought into alignment with the suicidal blow. Past and present, which carry the burdens of Othello's interior and exterior subjectivity, are forced into artificial coherence and synchronicity as the temporally divided selves – which he has attempted to keep separate until now – fuse in one terrible and climactic life-affirming and life-denying act. Othello takes charge of his destiny as he relinquishes his hold on life. His violence, like that of Oedipus, has given form and function to the life he has carved out for himself and is encapsulated in this vivid and powerful physical gesture. The memory of killing the Turk in Aleppo acts much like Oedipus's killing of Laius: it sets into motion decisive and transforming events that have led inexorably to the present. The memory is not accidental and fortuitous: it is exemplary. Killing himself, Othello also declares his discovery of epistemological coherence. This is not a tragedy of blame – Iago enables but is innocent of Desdemona's murder and Othello's death. This is the tragedy of a man whose active, vivid memory of the past has devoured his present and future.

CHAPTER SIX

King Lear and Memory

I

It is a curious fact that *King Lear*, which depends as no other play upon a decisive event preceding the beginning of the first scene, presents its past in a vague, usually shadowy light, through the use of allusions and references only ephemerally and fragmentarily realized. Yet the past is a powerful presence in the play, suggesting to Fredson Bowers, for example, that the real climax of the play is the decision to divide the kingdom, which Lear makes sometime before the start of the first scene.[1] In keeping with this recurring sense of previous experience, a kind of primitivism asserts itself throughout the drama by an atavistic impulse embedded in its linguistic and narrative structures. The language reverberates with biblical and pagan allusions and references that carry the burden of ancient time and incident, long preceding but intimately related to the drama itself. In addition, the images of bestiality and monstrosity have the effect and function of erasing the line between animal and human existence that augments the sense of primitivity that seems to lurk near the surface of the action of this play. On the more immediate level of the narrative, however, the play offers very little of lives formerly lived, of experiences endured or enjoyed – of how, in other words, the things we see came to pass. Yet the hints of those lives, their vividly realized texture, are there, folded into the fabric of the narrative, but perceptible chiefly through nuance.

Perhaps it is the sheer, terrible urgency that allows the characters so little time to reflect; for the traces of the past are strong, and earlier existence is given attention, its relevance to the present briefly illuminated. In its use of the past, *King Lear* makes a striking contrast with

Othello, which derives so much energy from memory and past history. The 'sequential discontinuity'[2] that John Reibtanz sees in *King Lear* results from the obfuscation of what existed before the play and produces a sense of the past as a shadowy, undelineated locale, lacking the harsh clarity that characterizes the play's present. The myths and stories of olden times are usually fragmented, randomly interwoven and incomplete. The sense of urgency and the concern with memory in the play may well derive from only recently resolved national anxiety over issues of succession. For many contemporaries of Shakespeare the nation's stability was dependent upon the viability of the traditional monarchy as they understood it, and a smooth, legal, orderly continuation of monarchical rule was generally desired. Thus, in the years around the composition and production of *King Lear*, there was a more than usually intense recognition of the ways in which the past in its various temporal and ideological forms affected the present and the future. Under such conditions of nervous expectation and national unease, the links of past, present, and future would have been more visible, perhaps, than they would under less contentious or fraught social conditions. In the play, Shakespeare seems to address the questions of the fragility of continuity and the friability of tradition by an interrogation of conventional assumptions about the nature of the past; of history, memory, and of memory's failure – forgetting – and the political and social consequences of that failure.

   King Lear possesses only twenty-four allusions and overt references to actual, lived experiences preceding the beginning of the play. The effect of some, but by no means all, of these moments within the play that take us and the speakers back into their pasts is to anchor the characters in an apparently real, personal, and political history that lends substance to the present. Chief among the beneficiaries of this retrospectivity is Lear himself, who acquires power from the simple act of locating himself in the trajectory of whole time – the cycle that includes past and future, birth and death. That retrospective view is essential to the tragic perspective: it enables the essential tragic mechanisms of victimage and sacrifice, which carry the burden of this drama. It engages history and memory, thereby activating the processes of violence and sacrifice without which tragedy is incomplete. The perspectives made possible by awareness of time – its passage and its prospects – bring into being in *King Lear* the sacrificial crisis that, René Girard implies, is the basis of the tragic experience.[3]

   A world in the kind of turmoil exhibited in the first scene of the play conforms to Girard's description of the sacrificial crisis, which he describes as a state of disintegration resembling the process of fragmentation of social categories made visible in *King Lear*. Girard refers to 'the disappearance of the difference between impure violence and purifying violence' as the hallmark of this crisis: 'When this difference has been effaced, purification is no longer possible and impure contagious, reciprocal violence spreads throughout the community.'[4] The evil, destructive violence of the play, most gratuitous but most eloquent, perhaps, in the blinding of Gloucester, is the play's index to that loss of distinction. In *King Lear* the brutality, the loss of distinction, the appalling cruelty that has seeped into the courts and castles of *Lear's* Britain, come about as a consequence of the decay and loss of memory. Lear's banishment of Cordelia and Kent comes about because of the king's desire to control the future without reference to the past and the structure of meaning and narrative with which it is burdened.

II

As Lear's tragedy becomes more manifest with the progression of the story, the past becomes more visible; the allusions, few as they are, become more sure and precise; and the characters in general become more confident and self-aware. Memory slowly stabilizes and allows the present to come into focus. Of the references within the play to pre-play, past lives, fully fourteen belong to Lear and three to Kent; one belongs to Cordelia, one each to Goneril and Regan, one to Edgar, one to the First Servant, one to the Old Man, and one to Gloucester. The force behind the references and allusions is memory; its activation results in the past's spilling into the present in different ways. Simply recalled facts give a kind of coherence to the present and seem to bring groundedness and order. More powerful is the consequent force of nostalgia that memory provokes; this force has a different and more emotionally charged effect on present events. Yet perhaps it is the undramatized assumptions of past life that are the strongest link between the present drama and the history of the lives under way. The very use and knowledge of language carry implications of history. The compulsive energy of the king as he attempts, by the exercise of speech, to control and direct the meaning of the present, indicates the continuous presence of remembered and codified past experience.[5] But this evidence of pre-play life is different from that developed by the deliberate and accidental use of memory. The latter is an allusive habit by which the speaker draws upon memory to settle something in the here and now. Sometimes the remembered event or item is conjured up to make a rhetorical point or to bring perspective to a present puzzle. Sometimes it appears unbidden, evincing a troubled mind through its random connection to the present.

The drama opens upon an emotionally neutral discussion between Gloucester and Kent about their past common misapprehension of how the king's affections and trust were distributed among his family. Each acknowledges his own misreading, and Gloucester offers what he wrongly thinks is the correct interpretation of the cagey king, whose later appearance only confounds the correction:

> *Kent.* I thought the King had more affected the Duke of Albany than Cornwall.
> *Glou.* It did always seem so to us; but now, in the division of the king-dom, it appears not which of the Dukes he values most.   (1, 1, 1–5)

This general allusion to the way in which the past has been appre-hended and rounded off into complete, remembered items or 'facts' and Gloucester's subsequent, more specific memory of Edmund's con-ception – 'there was good sport at his making' (1, 1, 23) – illustrate two kinds of history upon which the past is founded in this play. On the one hand, history is the thing done – the material but unorganized facts of past existence and experience; on the other, it is the ordered memory and presentation of those facts as they are recovered by mem-ory and knowledge, drawn on in order to anchor the present in the consciousness. That order is, of course, ideologically charged, and it is exemplified by the ways in which political and personal pasts are so often at odds in the minds and memories of the characters. Gloucester and Kent agree that they misunderstood the king; they agree that they remembered something one way, but it has been shown that they based their memories on unstable details, statements, or facts, however official or authoritative their sources. This information from the pre-play past is different in kind from another notorious 'fact' in this scene – the nostalgic recollection of pleasure by Gloucester in the 'good sport' he had at Edmund's making. The memory is personal and inarguable – whether the sport was enjoyed or not by the unnamed, interestingly inconsequential woman in question makes no difference to the accuracy of the recollection. Strength and confidence seem to be shored up by the remembered act, while mere assumptions about earlier social life challenge conceptions of the self in the present.

The scene illustrates the existence, within the mind of each individual subject, of a personal, private history; it is a history as ordered, narratively complex, and ideologically contingent as the so-called Grand Narratives of official and state historians. Each individual dramatic character is shown to possess a tendency to come to terms with the present by the act of remembering and controlling personal meaning by the use of linguistic processes not unlike those employed by professional historians writing the histories of empires and states. The personal history is, of course, limited in ways different from the metanarrative, but it is another and, I would argue, equally convincing example of the tendency or need to arrest and control meaning through language, and Shakespeare has effectively illustrated this human tendency in the play. Gloucester, for example, has made a salacious, comic, characteristically male story out of his seduction of the woman who is or was Edmund's mother. By the use of language, he has narrativised that piece of the past that lingers into the present and future in the form and person of his illegitimate son. His authority as man, old man, father, and duke gives him full epistemological control over the history of Edmund's conception.

III

The questions of identity and subjectivity, ideologically fraught though they are, depend upon the belief that a self can be constructed and partially known through the exploration of a text. They seem particularly urgent issues in *King Lear*, where the ontological questions dominate the play's various tragic quests. That text can be many things and be composed of many things, but whether it is apprehended as a life text or an art text, the self is a fictionalized, invented subject derived from the inevitable and contrived processes of selection and reduction. These processes themselves are the products of psychological, social, political, or economic motives, individually or in combination. The words the subject uses help to describe his or her means of connecting to the world in a complex coalescence of time, space, and ideology. The subject, says Paul Smith, 'is not self-contained ... but is immediately cast into a conflict with forces that dominate it in some way or another – social formations, language, political apparatuses and so on. The subject, then, is determined – the object of determinant forces.'[6]

The contradiction evident in the kinds of misunderstandings Kent and Gloucester display illustrates the potential collusion of the forces that make identity, and it suggests the whimsical and always uncertain nature of historical knowledge. Kent and Gloucester agree that they thought one thing but that present evidence contradicts the 'truth' of that thing. They were wrong, but they believed they were right. Gloucester's private sexual history, as he presents it here, is significant as an example of the representation of personal history: it is reductive and concise in the extreme, the account of an event that turns out to have the effect of changing the history of England. The reference to his sexual past – a conventional and typical form of male boasting – is often used as a black mark against Gloucester, who speaks with cavalier indifference about such intimate and private matters in the presence of the son who resulted from the coupling. A more crucial significance of the remark lies in its reflection of Gloucester's use of the memory to link himself to a past world that belongs to him alone, a world in which contradiction has been resolved. The statement is a means of reasserting his sense of the stability of the past and of re-establishing his locus in the present, which has been confounded by the king's unpredictable act.

IV

Lear's 'Meantime' (1, 1, 36) is a weighty introduction to his part. It signifies an attempt to balance past, present, and future. The word interweaves what was, what is, and what shall be, all in a manner that becomes incremental, as past and present are redefined and the future redirected in the course of the dynamic and transforming first scene of the play. That word signifies an action in temporary suspension. It precariously weighs the relationship between past and future, a fulcrum between the two temporal zones; the 'darker purpose' continues the sense of uncertainty carried by the ominous 'Meantime.' The king's words, which concentrate on present apprehensions of the future – ''tis our fast intent' (1, 1, 38) – are contingent upon the surely and completely known past action: 'Know that we have divided / In three our kingdom' (1, 1, 37–8). Lear unwittingly comprehends in these words the modes of response to his test provided by his daughters.

In the speeches of Goneril and Regan emphasis is placed surely in the present tense. Their styles are impersonal and general and rely on the asseveration of their love as evidence of its reality. The bases of their professed love are absent because, as it notoriously turns out, their 'love' has no basis in truth; it relates to no known or shared past affection. Rich and gorgeous though the speeches are, they are ungrounded in history or common experience with the king and might, with slight modification (and the willingness to accept hyperbole as a conventional part of such professions), be addressed to a lover. Each daughter asserts her love for her father, but each avoids the essential experience to which Cordelia compulsively and necessarily returns – that is, the past love by which they are and have been united, the function of that love, and the common experience of family that has brought the father and this daughter towards the confounding present. It is Cordelia's memory of and respect for the history of the love that she shares with Lear that forces us to reject retrospectively the exaggerations of Goneril and Regan's speeches and to see in that conventional rhetorical device a dangerous moral flaw. Writing about Lear's rejection of Cordelia's 'bond,' Lawrence Danson makes the point that the bond itself is 'expressive of traditional values, shared beliefs, of his history itself' and that the 'old way,' as Danson calls this shared past, has been radically dislocated.[7]

When Cordelia speaks at last, she must reach backwards in time in order to separate herself from her sisters and their hypocrisy and to bring into focus the relationship between herself and the king – to recover the personal and the universal experience of father and daughter with a shared past. It is noteworthy that in Goneril and Regan's speeches the only references to Lear are the impersonal 'Sir' and the generalized 'father' in the line, 'as much as child e'er lov'd, or father found' (Goneril, 59) and in 'your dear highness' (Regan, 76). Cordelia, on the other hand, strikes directly at the personal, precise details of the past lives of herself and the king:

> You have begot me, bred me, lov'd me; I
> Return those duties back as are right fit,
> Obey you, love you, and most honour you.   (96–8)

The thoughts are balanced, not merely by the symmetry of the syllables in the first and third lines quoted, but additionally by the logical conjunction of the two temporal spheres that place past and present into a sequential order: past begetting has brought present obedience; past breeding, present love; past love, present honour. There is a satisfying completeness in Cordelia's confident couplings, which bespeaks the fulfilment of love's obligations and feelings. The confidence seems to derive from the consciously remembered past, a past that is here publicly presented in terms of a shared experience and founded upon the complex and ineffable relationship between father and daughter. The crisp, mathematical precision of Cordelia's response derives in part from the way in which she assumes a linkage between herself and Lear in her memory; she recalls the hard reality of the facts that bind them and emphasizes these in the biting consonants of 'begot,' 'bred,' and 'lov'd.'

Lear's response to Cordelia vacillates between heroic abuse and passionate self-pity, modes that, because they are so violently yoked, suggest the spontaneous urge for balance within his mind. There is a vast intellectual and emotional gulf between the brutality and cruelty of Lear's words,

> The barbarous Scythian,
> Or he that makes his generation messes
> To gorge his appetite, shall to my bosom
> Be as well neighbour'd, pitied, and reliev'd,
> As thou my sometime daughter,   (116–20)

and the subsequent simple and spontaneous,

> I lov'd her most, and thought to set my rest
> On her kind nursery.   (123–4)

This outburst is a remembered return to that shared experience of love with his favourite daughter. The pain the words express here, and later as he contemplates his loss, is entirely contingent on his evident awareness of the past; the words carry the conviction that Cordelia has loved him. Nostalgia, according to Phyllis Rackin, is a longing for home or a longing for a lost time – particularly childhood. Indeed the word literally means 'a longing for home':[8] like remorse, therefore, it is a contingent term defined by the presence of a past or a history. It has meaning only and directly in relation to the existence of memory.

V

Nostalgia is a powerful force in *King Lear*, taking back the augmenting disasters and disintegrations of the present, constantly but compulsively, to a place of peace and certitude. It is nostalgia primarily that brings on Lear's madness. It carries the past into the present with unbearable but unavoidable power, producing pain by reference to the clarity and stability of the past. As the present becomes more fraught and dangerous, so the past becomes an inevitable refuge for the crumbling mind of the mad king. Lear's memory is a fragile and chaotic thing in these scenes of breakdown. His past life breaks through in sudden, disconnected, random flashes, undermining the security that narrative history supplies. In his madness, he casts off the staples of narrative, such as continuity, climax, and causality, in favour of an eruption of facts, images, and allusions that are available only through the exercise of memory and the continuous presence of a personal history.

Kent's intervention in Cordelia's banishment provides the antidote of specificity to the fuming chaos of the king's mad rage. He speaks with the force of his confident knowledge of himself and the king. His speech includes details that offer a direct perspective on the past perception of Lear and himself. He has known Lear as king, father, master, and patron:

> Royal Lear,
> Whom I have ever honour'd as my King,
> Lov'd as my father, as my master follow'd,
> As my great patron thought on in my prayers.   (1, 1, 139–42)

He has willingly risked his life for Lear:

> My life I never held but as a pawn
> To wage against thine enemies.   (155–6)

Thus, as Kent and Cordelia brave the present, they derive their strength to do so from their certainties about the past, which have brought this present into being. Their recognition of the sheer wrong of what is occurring is given authority by their perception of the crisis as part of the continuum of personal history. Each adverts to a historical relationship with Lear, a relationship that is direct, immediate, and personal. Cordelia, almost informally, sees herself bound to her father by the near equation of 'you' and 'I,' while Kent acknowledges his king by the repeated personal pronoun, 'my.' Goneril and Regan, by contrast, address their father as 'Sir,' as the generalized father of, 'As much as child e'er lov'd, or father found' (59), and 'your dear highness' (76). By this formality and generalization their speeches tend to separate them from the object of their professed love, while those of Kent and

Cordelia move in the opposite direction in their tendency to personalize matters by linking speaker and object in a vital relationship. That relationship is predicated on a shared history, evidence for which is only rhetorically and symbolically accessible.

Alone together at the end of this scene, Goneril and Regan take the opportunity to discuss their version of history in relation to the present; to make of the pre-play past a justificatory myth by which the future can be twisted into self-serving formulations and directions. Their temporal arena of operation is the present, with a ready eye to the future; their vision is clearly focused on gaining control of their world by looking at what is, rather than what was, in order to determine what will be. Goneril knows, in common with everyone in the court, that Lear 'always lov'd our sister most' (290) and Regan that 'he hath ever but slenderly known himself' (293–4). These two 'facts' about the past are expressed not as evidence of their knowledge of or shared experience with the king but, on the contrary, as demonstrations of his vulnerability to them. Their factual accuracy is borne out by events and is not contradicted by Cordelia or Kent. Yet, used in this way, their sense and knowledge of the past, of their domestic history, of their childhoods and family lives, the information becomes charged with malevolence and acquires the function of a domestic myth used to justify an abuse of power. They perceive in the banishments not the maniacal inconsistency that Kent and Cordelia see, but a further example of how and, on a curious and self-justifying moral level, why the good of all will be served by his subjection to themselves. Lear's unpredictability and inconstant starts give them something we don't expect them to need, a moral rather than merely expedient reason for hitting together against the king, their father.

That these two characters should feel a need to justify their conspiracy on the level of morality and national unity is remarkable in itself and shows them, at least this early in the play, as being aware of a need to seem to being doing a right thing. Their last words in the scene reach into the future: it is as though the past and its connections have served their purpose and can be put aside to make way for the time to come:

Reg. We shall think further of it.
Gon. We must do something, and i'th'heat. (307–8)

The expression 'i'th'heat' is dramatically perfect. It means now, while the iron is hot, quickly, efficiently, without delay, and it effectively removes the pretense of altruism or good motive. It conveys urgency, expediency, and opportunism and is a ready index to the real motives – as if there were any doubt except in their own minds – of power brokering.

But the past that haunts and tortures Lear belongs to the play itself; it is the catastrophe of the first scene. It is this, the recent memory of his wrath and righteousness and their terrible consequences, that threatens his present and future, this that unbalances the equipoise he strove for in his careful and thoughtful, but ultimately disastrous, attempt to determine future history and prevent future strife. The madness he persistently fears, while its apparent source is the banishment of Cordelia, has deep roots in that vaguely but profoundly felt and profoundly complex lifetime of knowledge and love of Cordelia. His present pain threatens to destroy him because as yet he is incapable of seeking beyond the act that has led to it. Lear cannot acknowledge the violence he has done to the history of his paternity. While the father and his three daughters come to us whole, their words and actions carry the formal evidences and textual and cultural paraphernalia of that artificial ideological construct, the family. A family, according to the norms governing its existence, includes relationships (interestingly and symbolically known as blood relationships, with all that the term implies) and its own unique yet essentially imitative history. The ways in which Lear's family is like and unlike other families is the evidence of its dependence upon imitation as its chief survival mechanism. The play is the performance of the last act of that history. Lear the father's banishment of Cordelia the daughter opens to view the fragility of the ideology upon which familial relationships depend.

VI

Lear's story, from the interrupted sojourn with Goneril until the death of Cordelia, is one of a series of dangerously augmenting crises, each of which has to be faced on the available present terms and with current understandings of peril. The circumstances of present life consist of sudden plunges from one adversity to the next, and only the present is allowed to matter. The pre-play past is in evidence, but to Lear its connection with the situations imposed upon him by the persistent danger of the present is ephemeral. Sometimes the past is thrust into active presence by the apparent imperatives of emotion, imposing itself on his consciousness unbidden and unconnected to the present. When, for

example, he instructs Regan on her filial obligations, he muses venge-
fully,

> I know what reason
> I have to think so: if thou shouldst not be glad,
> I would divorce me from thy mother's tomb,
> Sepulchring an adult'ress.   (2, 4, 130–3)

He uses his deceased wife – their mother, their common bond – as an
instrument of debate. This unnamed woman, a cypher in all of their
pasts, has become a mere evidentiary detail, winnowed from that
amorphous experience of both father and daughter and here distorted
by the present into a symbol of his ill treatment.

It is not until much later that Lear is seen looking farther back than
the beginning of the action, beyond his immediate plight and its immediate cause. It is only minutes before the encounter with Poor Tom that
he acknowledges that past in a single, passionate exclamation, which
brings with powerful certainty a reminder of that life and its failures:

> O! I have ta'en
> Too little care of this.   (3, 4, 32–3)

Whereas the previous allusion to the past ('I would divorce me') was
conditional, and as it separated Lear from the past by bringing the allusion into the present, this present reference propels him back into the
past, consciously making both him and it a single part of the same long
lifetime. The sentence is a recognition of a specific historical locus. It
acknowledges power, authority, and humanity in a way that has not
been evident in Lear's self-expression until now. Indeed, this very
remark is the basis for Jonathan Dollimore's powerful argument about
the pervasive sense of political futility that informs the play as a whole,
a futility, it may be added, that is contingent upon the exercise of memory and its essential function in the projection of human consciousness
in time. To Dollimore the play refuses essentialist mystification by
which 'human values' are reaffirmed and offers instead 'a decentring
of the tragic subject which in turn becomes the focus of a more general
exploration of human consciousness in relation to social being – one
which discloses human values to be not antecedent to, but rather
informed by, material conditions.'[9] Values, Shakespeare insists, cannot
exist outside time and memory.

The present, as suddenly and vividly apprehended by the suffering former monarch, radically challenges preconceptions about what the past really was. In this sense the memory stands apart from the speech, even though it serves as a foundation for the ideological generalization which is built upon it. It is significant, also, that Lear's first such recognition has reference to himself, not as the father of the wronged daughter, but as the king. In his earliest recorded memory the political takes precedence over the personal. This recognition is one of Lear's many modes of self-construction: he likes to present and believe himself as organically connected to his nation's history. The moment relates to the play's opening lines, where past error is revealed and the possibility of change is acknowledged. Thus, in the process of linking the personal to the political past, an old assumption, a past 'truth,' is subjected to radical revision, which in turn makes necessary a radical reconsideration of the formerly stable self.

Through the miasma of his madness, details of that old life leap into sudden focus, informing the lexis of insanity with a precise relationship to that old fragmenting self. The affectionately named and remembered dogs, 'Tray, Blanch, and Sweetheart' (3, 6, 63), link the king to that other part of this early self, the domestic, paternal, ordinary man. In such moments, when the past acquires clarity for Lear, lies a recognizable consistency: for just as the present is fraught with a paranoic certainty of the adversity of all forces, human and natural, so does old experience take the forms of aggressive challenge. The slowly growing knowledge of himself as a traitor to himself, his family, and his kingdom is lent authority by such lucid yet disconnected flashes from the histories that have determined him.

Between the memory of his dogs and his next, much later memory of the world he inhabited before the drama, are two recollections of that old time by two nameless characters whose memories supply them with motives for selfless acts of resistance. Cornwall's servant, enraged by his master's cruelty – 'take the chance of anger' (3, 7, 77) – kills that master and is rewarded in this perverse place by being killed for his pains. He harks back to an older, morally clearer, and more demanding code of loyalty:

> Hold your hand, my Lord.
> I have serv'd you ever since I was a child,
> But better service have I never done you
> Than now to bid you hold.   (3, 7, 71–4)

There is also the Old Man, who risks 'hurt' to lead the blind Gloucester out of the terrible place of death and violence, moved by compassion and a code inspired by nothing more than the memory of a kind of (possibly benign) serfdom, which has linked his family to Gloucester's over a long time. He is not, evidently, prompted by sentimental attachment to a kind old master; his motive is nothing more than memory and empathy:

> O my good Lord!
> I have been your tenant, and your father's tenant,
> These fourscore years.   (4, 1, 12–14)

In these two brief but intense and transformative passages, when the feudal values of the old times are seen asserting themselves so vividly, we discover one of the deepest consistencies of the play. In each case, the defiance of authority and its attendant risks are motivated by feelings that are personalized and validated by history. Yet the fragility of the old ideologies of loyalty and sympathy is demonstrated in the death of the servant and the feebleness of the Old Man. Though imperilled in the present, however, these modes of belief and action, because they are related so intimately to remembered experience, are ultimately as irrepressible as the human nature that expresses them. Nostalgic memories provide the play's few hopeful, if doomed, actions. The impulse to help, to rescue another from hurt and pain, gives social and passionate force to instances of nostalgia.

VII

In contrast to the moral and mental lucidity of the two anonymous servants, Lear's madness in act 4 reflects dreadful confusion as his memories erupt in disorder, thrusting and twisting against each other. Lear looks to his past as a firmly structured and ordered place of factual certainties:

> Gloucester's bastard son
> Was kinder to his father than my daughters
> Got 'tween lawful sheets   (4, 6, 117–19)

The past in this instance is a source of information; it validates Lear's understanding and interpretation of the present.

In the meeting of Lear and Gloucester two phrases adverting to the past echo poignantly. Gloucester encounters the mad king and, though blind, knows him:

> The trick of that voice I do well remember:
> Is't not the King?   (4, 6, 109–10)

The sense memory brings comfort to the old man, whose bearings are lost but who is suddenly and simply able to glean comfort from the sound of a previously heard voice. The recovery of the past through the sense of hearing brings order of a kind to the lost, wandering old man. Lear's equally grim plight is given added force by his mad echo of Gloucester's recollection; for him there is no possibility of rest as his own crazy recognition drives him towards further confusion. Indeed, he knows Gloucester – 'I know thee well enough; thy name is Gloucester' (4, 6, 179) – but the manner of knowing him is bizarre: 'I remember thine eyes well enough' (138). He knows Gloucester on a deeper level than either suspects.

When Lear appeals to Gloucester's sympathy, he does so on the basis of a shared human memory: 'Thou has seen a farmer's dog bark at a beggar?' (4, 6, 156). He makes, or assumes, a sympathetic alliance with Gloucester on the basis of the experience of common life. The question is an appeal to the past and the unremembered but known experiences that their long lives imply; but it touches the audience in the same way. How would it touch an audience of beggars, one wonders.

> thy name is Gloucester;
> Thou must be patient; we came crying hither:
> Thou know'st the first time that we smell the air
> We wawl and cry.   (4, 6, 179–82)

The past is invoked here as part of sensory memory – the sounds and sights of shared, common, everyday experiences; it contains, as well, the unremembered but observed experiences of normal human life. As Gloucester's recognition of Lear's voice brings a vestige of order to his mind when it connects with the structures of the past, so even Lear, clad in what Cordelia later calls the 'weeds' of recent memories (4, 7, 6) and fretted in mind, nevertheless finds beyond his madness a kind of order in his memories. It is from these bases in personal and political history that arise the commanding horrors that fuse his personal plight with that of the suffering nation.

VIII

Less literally related to Lear's actual memory, but more painful by far, are the conflations of the normal with the monstrous, producing images of horror from the fusion of memories with fixed mythological information. Goneril and Regan are transformed into 'unnatural hags' (2, 4, 280), 'pelican daughters' (3, 4, 75), and Centaurs 'down from the waist' (4, 6, 126). In such moments the memory of his daughters is only a trigger of gruesome and haunting imaginings of monstrosity. The transfigurations of the observable world into monstrosity are part of a process that relies upon memory. Monsters, Girard posits, 'are surely the result of a fragmentation of perception and of a decomposition followed by a recombination that does not take natural specificity into account. A monster is an unstable hallucination that, in retrospect, crystallizes into stable forms, owing to the fact that it is remembered in a world that has regained stability.'[10] The recombination to which Girard refers results in the literalization of monstrosity; it acquires imaginary form and then a real name – Goneril or Regan. The 'unstable hallucination' is remembered, but not in a world that has regained stability. Rather it is remembered at this moment in the play in a world where the only stability is monstrosity, where evil deformation has become the norm.

In the last moments of the play's final scene, Lear's past, as both mad and rational monarch, merges with his present in a short, concentrated series of wrenching exclamations. Lear, '*with* Cordelia *dead in his arms*,' brings into conjunction those temporal spheres which have wandered in disorder through the play. The pre-play past and the play's internal past, the present and the future all are contained; both the detailed and the generalized knowledge of personal history tumble to the fore of the king's consciousness in a way that is only apparently random. Old and new history and new and old memories give new groundedness and stability to Lear in a form that seems once to have been natural. The old Lear of the first part of the first scene knows when one is dead and when one lives, with the terrible certainty of experience and memory. From the recognition that Cordelia is 'dead as earth' (5, 3, 261) flows the remorseless knowledge of that fate worse than his own death, that certainty of having been eviscerated by a tragic reality that compels him to reckon with the fact that the death of his own child has preceded his own. 'She's dead as earth' is a statement of simple and absolute truth; it is a declaration that acquires authority, emphasis, and status as truth by the metaphor to which it clings and by the meaning through which that metaphor manages to encompass the entire play. It is the surest, possibly also the simplest, statement that Lear makes in the course of the play; it is a felt and known assertion that includes both the object of his passion and the entire world that contains it. For Lear and those assembled in the exquisitely realized deathwatch in this tragedy, Cordelia's death is like the realization of the end of life on earth; it is Shakespeare's spectacular apocalypse. The idea and, to Lear, the reality of the 'death of the earth' signals the apocalyptic end of all value, all existence. The audience is presented with the idea that those who have killed Cordelia have also killed the once fecund earth. All vitality seems crushed in this image. The killing of Cordelia is a crime against nature itself. The present physical finality is extended, in his remaining words, to the dimension of time. Kent, Edgar, and Albany perceive the moment as the last horror of life, as the coalescence of the future with the present. To them the future has died in the present catastrophe.

Yet, while to these three observers of the scene life appears to have lost all meaning, it is left to Lear to rediscover purpose and validity. His words of grief, far from the nihilistic dogma of the three survivors, assert, anomalously, the value of life. He discovers the possibility of redemption and defines its exact worth:

> This feather stirs; she lives! If it be so,
> It is a chance which does redeem all sorrows
> That ever I have felt.   (5, 2, 265–7)

The past – the whole of Lear's life – crowds into the present and gives it a perceptible form. Cordelia's life has an equivalent: the sum total of Lear's agonies, which he offers in exchange for Cordelia's life. All of the felt sorrows of a long life that is about to be consigned entirely to the past, and the memories of those left behind, suddenly have tangible, measurable meaning; like love itself in the first scene, these griefs and sufferings are comprehended in the terminology of exchange. Lear's 'redeem' possesses a nice, clear mercantile sense as well as a religious one. The amorphousness of the past is distilled into a bitter drop of pure pain and offered like a sacrifice in exchange for a single consoling breath from the dead: a funereal ritual takes possession of the stage, with all of the protagonist's sorrows comprising the sum total of his history. But Cordelia, of course, is dead, and the usual systematic methods and means of consolation – words, rituals, history – are futile.

The word 'ever' in the phrase, 'that ever I have felt,' leads the king to further recognitions of eternity, recognitions that culminate in the great antithetical but logical swing to the repeated 'nevers' that he utters seconds before his own death. When Lear exclaims a few lines later, 'now she's gone for ever!' (270), the single word 'now' calls him back into the present from that realm of his past where the sorrows of his life are summoned into a single defining form of a measureable value. It is in his recollection of the quality of Cordelia's voice that Lear asserts control over his own history. He states a fact, which leads to a generalization, which becomes in the process a limpid truth:

> Her voice was ever soft,
> Gentle and low, an excellent thing in woman. (272–3)

Cordelia's *presence* is related to personal and general history. As Gloucester found comfort in the sound of his king's voice and the memories it recalled, so Lear finds in the memory of Cordelia's voice a way of reconciling the present with what once was. Clarity increases for Lear as he begins to situate himself in relation to his and Cordelia's past lives. In this awareness, tragically late in coming, he seems to be taking the opposite direction from those other Shakespearean characters, described by Alvin Kernan, who are 'caught in the movement of history, driven by their own passions and the historical forces at work on them,'[11] and who lose sight of the direction their world is taking. There is, Lear's memory tells him, a phenomenon of continuity by which individual life makes itself felt and is made a part of the whirling events of the past.

It is this realization that surely must account for the otherwise amazingly irrelevant recollection of his own prowess as a warrior and swordfighter. In one of the most effectively naturalistic leaps of his mind, Lear, with Cordelia dead in his arms, calls up a boast from his memory:

> Did I not, fellow?
> I have seen the day, with my good biting falchion
> I would have made them skip: I am old now,
> And these same crosses spoil me. (275–8)

In his rejoinder to the officer, the recent memory of his attempt to save his daughter recalls to Lear his old skill, whose loss is brought home by modern fencing practice[12] and his present troubles. In this sentence the cohesion of the modes of past time – both within the play and preceding it – in opposition to the present, give the remaining lines of the play their dynamic form. Lear's mind finds a resting point just as it begins to wander over the present. His memory of his old competent self seems to give him the strength briefly to face the fact of what is. The boast is like a respite from calamity; it takes him away from the here and now and lends him momentary assurance through a self-defining recollection in which the present and past conform to and confirm each other.

IX

It is the present only that remains to be faced; divorced from the past, it is made tangible and real through language and spectacle. This fact necessitates the second ending of *King Lear*. The structures of history and memory, while eternally present, are revealed as useless, constructs merely of illusion and desire. The forms that life is supposed to possess – individually yet consistently assumed in the mind of each character – are linguistic and functional. Characters in this play, including Lear, who connect through shared assumptions are connecting, after all, on the basis of words and ideologically and culturally constructed feelings. It is, indeed, to words and the kinds of consolations they habitually are understood to contain that Edgar resorts in the end. He is a kind of dramatic chorus, usefully removed and emotionally distant from the intense feelings driving the appalled others in this scene. By his attempt to define the disaster, even in his awareness of its resistance to definition, he is the restored agent of narrative wholeness charged with the task of giving form and meaning to what has occurred – that is, to assert some kind of human control over human catastrophe. To Edgar Shakespeare gives the task of supplying a perspective on the tragedy, even in his assertion of its incomprehensibility. Edgar's words acknowledge the paradox of the inadequacy of language and the plurality of meanings that are the inevitable by-product of speech. His words, in obedience to the demands of decorum, give the play conventional wholeness and dramatic form, just as their helplessness and faintness advert to his own failure to comprehend the moment and to give meaning to the tragic reality with which all who observe are here faced.

Edgar's final utterances are at appalling odds with those of the king. Lear's sound like uncompleted, almost instinctual or reflexive gasps of incomprehension, whose echoes linger much longer than the official ending of the play. They buffet against the closure that Edgar's historical perspective attempts to supply, and because of their greater feeling – amorphous and unclear – they rupture the very human desire for neatness and closure that Edgar verbalizes. Edgar's words also stand as a conventional attempt to restore memory and history to the collective mind. They speak to the consequences of a loss of memory and a degradation of history; indeed, it is the loss of these indices to the past – history and memory – that have made the tragedy. Edgar looks backwards and then forwards, bringing past and future into realignment:

> The oldest have borne most: we that are young
> Shall never see so much, nor live so long.   (5, 3, 325–6)

Lear's last words transcend the historical and linguistic dogmas by which characters in this play position themselves in relation to the events of the present. He digs deep into the very idea of a systematic universe, into the world of nature beyond history and time, and finds nothing. Why should a dog, a horse, a rat have life? The answer Lear seems to hear, and that his last agonized sounds point to, is a mocking silence.

CHAPTER SEVEN

The Past of *Macbeth*

What is true of endings is also true of beginnings. Lady Macbeth's myste-
riously missing children present an ominous, unknown, but undeniable
time before the beginning. Doubtful beginnings are also incidentally
inherent in such details of the play as Macduff's non-birth. Indeed the
beginnings, sources, causes of almost everything in the play are at best
nebulous.

Booth, 'King Lear,' 'Macbeth,' 94

I

Lady Macbeth's children, present either in her mind as a figment, or in
her memory as a piece of her history, allude to something singular and
usually unnoticed about the play. The characters of *Macbeth* are presented as possessing almost no personal history. There is only sparse
and scattered mention of the events and the time that precede the
beginning of the drama. For a play that centres vividly and painfully
on the effects of remorse – a feeling that by definition is possible only
through the exercise of memory – this is an astonishing fact. Indeed,
Lady Macbeth's words about having suckled her infant is one of
remarkably few specific memory references to a time earlier than the
events of the play. Memories like these lend sensory focus to the
present; they fill it suddenly and disquietingly with what are constructed as remembered feelings. More usually in *Macbeth* those feelings are of fear and danger and produce the sensation and threat of
panic in the actors in the tragedy.

Robert Louis Stevenson remarked, 'It is no wonder, with so traitorous a scheme of things, if the wise people who created us the idea of Pan thought that of all fears the fear of him was the most terrible, since it embraces all.'[1] Tragedy is, I think, a response to the human tendency to panic in the face of dread. The fear of disintegration is constructed as a means of warding off, controlling, or mastering the panic impulse. Tragedy is panic with circumference and form. The deconstructionist notion of immanent displacement, where the wholeness of the work is illusionary, is well exemplified in the constructions of tragedy. The success of tragedy is contingent on disaster and the danger of the narrative emotionally overwhelming the boundaries of completeness, which are only ostensible. What lingers beyond these boundaries is the power of the tragic – and panic – experience of calamity endured. Macbeth carrying two bloodstained daggers and confronting his wife, minutes after the central murder of the play, asks, 'Didst thou not hear a noise?' (2, 2, 14). He has heard the stamping of the hoof of Pan; the abyss yawns and he must act to avoid it. Evident here is a clear link between tragedy and memory: the memory that produces the impulse to panic is among the most powerful stimuli of the dread by which tragedy is animated and, at the same time, that it seeks to contain.

II

The characters of the play make only about a dozen direct references to personal experiences before the action of the drama begins.[2] These references fall into two categories; there are specific memories of particular events or people, and there are vague allusions to possible and probable memories of feelings and sensations that seem to have preceded the action. The categories are capable of resolution into subcategories and types, such as, in the first instances, the difference between persons actually known and remembered and those known by report. In short, the world that existed before the first line of the play is presented as nebulous and curiously disconnected from the present action. The play exists solidly in the present; its protagonists lean hopefully and desperately towards the future. This tendency away from the present and towards a better time is appropriate for a play so specific in its complimentary references to James, the reigning monarch, a play that, John Turner argues, explores 'the language, metaphor and myth of a society which we are encouraged to identify as the prehistory of the present.'[3]

The implications of such selective and limited temporal focuses offer subtle insights into the workings of the drama as drama, and drama as history. On the dramatic level, the excitement of the play is made more intense by this absence of the personal. On the historical level, the past cannot be measured or invoked as a moulding force in the lives of the characters with anything like the depth or power with which it operates in other dramas. In *Othello*, for example, every crucial action is almost literally informed by specified pre-play experiences, remembered actual events, and registered, if often distorted, history. This presence of the past richly informs and determines the play's character and direction. *Othello*'s past is replete with remembered detail and is a source of energy in the present, while *Macbeth*'s past is sparsely and randomly delineated; the difference in each case is a strong determinant of action.

This is not to say that the twelve references are the only evidence of past life. Clearly, other ways of presenting history and the merely personal past in *Macbeth* do exist. Certain historical realities are vivid. A multiplicity of facts, allusions, practices, habits of address, modes of discourse, modes of speech, and customs of verbal and physical behaviour indicates the reality of the past and the groundedness of the play in a vital history. Indeed, the drama insistently implies continuity with the history it enacts and with which it continuously becomes a part. For example, his title alone tells a great deal about Macbeth the individual subject and Macbeth the social and political personage. The title, Thane of Glamis, indicates a locus in a social order that itself is imbricated in an established political and historical tradition. Of Macbeth's history within this context we learn much within minutes of hearing his name: he is, according to the textual and paratextual information provided, a valued and loyal soldier of his monarch; he has wealth and friends; he is married; he is, more simply, a man of a certain age – young enough to be a vigorous warrior and old enough to command men; he inhabits an old country; his nation evidences a stable and long-established political system.

In other words, Macbeth, like every other character in the play, is making and participating in the making of history. These are material facts about Macbeth that the audience absorbs spontaneously because they are based upon justly unquestioned assumptions about drama and culture and social living. They help to preserve the illusion that this play, like all other plays, is a slice out of the past. The illusion is the more ambiguous in the case of *Macbeth*, since the drama is so specifically concerned with the monarch for whom it was to be performed and with the issue of treason, which remained so close to his own experience. As Steven Mullaney has written: 'at the heart of *Macbeth*'s dramaturgical concerns lies the developing absolutism of the Jacobean state. If sixteenth-century political cosmology precluded the possibility of a fully intentional treason ... that same cosmology radically restricted the power of authority to control or contain treason's amphibology ... James was endeavoring to extend the threshold, to redefine the boundaries of rule, and his claims for absolutism were ... grounded in the figure of a king who could, from his quasi-divine perspective, spy into the mystery of things, including the indecipherable countenance and amphibolic tongue of treason.'[4] The actual treason of the Earl of Gowrie and the strange correlatives of the story of that treason – such as the refusal of the traitor's corpse to bleed until the written evidence of its treachery was discovered on the body in the form of allegedly magical writings – made of *Macbeth* an uncanny, bordered mirror into which the king must have gazed with mixed but mainly satisfied feelings.[5]

Nevertheless, the facts are the mere givens of the drama. Its discursive constructions of the history or story that it tells are generally silent on, or only allude to, those features of the past that imply its own history. Indeed, my point very largely is that one of the singular aspects of the various discourses of *Macbeth* is the force of that very silence and the heavy emphasis on present and future that displaces it. The impetus of *Macbeth*, its energies and motives of violently gaining and violently keeping power, is *felt* and carried by a relentless tension between the present tense and the unremittingly hopeful anticipation of security supplied by the future. Part of the mystery of the witches of *Macbeth*, and of preternatural characters generally, is precisely that they are not subject to time or the constructions of history or, for that matter, to the changes that history and the past enforce. Paradoxically, however, just because they are old, it follows that they must be subject, in some usually undefined fashion, to the temporal workings of nature, even if not in a normal or recognizable human sense. The witches crucially define the drama: their presence in the first scene establishes the commanding authority of the uncanny as the new and essential realm of habitation and action. From the moment he sees them, Macbeth is made aware that he has ceased to live in a world of rational matters. This being the case, the irrational becomes valorized and the unthinkable and unmanageable suddenly acquire realizable possibility. This has become a world where the abnormal and absurd have the power to speak and to predict – all earlier bets are off. The witches are terrible evidence of the contamination that adheres to 'the warrior returning to his homeland, still tainted with the slaughter of war,' according to

René Girard, who goes on to explain that the 'returning warrior risks carrying the seed of violence into the very heart of the city' or among his people.[6] Macbeth moves forward from his encounter with the witches without having cleansed himself of the blood that clings to him after the battle. His plunge into murder is an almost logical progression by which he seals his connection to the present and his distance from the past.

III

The very first direct reference to any life experience prior to the beginning of the play appears in act 1, scene 4. Malcolm is reporting a version of the Thane of Cawdor's death by 'one that saw him die' (5). The speech alludes to the trust, faith, and friendship that existed before Cawdor's earlier treachery:

> That very frankly he confess'd his treasons,
> Implor'd your Highness' pardon, and set forth
> A deep repentance. Nothing in his life
> Became him like the leaving it: he died
> As one that had been studied in his death
> To throw away the dearest thing he ow'd
> As 'twere a careless trifle.   (5–11)

It is not clear that Cawdor is already dead at the start of the play – but it is possible. This second-hand report, however, strikes a peculiar note. The strangeness and violence of language and action of scenes 1, 2, and 3 are given a kind of respite here: it is a still moment of reflection that interrupts and thus momentarily transforms the process of history in the making that the play so egregiously is. Duncan's response to the speech, possessing the rhetorical hallmarks of yearning and disappointment, is deeply ironic:

> There's no art
> To find the mind's construction in the face:
> He was a gentleman on whom I built
> An absolute trust –   (11–14)

The past for Duncan was a good place with good men in it. We see here the beginning of the process of unravelling the present. The lines imply an impulse of reflection, which is a necessary precondition of the making of history: the speaker seems to reconstruct himself in the immediate present as a being outside his present self, as someone whose earlier self – unenlightened, unknowing, and innocent, but whole and comprehending – is being contrasted with his present self. This clash of selves, first heard in Duncan's sorrowful recollection, is the source of Macbeth's manic energy. As the Elizabethan theatre was forced to explore its own contradictory and anomalous place because of its marginal location in the city Liberties,[7] so the characters it created often enacted that marginality, compulsively driven by the need to bring the past into the present view. The divided nature of Macbeth's selves is not, however, contingent upon time, upon the past's habit of ambushing the present – as might be said of Othello; rather, it is the clash of interior with exterior realities that become tragically irreconcilable in him. The division of consciousness and of experience in Macbeth himself, and in the play more generally, is remarked by Graham Holderness, who writes of a 'central historical contradiction' at the heart of the play. 'Ambition in this society is not some eccentric personality-disorder,' he notes, 'but a central historical contradiction: a natural extension of the militaristic violence which is both liberated and restrained by the feudal pattern of authority.'[8]

Even Lady Macbeth, in the play's second allusion to the past, recalls a time when virtue held sway, and she contrasts it with the present, from which the past needs must become detached for her ambitions to achieve fulfilment. To her, Macbeth's formerly evident goodness has become an impediment to the present endeavour: it is old-fashioned. As we shall see, this is not the first time that life before the play impinges on the urgent demands of the present. In act 1, scene 5, she recalls her husband's potential insufficiency for evil deeds.

> Yet do I fear thy nature:
> It is too full o' the milk of human kindness,
> To catch the nearest way. Thou wouldst be great;
> Art not without ambition, but without
> The illness should attend it.   (16–20)

This passage, too, is only indirectly about what was. It refers to a wife's old knowledge of her husband. Thus, while the past is allusively incorporated, the use of the historic present contributes to the senses of urgency and immediacy that characterize the greater part of the drama. The 'wouldst' stands as an obstacle to the 'should' and generates a tension within the wife as she attempts to correct the contradiction between the selves of her husband.

Without doubt, the memory – specific, precise, tactile – of a pre-play experience that has prompted the greatest, deepest, most extensive speculation is that of Lady Macbeth in act 1, scene 7, when she recalls the experience of nursing her own baby: 'I have given suck.' (54). The reference to mothering her own child, and the warm, loving feelings and physical memories of being sucked on and releasing milk from her breast in a timeless rhythm, is contrived to seem grounded in felt recollections that have the power to evince the sensory memory of 'How tender 'tis to love the babe that milks me' (55). This is not mere rhetoric: the line's monosyllabism is a typical Shakespearean means of representing authentic emotion. Robert Weimann notes that it is the contrast between the elevated metaphor and simple everyday speech that sharpens the effect of both. Within the range of expressive modes, the 'everyday syntax and diction' can carry the force of tragic experience as powerfully as the elevated.[9] That Lady Macbeth should use the memory of that experience to drive home and recover her capacity for violence is her way of suppressing the gentle and 'natural' in favour of the possible: the Crown.

It is surely no accident that Lady Macbeth's next memory of her life before the play links her with equal force and solidity to other familial and tender realities. In act 2, scene 2, yet another specific, defined, and grounded memory gives the action a terrible and transforming jolt. Lady Macbeth has looked at the sleeping king:

> Had he not resembled
> My father as he slept, I had done't. – My husband!
> *Enter Macbeth.* (12–14)

This is one of those Shakespearean moments when the stated obvious merges with the unspoken in a complicated knot of connected linguistic and psychological implication. The primary force here is memory, but it is memory animated and transformed by nostalgia. The image of her sleeping father, reproduced in the sleeping form of the king, arouses remorse and conscience in this unlikely woman. Though we may be surprised that she has children, the moment brings to reality the obvious and unsurprising fact that Lady Macbeth is the daughter of a father. We must not, however, let what is obvious obscure what is true and strange: the sudden paralysing recognition of her father's face in that of her victim is a chilling return to the reality of psychological motive and scruple.

The moment radically reverses the movement of the drama. The past lives of these characters, only nervously present up to now, are shown to have a violently tranformative power and, in being so shown, indicate a powerful reason for the absence of the past or, more sinisterly, a reason why these characters may be avoiding it. Through the spontaneous exercise of memory, the past seems to leap unbidden and unwelcome into Lady Macbeth's conscious mind from that place in the subconscious where it is kept, only to be prompted to life by familiar images and likenesses. The drama is made fearfully intense here by the momentary possibility that Duncan's life, whose loss is signified by the bloody hands and daggers of Macbeth, might have been saved by the single coincidence of his resemblance to Lady Macbeth's father. Terrible nostalgia is contained in these words; it enforces upon Lady Macbeth a crippling coalescence of memory and feeling that forbids her to act out her desire. Our eyes, filled with the sight of Macbeth covered in blood, tell us that Duncan is already dead; our ears tell us that he might have been spared. The moment is suffused with tragic helplessness; the verge of going back has been traversed – from now on the idea of what might have been springs into awful life, only to be crushed by what is.

The scruple – Lady Macbeth would not have killed her father – adds something to the moment as it interrupts the rapid pace of the plunge to achievement and destruction. The moment is also pregnant with a sign of the weakness of the whole enterprise: that weakness, as the play intermittently and vaguely shows (and conceals), is the continuous presence of the buried past. The moment is punctuated by the recognition, made visible, of Macbeth's bloody appearance. Images and signs coalesce with the dominant words of the short speech giving way to the short parade of significant male figures: the king – the 'he' – becomes 'my father,' and 'my father' becomes 'my husband!' Male identities merge in the powerful image of Macbeth, who stands bloodily before his wife, as the two other male figures, father and king, are reconsigned to memory.

Yet the past, as constructed here, is not separate from the present. It is shown to be a crucial part of it. The fifth example of the use of the pre-play past is more purely and conventionally historical. In act 2, scene 4, the Old Man looks back to a less confused and turbulent time. He recalls:

Threescore and ten I can remember well;
Within the volume of which time I have seen
Hours dreadful and things strange; but this sore night
Hath trifled former knowings.   (1–4)

The human habit of trying to make sense of the present by comparing
it with the past is a way of supplying a comforting perspective to
present events. It is a familiar cry, perhaps more justifiable here than
usual. The old days were innocent by comparison. The past gives
authority to this grim evaluation of the present horrors. The Old Man
and Ross proceed to catalogue the recent eruptions and deformations
of nature as prognostications.

Macbeth's second reference to the past – and only the sixth overt one
in the play – uses the idea of history, the authority that the past is supposed to carry, to manipulate the present. Macbeth tells the two murderers hired to kill Banquo that

it was he, in the times past, which held you
So under fortune, which you thought had been
Our innocent self?   (3, 1, 76–8)

He asks them,

Are you so gospell'd,
To pray for this good man, and for his issue,
Whose heavy hand hath bow'd you to the grave,
And beggar'd yours for ever?   (87–90)

We and the murderers become ensnared by a possibly falsified version
of the past. There is, of course, no way of confirming this version of the
events before the play. What signifies, however, is Macbeth's perceived
need to use or invent history to advance his purpose. Thus, while he
strains to determine the future by the intense and violent perversion of
the present, so, inevitably, the past becomes corrupted and compromised, a thing of use and a means of stabilizing Macbeth's uncertain
rule. The murderers represent themselves as qualified for their task by
virtue of their personal histories, their subjectivity – in more than one
sense of the word – and their fitness for this work, as determined by
what they present as their lives to this moment. The Second Murderer
has been made 'reckless' by 'vile blows and buffets' (108), while the

First Murderer is 'weary with disasters' (111) and ill luck. Both are ready for labour, however criminal or violent. Private history, they assert, has moulded present disposition – an indirect but credible allusion to the social roots of crime.

The banquet scene supplies yet another occasion for the fusion of lies and truth; the past is pressed into the service of the present. Macbeth's access of conscience is explained by his lady as a manifestation of an old condition. When the ghost of Banquo prompts the plea (or threat), 'never shake / Thy gory locks at me' (3, 4, 49–50), Lady Macbeth attempts an explanation whose feebleness adverts to the schism between truth and falsehood that the Macbeth enterprise has caused:

> Sit, worthy friends. My lord is often thus,
> And hath been from his youth. (52–3)

The excuse is palpable and unconvincing: the hallucination is clearly fired by the recently suborned murder. The history Lady Macbeth here invents becomes an inadequate buttress of the present; it is invoked in order to give Macbeth's current behaviour a link to an innocent, past, pre-regal self. Furthermore, it argues the existence of a youthful, innocent Macbeth, possessed, even as a child, by private demons. The haunted, raving monarch is thus connected to a haunted, raving boy, untrammelled by the responsibilities of power and official authority. It is, of course, doubtful that such a youth ever existed. However, the effect of Lady Macbeth's invention is the creation of a parallel past, one that never was in reality, but that has acquired discursive existence in the present drama. The deformed and poisoned present of the play thus stands on the shifting sands of real and also invented history. The effect of such simultaneous histories – one true one false – is to drive the infinitely unstable present further into the wild, strange, and violent realms Macbeth has carved out for himself.

Macbeth himself, partly raving, partly lucid, harks back over the ages to a long and terrible history of murder in which he has become an infamous actor:

> Blood hath been shed ere now, i'the olden time
> Ere human statute purg'd the gentle weal;
> Ay, and since too, murders have been perform'd
> Too terrible for the ear. The time has been
> That when the brains were out, the man would die,

And there an end. But now they rise again
With twenty mortal murthers on their crowns,
And push us from our stools. This is more strange
Than such a murther is.   (3, 4, 74–82)

This is the clearest attempt so far in the play to locate the present in a sequential historical pattern. The 'olden time' is prehistoric, a period before the existence of law; it was, by Macbeth's desperate reckoning, a time of dreadful brutality. But even then the laws of nature were in effect: human life is linked through time by murder and violent death and a string of victims who, unlike the present victim, remained dead. The past, in other words, was a stable place, one in which cause and effect – savage killing and sequent death – supplied the safety of predictability: a man whose brains were bashed out was a dead man. In this moment, in which Macbeth recognizes Banquo, the play realizes its own temporal indeterminacy. Only a ragged and uncertain future can emerge from a present that is impervious to the laws of certainty, themselves another construction of the laws of nature. Macbeth's terror derives from the unforeseen reign of the unnatural, where nothing is but what is not. In *Macbeth* the laws of nature are in a constant state of transgression.

Macbeth's sense of history is shadowy and sweeping. He seems to prowl outside the cage of his past life, perceiving it as a menacing object that threatens to contain his entire being. His response to the threat is to immerse himself in the tide of the present time that is sweeping him to the future. The present in the play seems driven by a historic force, famously encapsulated in the repeated word, 'tomorrow.' He constructs history as a terrible and overwhelming force as he faces tomorrow: 'all our yesterdays have lighted fools / The way to dusty death' (5, 5, 22–3).

The contradistinctive historical force is invoked by Macduff in his English scene with Malcolm, who recalls stable and sure values embodied in the deceased persons of Duncan and his queen:

Thy royal father
Was a most sainted King: the Queen that bore thee,
Oft'ner upon her knees than on her feet,
Died every day she liv'd.   (4, 3, 108–11)

The past, as recovered or remembered here, acquires the sharp edges of persons, behaviours, actions, and precise Christian values. Macduff is both telling and showing it: he remembers king and queen in order to shape and comprehend the present.

His speech harks back to an apparently better time, to a more benign patriarchal world, a surer and more firmly set history that includes national myths and moral touchstones by which the nation has been directed and from which it takes its heroes and villains. From these myths and stories of Scotland's past Macduff draws a moral perspective on the present: he remembers and reminds Malcolm of what Scotland was and may be again.

By contrast, Macbeth's last memory of the world he once occupied and has now lost is contained in the dread-infected speech in which he recollects his capacity for ordinary human fear:

> I have almost forgot the taste of fears.
> The time has been my senses would have cool'd
> To hear a night-shriek, and my fell of hair
> Would at a dismal treatise rouse, and stir,
> As life were in't. I have supp'd full with horrors:
> Direness, familiar to my slaughterous thoughts,
> Cannot once start me.   (5, 5, 9–15)

Here, the past merges with the present in a virtually undiscernible shift. For four and a half lines Macbeth recalls a time gone by in his recollection of the person he once was: the time when he, like others, was susceptible to the feelings of fear; when he, like others, responded to a night shriek in normal terror; when his physical being – his reflexive instincts – responded involuntarily and naturally to the world of sensation. Gary Wills comments that this evident desire of Macbeth to overcome his own fears, and thus to triumph over his own memories, is part of a process set in motion after the murder of the king: 'Macbeth engages in a self-refashioning that amounts to sabotage committed upon himself. He systematically disconnects the systems of reflection.'[10] Systems of reflection are, of course, entirely dependent upon memory. Macbeth refashions a self almost without memory; his vain mission is to distance himself from the source of his pain. But his memory is, in the end, inescapable. It manifests itself in a myriad of ways, and no evasions can put it outside the pulsating interior self that gradually consumes everything it touches.

The final direct and specific reference in *Macbeth* to the world that existed before the play belongs to Macduff, as he brings into life the nightmare curse:

And let the Angel, whom thou still hast serv'd,
Tell thee, Macduff was from his mother's womb
Untimely ripp'd.   (5, 8, 14–16)

The brutal language here produces a curious and mixed effect. Nemesis in this play is necessarily a figure of violence; every dramatic detail has conspired to deny Macbeth a peaceful or a solitary death. The violence of Macduff's birth seems here to be evidence that the ordained mission of his life is to kill Macbeth. Mothers and motherhood in this play are ambiguous states in which suckling and giving birth are surrounded by images and details of violence and death. Macduff's invocation of his birth is a discursive and active means of realizing the hideous dream. Of course, the whole is predicated upon a sleight of hand: certainly Macduff was born of woman, unless the word 'born' is given an entirely original, etymologically unprecedented meaning. But there has been a rent in nature's design in a world of long ago; it is this detail that convinces Macbeth that Macduff's is the hand that will slay him. The past, that world of which Macbeth is an inevitable part but that he has sought assiduously to deny, is what defeats him in the end; a small tatter in nature's plan from a world he has almost successfully avoided is the blow that crushes the tyrant.

IV

The paucity of references to the pre-play past lends immediacy to the dramaturgical discourses of *Macbeth*. From a devastated present, the outlook for most of the play is more devastation, violence, and loneliness. The presentness of the action leaves, as the play's most powerful impression, a sense of dislocation – a dislocation heightened by the nearly ubiquitous imagery of disturbance. The great rush that the Macbeths are making towards the future gives a sense of panic to the enterprise, a sense intensified by the apparent absence of a world of past certainties upon which the present can safely rest or depend. Panic is the dominant mood of the early scenes of the play, a feeling that hardens into recklessness as the drama progresses; but recklessness built on panic is fragile. The early scenes of the play are in a constant state of anticipation of disaster. Action is the antidote to panic in this play, but it is not always efficacious; for here the panic born of the possibility of success leads to action that produces only more panic.

The play in large measure is about what it feels like to have killed the king, in the same way that *Hamlet* is about what it feels like to *have to* or to want to kill the king. The two plays depend for their terror very largely on nostalgia. As Hamlet hankers for the days of innocence before his father was dead, so Macbeth more intensely hankers for the moment, the second, the instant, before he took the fatal step. Thus, while the speech

> Had I died but an hour before this chance,
> I had liv'd a blessed time; for from this instant,
> There's nothing serious in mortality.   (2, 3, 91–3)

can look like cynical pragmatism, many will see in it nothing but the purest and most fraught expression of remorse in the language. These words are an attempt to surround and contain the invasion of panic and terror. This moment bites back at Macbeth for the rest of his life as though it were the moment he came into being; what alters as he ages in the course of the play is his manner of recollecting it.

The history of Macbeth's life loses meaning in the presence of the central murder. What matters is the present: to deal with, to cope, to do. These needs, after the crisis of murdering the king, are matters of great urgency that belong to the here and the now. The history of Macbeth is absorbed into the shadows that the present and future throw over the world he strives to hold on to. Macbeth's life as an outlaw starts after the play has started; his criminality is a feature of that present reality, one that appears to resists historicization; a resistance that is self-consciously centred in the hero himself, who possesses a defiantly individualistic, somewhat ahistorical and apolitical perspective on his own plight. Although his present life strews everywhere evidence of a past, in his conscious mind, in the words he speaks, Macbeth cannot linger in that old place. Yet, of course, Macbeth – the subject, the character, and the historical figure – is represented as having had both father and mother. His father, Sinell, is remembered only because his death authorizes Macbeth's thanehood; but his mother has no existence in the play: the marginal paternal presence and entire maternal absence are appropriate signifiers in this male-driven narrative. No word in the drama adverts or alludes to a place or time in which the parents of Macbeth existed or were relevant except, of course, in the probably fabricated history his wife provides to explain his hallucination at the banquet. By withholding references to normal, connective, familial bonds in the life of this character, Shakespeare has contrived a means of representing formidable and alarming dramatic pace through the agency of panic and a discourse that maintains its pace by notionally jettisoning the past.

By not providing Macbeth with a fleshed-out, substantial past, Shakespeare creates an impression of alienation: Macbeth seems not to belong to anyone; he is estranged even from the roots that personal history provides. He is a prime exemplar of Girard's 'surrogate victim,' the victim/scapegoat who comes from inside the community.[11] Macbeth is the scapegoat who is guilty of the crimes with which he is charged and for which he is sacrificed: the violence of Scotland and its raging, bloody mayhem achieves apparent resolution in his death by the massive exercise of communal violence that typically seeks to extirpate the seeds of its own self-destruction by locating them in the person of the nation's most visible villain. His dependence upon his wife is broken at the moment when he kills Duncan. Lady Macbeth, who remembers her father at an utterly crucial time, is weakened by the memory, but she is also, in a small way, redeemed by it. Her appalling intentional cruelty is momentarily interrupted by a sudden access of human feeling brought on by a potent and literally transforming memory: her role as murderess is changed to that of a woman with a conscience. Her inability to kill the king connects with the self-lacerating expressions of remorse and regret of her mad scene, where her subconscious mind reveals the existence of a latent humanity and moral instinct. Macbeth's tribulation is that the *agōn* between moral instinct and evil ambition is played out on the stage of his *conscious* mind: he knows, sees, and confronts the horror and evil within himself. The range and extent of his crime is manifested in the intensely present mood of his struggle. Macbeth's reflection is moral and emotional rather than historical: he doesn't yearn for an easier or more innocent time; rather, he longs to recover an easier and more innocent feeling.

V

Feeling is no less contingent upon memory than it is upon moral and historical knowledge. The play is filled with evidence of ancient historical memory. Notwithstanding the characters' almost pathological inadvertence to their own past lives, there are intricate layers of historical memory and detail everywhere evident in the discourses of the drama. Obviously, each of the characters (or subjects) exists in a historical context that each persistently and consciously recognizes. Those contexts include the linear history to which each sees himself connected: Macbeth locates himself in a line of Scottish kings, Lady Macbeth in a line of Scottish queens; Fleance is destined to continue an established line, while Malcolm's position is to succeed to it. In short, the past is systematized through the forms of living that the present takes. King James himself is one of the more vivid, if unacknowledged presences of the play. Gary Wills offers a multiplicity of details describing the play's homages to the monarch. He includes references to the ways, for example, that James – a Scottish monarch, after all – was *not* to be confused with Duncan; for James possessed a much touted ability to find, almost magically, the mind's construction in the face: 'He was like an angel looking through appearances, according to Coke.'[12] Moral certainty itself is measured by its deviation from or its adherence to established norms. In addition to the established laws of the land are the uncodified but iron-bound laws of custom – notoriously the law of hospitality – which reify the presence of that past.

In addition, the mythological pasts bring into being the ancient Scottish, pagan, and Christian 'history' in simplified moral form to add weight and authority to the discourses of disaster with which the present is informed. Golgotha, Bellona, Saint Colm, Hecate, and Tarquin are among those references whose shadowy presence in the drama helps to support a metaphorical structure by which history and metaphor are intertwined. The past becomes, in references like these, a non-material but substantial locus of precedent for the present. The past, in other words, looms ubiquitously in the play: it is large and it determines events, behaviour, and attitude to a considerable extent. It possesses chiefly a kind of abstract precision – it is a touchstone and a referent; but it seems, almost contradictorily, to have little materiality. Such materiality or literalness as the past does possess in *Macbeth* is limited and discrete, confined to remarkably few moments.

PART III

CHAPTER EIGHT

Messengers of Death:
The Figure of the Hit Man

I

A paradoxical kind of functionary, the messenger is both defined by the presence of borders and a means of defining them; his presence proves their existence. In pursuing his function, he separates and merges the opposing or alternative areas between which he operates. The messenger is a kind of cultural artefact who has become an index to the complexity of the culture in which he exists. He is a delegate who performs his task by negotiating different and often opposing spheres – that occupied by his employer and that described by the area his employer attempts to enter through his agency. His literary proto-type is Hermes, a unique god, who traverses the divide between upper and lower worlds,[1] while belonging to both and to neither – a god, that is, of the boundary. Boundaries can be fixed or flexible, impermeable or porous; they can be physical or hypothetical, ideological or geo-graphical, natural or psychological, individual or social. The job of the messenger is to penetrate boundaries, ideally, by free and easy move-ment across them: frequently, however, such movement is difficult and contingent. The messenger is a servant who is willing (for money or loyalty, or both) to move between, to mediate areas between characters that are rarely clear and most often unspoken, fraught with the dan-gers of intentions hidden or partly revealed and certainly apt to be misinterpreted by those to whom the message is delivered. This is why Hermes, the messenger god and the god of messengers, is colourfully mythologized in Homer's *Hymn to Hermes* as having, on the day of his birth, stolen Apollo's cattle, invented the lyre, and fooled Apollo by returning to his cradle and pretending to sleep.[2] His originary association with trickery, dishonesty, speciousness, acting, and performance lends some credence to the concept of message-carrying as an occupation that possesses an inherent taint. In some sense, this taint may have to do with the fact that all message-carrying implies reward for the messenger – possibly by the simple fact that the messenger is defined as being in the permanent or temporary employ of someone with more money and power than himself. He is, in other words, a usually willing servant chosen to do an often dirty job.

The plays of Shakespeare revel in the serious and comic possibilities supplied by the messenger figure. As well as his tricksterism, they construct the messenger's sinister side, encouraged, no doubt, by the disturbing contemporary presence of state-sponsored spies, agents, and assassins with which Elizabethan and Jacobean society was rife. Patricia Parker, for example, notes that there is a wealth of contemporary references in early modern England to 'delators as secret or "privie" informers (those who report *about* the secret and inform *in* secret) as part of the "floating population" of informers and spies in the years before more full-scale development of police and the policing apparatus of the state.'[3] The task of such delators clearly is the carrying of messages that have the power to do harm to their subjects. In Shakespeare's England, that is, Hermes the trickster has been overtaken by the cultural complexities and exigencies of the power-driven, paranoic modern state. The hired killer is very much a version of the sinister messenger. He moves between worlds; he, too, is a delegate and a crosser of boundaries, and though his work is violent and his message is both the death he causes and the meaning of that death, he remains integrally associated with the dark side of Hermes. Hermes is typologically dressed in a broad-brimmed hat and sandals and carries his caduceus, his snake entwined wand: the hired assassin's 'hat' persists symbolically in the necessary concealment of his mission, his 'sandals' in his need of entry and escape, and his 'caduceus' in the sword or club or pistol, which refer to the bloody message he carries.

The 'delators' to whom Parker refers are, of course, part of the apparatus of state. Grim, distasteful, and occasionally brutal though their jobs often are, they have the sanction of legitimate power standing behind them, however illegal or immoral their tasks. The suborner of murder exists or places himself by his action outside the law. He himself can come from the ranks of criminality, or he can be a representative of the highest legitimate authority of the state. As we frequently see in Shakespeare's plays, the monarch himself may hire a murderer from the outskirts of society to commit murder upon someone close to its centre and thus move his sphere of action from legitimate possession of authority to the realm of criminality. When a king hires a killer, he simultaneously employs means beyond the scope of lawful authority and preserves that lawfulness itself, objectifying (and, in a sense, abjecting) the 'illicit' in the person of the killer. For the figure of authority, the fact of murder indeed renders an illegitimate act 'legitimate' in the service of a greater cause. We all accept (without necessarily liking the fact) that spying and secret information gathering are necessary and even legitimate activities of government. We think, perhaps, that we are being realistic, rather than moral when we offer this acceptance, but we seldom condemn such activity, since practical necessity and occasionally simple survival seem to demand it. We may believe that there are limits to how much of such activity we are willing to accept. But the permeability of these limits – our willingness to stretch and to contract the bounds of 'acceptable' activity – is attested to by the chimeric figure of the messenger who sneaks through and beyond them, returning with his mission complete, never having needed to articulate what we often cannot afford to declare for ourselves.

II

A function of this chapter is to define and develop this porosity by concentrating on three messengers in Shakespeare's plays: *Richard II*, *King Lear*, and *Macbeth*. Although the messengers in these plays are subject to the wills of their masters, all have different relationships to payment, some defining it through money, others through service. For all of them, it is *words* that they carry, words that at once clarify their tasks and, because of the vagaries of this very medium, indicate their porosity. By this I mean that it is all too often words that betray the duties they perform, words that can cut their recipients in return, falling 'on the inventors' heads' (*Hamlet*, 5, 2, 537).

All message-carrying involves the superior and the subordinate in a kind of contract driven by two competing imperatives: it demands that the subordinate submit himself to the will or desire of his superior, but it also demands that the superior adhere to a moral understanding that renders the bond legitimate. While the act of using a messenger to communicate news or information may be innocent – a means, for example, by which the superior traverses geographical distance – the act of hiring a killer is more complex: it is usually intended to increase the distance between suborner and victim by interposing the messenger-killer between them, thus increasing, in a real sense, the physical and social distance that divides the suborner of murder from his victim. Between them stands the messenger of death, the hit man. The employer is connected to the intended victim by motive. The messenger-murderer himself, inhabiting that unclear space of in-betweenness that is fraught with motive, intention, interpretation, is almost always driven by one clear function – service in return for capital, be it in the form of money or advancement.

Murder is very nearly as old as human life. But while the hired assassin may be as old as history, he becomes a dramatic type in the early years of Elizabethan drama, first appearing in Thomas Preston's *Cambises* (c. 1561).[4] By the time of Shakespeare, the hired killer had become a staple of the Elizabethan stage, making appearances in no less than fifteen of Shakespeare's plays.[5] In Shakespeare, the hit man is usually a bit part, who is, nevertheless, the means by which the irreversible can be set in motion, often with tragic results. It is a truth universally acknowledged that anyone can be killed. Once that truth became firmly established in the human mind, it followed logically and inevitably that killing would become an enterprise and a trade. And because, as a rule, the victims of killing are unwilling, it followed further that the trade of killing would inevitably require skill, ingenuity, and even sophistication equal or superior to those skills necessary to avoid its successful execution.

The impersonal nature of his motive, that is, the mercenary essence of his contract to his superior, is perhaps the fundamental element of the hit man's value. His willingness to cross social and local boundaries is a by-product of that motive. The killer's efficiency at his trade is a significant qualification, although it is remarkable that the fixedness of the idea that anyone can be killed often produces the only apparent corollary that anyone can kill. Hence, we are presented fairly often with the drama of a mere messenger or body servant being charged with the job of killing, even though he has never shown any particular talent for it. Shakespeare gives us Pisanio, among others, as Sophocles gave us the Shepherd, charged with the murder of the baby Oedipus. Experience at the trade, in other words, counts. King Richard III's attempt to suborn Buckingham to kill the little princes, leaving the duke asking for 'some little breath, some pause' (4, 2, 24), convinces him to opt for experience over greed as a way of ensuring efficiency, and he uses Tyrrel instead. Richard discovers that it is preferable to hire a killer with no personal stake in the business beyond an acceptable salary. The choice of Tyrrel represents an interesting shift down the social scale to a working killer and away from the stratum of nobility – a stratum that in this case also implies qualm and conscience, which derive, apparently, from a refined sense of history and morality seemingly absent from the processes by which the poor are acculturated.

The usual differences between Shakespeare's aristocratic hit men and his ordinary or plebeian hired murderers are significant cultural markers. The dramatic formation of the suborned murder – its circumstances and its performance – are contingent on the language with which it is constructed. Shakespeare's well-born killers, when charged with the task of murder, tend to be shown reacting to the order or request, then considering it, and finally performing it. The language of reaction, consideration, and performance expresses class through style. We learn, as we observe this process, that there is something we might call a patrician conscience and, what is more interesting, that it differs from a plebeian conscience. That environment has a role in forming a conscience is not news, of course, but that social class is a factor in making that conscience more or less 'moral' is surely arguable. In Shakespeare, however, access to a refined language of interiority, as possessed by the socially superior characters, is often an index to a higher moral character. In the encounter between the hit man and the victim, a set of assumptions and subjectivities comes into play.

III

In *Richard II*, a play that avoids the demotic as its immediate successor plays indulge and revel in it, the act of murder, performed by a surrogate of the king at the king's veiled urging, contains some of the evidence of the existence of a class conscience as well as class consciousness. The murder of Richard is the great act and detail of the play. Around, within, and towards it, all other actions tend and are subordinated. The play asseverates and demonstrates that the killing of a king is unlike any other murder. Yet it is also very much like other murders, this same play grindingly insists, in that a man is violently deprived of his life. The consequence of the act forms its own gestalt: it includes the implements of murder, the accomplices to murder, the blood of the murdered man, and his dead body, which is the brutal but inevitable detritus of murder. These material facts are obvious to any caveman present at a similar event. More complex are the abstract realities that accompany these merely physical details. The abstractions, not all easily separable from the physical realities, include the sentient, speaking human beings involved: the protagonist and employer of the murderer (Bolingbroke), his antagonist and victim (Richard), and the messenger-mediator of murder (Exton and his helpers). Motive forms part of the immaterial, if not quite abstract, element of the gestalt. Violence, too, while visible, partakes of the physical reality while it also powerfully imbricates motive, language, spectacle, desire, doubt, and fear. Fear and its attendant emotions in this highly charged and complex spectacle is one of the means by which drama indicates and alludes to the boundaries within which the prisoner-king exists. The emotional effects of killing are a primary conduit to cultural and political realities.

There is no scene in *Richard II* where Bolingbroke actually delegates Exton to take his message of death to Richard, and both play and history are unclear about the extent of Bolingbroke's involvement – a confusion that provides Shakespeare with an opportunity to dive deep into the ambiguities and discontinuities he so relishes.[6] Exton's social position makes him a specialized descendent of Hermes. He asks his servants to confirm the evidence of his ears. Did not Bolingbroke ask, 'Have I no friend will rid me of this living fear?' (5, 4, 2). Does this mean he has been hired? Exton urges again in the next line, 'Was it not so?' Exton is no mere messenger and no ordinary hit man; he must have motives of his own for so emphatic a wish to benefit the new monarch. But these are left unspoken and so intensify the sense of uncertainty charged with fear that becomes the dominant mood of the last scenes of the play. Exton knows that murder is serious, and he indicates this knowledge in the euphemisms for murder in his speech. In the end, Bolingbroke does not deny Exton's assertion, 'From your own mouth, my lord, did I this deed' (5, 6, 37). Neither does he actually confirm it. Bolingbroke has referred to being 'rid' of Richard. The scene in which Exton, in his imagination, writes his contract with Bolingroke is shadowed with an ambiguity that must later be reconciled with the reality of Richard's violent death. Exton's doubt and fear are palpable; he seeks reassurance: 'He spake it twice, / And urg'd it twice together, did he not?' (5, 4, 4–5). Twice the servant confirms his memory of the delegation. But no words, spoken two, three, or four times, can shore up the act of murder. In the very act of announcing conviction, words also betray the gap between 'terror' and a 'heart,' as Exton strives, with the force that only doubt can supply, to interpret his new monarch's words and looks, even going so far as to translate his looks into language:

> he wishtly look'd on me,
> As who should say 'I would thou wert the man
> That would divorce this terror from my heart.'
> Meaning the king at Pomfret. Come let's go.   (6–9)

Again that word 'rid,' as effective in its equivocality as the word 'divorce,' accompanied here by compelling ethical forces of friendship and animosity. Exton, like any messenger, is driven by a form of moral imperative and allows himself to participate in a moral contract that, he argues, legitimates his bond to his employer: an upper-caste ally of the king, he needs to convince himself that he is doing the right and good thing for king and country. He reconfigures his contract with his evidently quite taciturn employer in terms that answer his own moral and emotional need. Like most of Shakespeare's patrician murderers (Hubert de Burgh comes to mind), Exton has the rhetorical ability, and the need, to word his desire for advancement as a matter of the public good.

IV

Murder by messenger is always premeditated murder; it reflects the desire to impose a new order on the world. This order, deriving from an evil act, is always represented as a countervailing force that threatens society. When, in Shakespeare, the social formation is altered by a crime, evil consequences follow. Whether the form of order it attempts to replace or unhinge is in itself good or evil is often left unexamined but, as in *King Lear*, loud in unspoken questions. For example, Jonathan Dollimore's version of the futility and hopelessness of the ending of *King Lear* has the unfortunate effect of suggesting that all the killings of the play are equal in their incapacity to produce moral or social melioration.[7] Legitimate order is powered by the apparatus of the state; illegitimate order is exclusively theoretical, since it is any order or idea of order that would overthrow and replace the legitimate. Although Exton is motivated by ambition, he acts on the rationalist belief that legitimacy is a construct separable from morality – a belief that the play does not endorse. As a messenger from the king, Exton recalls his contract with the king as a murder for hire. The discussion with his servants takes him from talk and validation to the act itself.

The murder scene is the delivery of the king's message. Like most messages, especially those as freighted as this one, it is subject to considerable interpretation. Hermeneutic pressure informs the scene of the killing of this king. The action is more than itself: it is a series of layered actions that contain a multiplicity of meanings and implications. Just prior to the entrance of Exton into Richard's prison cell, the Keeper arrives with poisoned meat. Although the Keeper belongs to this place, the meat itself is his message, and by his contract with Exton he is transformed into a messenger of a messenger. By the creation of this threshold within his own prison he becomes a surrogate killer in the employ of and inferior to a surrogate killer. To Richard's order that he taste food he has brought, the Keeper answers,

> My Lord, I dare not. Sir Pierce of Exton, who
> Lately came from the king, commands the contrary.   (5, 5, 100–1)

The portals of Richard's prison are the ominous threshold across which the spectre of death casts a long shadow. The Keeper's words contain the implication of death by poisoning, and while this play is notorious for the way it keeps primal emotion at bay, here is it suddenly and powerfully invaded with surprise, fear, anger, and grief. These feelings are enacted in the devastating murder that accompanies the messengers of violence. The 'rude assault' (105) of Exton and his hired helpers brings into play a new set of dramatic rules and practices. Richard's deep, primal sadness, magnificently displayed in his great soliloquy, is followed by a terrible spectacle of explosive savagery. Richard's reaction to the incursion of murder functions as a curious biological index of a renewed will to live, a will to survive in a world that has become the quintessence of despair and dread. The Keeper – a messenger of the messenger – bringing death, triggers an emotional exploration of kingship and its cultural overlay. The killing of the king resolves moral doubt as it throws the question of kingliness, of monarchy and its parameters, open to the murderers themselves and to the audience bearing witness to this slaughter that is also palpably a sacrilege. Yet the fact that the keeper is the messenger of a messenger shows that, while the king may be remarkably sentient, those employed to do his work are most often not – they act in a a moral vacuum. The intensity of the emotion almost blurs the distinction between stage and world, when the primal feelings and the learned feelings, and the carapace of history and ideology within which they are packed, are released into the open, if fetid, air of this prison.

The power of the messenger to transform the world by crossing a threshold is vividly reflected here. But the messenger's task is completed only when he can report the success of his mission. In the scene of Richard's death, the rage and the violence come as a kind of relief. Rage and violence have been implicit in this play from its opening scene; it is only here that they finally are given voice and here that that voice is enabled by the messenger figure, whose message has the capacity to transform the world he invades. Shakespeare constructs the scene's two acts of killing with an eye to the moral and human details of murder. The Keeper's cry for help brings the murderers to the scene almost as if they are rescuers rather than murderers. Exton is silent and speechless until after Richard has been killed, almost as if he is aware of his awesome place in history. He becomes, paradoxically, the unwitting agent of a historic relegitimization of King Richard, the means by which the Crown reassumes its moral and political value. The power to do this deed makes Exton the vital agent of the play: the killing of the king has consequences and ramifications and reverberations far beyond anything – any action or statement – in the play. The messenger is catapulted to the forefront of history. The assassin and his royal victim are symbiotically connected forever after. Assassination has a way of relegating the questions of right and wrong, of good kingship and bad, to irrelevance. What remains relevant about Richard is no longer whether he was a good, bad, or indifferent monarch: it is the fact that he was murdered. The intense emotions generated by the murder link the king to his English audience with renewed integrity.

Exton's response to Richard's last words burdens him with dread: 'this deed is chronicled in hell' (116). They reach deeply into his guilty soul and complement the searing clarity of Richard's ecstatic demise; they lend Exton terrible stature at this crucial moment. The magnitude of Richard's imagination transforms his murderer. The killer receives a revelation from the self-assertion of his victim: 'thy fierce hand / Hath with the king's blood stain'd the king's own land' (109–10). Exton is one messenger who possesses the imagination and compassionate power to utter his remorse in the true tone of tragedy. His dread threatens to engulf him when he comes to terms with his crime; Exton is the agent and the sharer in Richard's tragedy, acquiring in his agony an almost heroic stature that makes him worthy to be the king-killer of history.

Bolingbroke's repudiation of Exton marks this king in a way little else does. In exiling his own messenger, in punishing the surrogate doer of his own evil, Bolingbroke articulates an unspoken contract that obtains between all messengers and their superiors – that, if necessary, the messenger will embody the shame of the deed he has done so that 'authority' can proclaim itself. The new king's almost apocalyptic pronouncement of exile on his hit man sends Exton into a limbo of isolation and strangeness that even death cannot cure:

> With Cain go wander thorough shades of night,
> And never show thy head by day nor night.   (5, 6, 43–4)

The 'curse' is Bolingbroke's attempt to distance himself from the message. The theatricality of the freighted biblical imagery has the hallmarks of a hieratic ritual of cleansing. The king plays the part of a shaman casting out the force of evil and violence as he attempts to cleanse his world of its destructive energies; and he consciously casts the messenger as a scapegoat into whom are concentrated those undifferentiated forms of savagery that threaten continuing social discord.[8] The moral calisthenics involved in blaming the messenger for successfully delivering the message are extraordinary, and the messenger himself returns to haunt the new king with the message of his guilt. Oppressive guilt hangs over the conclusion of the play; it is conveyed by the king's reference to 'my guilty hand' (50) and implicates him fully in the murder. The word 'hand' can be taken literally and metonymically, in the latter case as a reference to Exton as a figurative extension of the king's person. Exton thus becomes the literal agent of his employer. Bolingbroke's imperial curse and his promise of mourning, of penance, of a crusade, of weeping, are suffused with imagery and agency of performance. The banishment of his messenger is only the most dramatic of the gestures left to him; this act constitutes the performance of remorse without being the thing itself. The messenger's fate is his inferiority.

V

King Lear's death-messenger is among the most notorious in drama. The Captain, surely the biggest bit part in Shakespeare, is given almost literal possession of the tragedy. His role as hired killer involves issues of class with chilling specificity. A man without money is given the task of doing a terrible thing for money. It is as simple and as complex as that. Unlike Oswald, whose messengership is a matter of crossing territorial boundaries and who has a real part in the play, the Captain seems to happen into Edmund's path, and his fortune is to be chosen as the bearer of tidings of death without his having been born to it. The killing of Cordelia takes place in the shadows of illegitimacy and crime, against a background of carnage and violence. Though it occurs offstage, this murder, delivered very much in the form of a message, expresses the explosive social and political wars around which the action constantly circles. The murder reminds us of efficacy and the terrible clarity of killing as a political weapon, and the message ramifies through the world in which it happens. The spectacular display of the morality and the social and ethical illumination implicit in the death of Richard are denied here. The Captain is unnamed; he is drawn from the ranks; he is promised fortune and advancement, even, as M.M. Mahood notes, to the point of ennoblement.[9] And he is ordered to murder prisoners. Like Richard, Cordelia is a prisoner when she is murdered. Edmund's instructions are blunt and to the point. No hint of moral compunction informs them. Yet there is, perhaps, just a hint of awe in his description of the job as a 'great employment':

> Come hither captain; hark.
> Take thou this note; go follow them to prison.
> One step I have advanc'd thee; if thou dost
> As this instructs thee, thou dost make thy way
> To noble fortunes; know thou this, that men
> Are as the time is; to be tender-minded
> Does not become a sword; thy great employment
> Will not bear question; either say thou'lt do't,
> Or thrive by other means.   (5, 3, 26–34)

The Captain bears a note, a message to Cordelia and Lear's jailers, that will give him the power of death over them.

Phyllis Rackin has described Renaissance history as 'a masculine tradition, written by men, devoted to the deeds of men, glorifying the masculine virtues of courage, honor, patriotism, and dedicated to preserving the names of past heroes and recording their patriarchal genealogies.'[10] To the list she could have added vice, evil, and the names and deeds of villains. For the heroism and virtue contained in that masculine tradition has and depends upon that other side of history, also written by men – the tradition of crime and violence by which so much of the heroism is set up to be judged. Sir Piers of Exton clearly belongs to that countervailing tradition, as does the Captain. The Captain, however, has no name; and it is the possession of a name that makes a man more than a cypher. A man with a name is the bearer of a Name, as though a name itself were a message to the world that the man is a representative of a house or family and is, as its possessor, capable of transcending death by keeping that name alive in his descendants. Unlike even patrician villains, nameless men lack the capacity for transcendance; they are reduced to numbers and deeds, body counts in war, masterlessness and anonymity in insurrection. And they are reduced in these ways by the political and ideological needs implicit in traditional chronicling described by Rackin. Named messengers – especially when their message is death – are aggrandized by history. Their deeds are large, their victims worthy, while the nameless hit men of history and drama are diminished and degraded by the fact of their utility and by being denied the historical validation that a name carries. Edmund's offer of ennoblement to the Captain is precisely the offer of a name and a place in the history of the future.

In this murder-by-messenger Shakespeare strikes at the heart of a brutal reality by employing surrogacy as means of killing. 'Men / Are as the time is' (5, 3, 31–2), avers the cynical Edmund as he triggers the event that will bring this world to its knees. Lynching Cordelia offstage produces the impression but not the spectacle of its brutality. Her dead body, borne onstage by her dying father, is the symbol of the triumph of violence and the image of the efficacy of murder. Edmund's instruction to his messenger carries exactly the tone of the world as he would like it to be. The Captain, says Mahood, is a 'serviceable villain who can be flattered, threatened, and cajoled into doing the worst of deeds ... a man at the very extreme of depravity.'[11] He understands manliness as the capacity to do evil without flinching; he is the creature contained in Edmund's chilling construction of the present world in which, 'to be tender-minded / Does not become a sword' (29–30). Like Exton, the Captain is metonymized by his employer. A man who is employed is defined by his employer. He is his function. (Yet Cordelia's body, which her father tries pathetically to make 'speak,' indeed speaks its own words of pity and tragedy, and of the whole mystery of death.)

I cannot draw a cart not eat dried oats;
If it be man's work I'll do't.   (39–40)

These lines address the issue of the relatedness of work to living an amoral life. They refer to a labour that is separate from ethical considerations and subordinate to the demands of survival and advancement. 'Man's work' – the murder of a man and his daughter – implies only its exchange value. Thus, I am not sure that Mahood is right about the Captain. Rather, I would propose him as the apposite and predictable product of this world of carnage. His namelessness tends to suggest a near-randomness in Edmund's choosing him and the possibility that many other men of no means would have regarded the contract in the same way.

The hiring of messengers always implies issues of class. The representation of these issues reveals ideological notions contained in the presentation of class. It remains the case that even in the representation of a hired murderer, the social class of the murderer is usually, and with notable exceptions, an index of his capacity for empathy. Both Exton and Hubert de Burgh, articulate and educated in speech, reveal highly wrought consciences when they are put under pressure by their tasks. The message that they deliver, however it may emanate from a place even higher than theirs in the social scale, produces in each of them heightened awareness of the suffering they cause and awareness of the moral implications of their deeds. Working- or lower-class messengers, including both the Captain and the many murtherers in the plays, are, with exceptions, crudely insensitive on both scores. The Captain's rough and ready response to the order to kill shows him to be socially adapted to the new order, where cruelty is more usual and normal than kindness and where the consequences of both are random. He has a kind of accidental identity in being chosen for the task – Edmund clearly does not know with any certainty whether the Captain will agree to do it or not. Lear's condemnation, 'A plague upon you, murderers, traitors all!' (269), declares the collapse of moral categories, lending strange credence to Dollimore's sense that things have come to seem distressingly equal in this world of disintegrating political sensibilities. Rather than being the rant of a disturbed mind, Lear's rage accounts – in some excessive but comprehensible way – for the horror that has befallen all the inhabitants of this world: no one is innocent.

In a perverse and unwilling fashion, Kent, Albany, and Edgar are part of the same male-driven engine of destruction as the messenger of death who hanged Cordelia, leaving the impression not merely that the messenger carries the message imposed upon him by his superior, but also that he and his message are the centre, the very meaning, of the world in which he operates. The death of Cordelia raises questions about the unintentional complicity of Lear's friends in the murder of the French queen. One question that grips every member of the audience of every production of *King Lear* is why these men don't get down to the business of rescuing Lear and Cordelia, and another is how on earth they are able to forget the 'great thing.' There is surely a level on which Cordelia is the victim of a larger political machine than the apparently simple conspiracy of a bad man who sends a bad man to kill her. What are lost or forgotten for a short but crucial space of time, as the younger men of Britain take breath after their battles, are, significantly, the old man and the young woman; they are visibly marginalized and forgotten in this masculine world of death. The centre of this stage of history belongs to those who will write it, and Lear and Cordelia are not among them.

Edmund's almost casual employment of a messenger to do his work of killing as a matter of simple political expediency is dramatically different in its way from the guarded and guiltily indirect manner of Bolingbroke. Killing in *King Lear* has become an apparently necessary, even normal, part of the political process. Killing is possible and it is definitive. In its final dreadful scene, the entire *Lear* world pivots dangerously away from the gravitational pull of the ideological forces that are presented in the morally polarized play as universal truths.

Edmund's use of a soldier, a relatively poor working man, highlights the business aspect of the contract by which messengers are hired. All the killers who possess social standing in Shakespeare express a need to acknowledge a higher cause than mere cash. They refer to patriotism, loyalty to their masters, and the security of the state to justify their work. Messengers, when they are poor, tend to be pragmatic. The poor were the majority in the world in which Shakespeare lived, but they are a minority in the plays. Cultural artefacts like drama leave the suggestion that the poor, despite their numerical superiority, are somehow peripheral to the social formation. Their relation to crime is a function of their poverty.

VI

Patrician crime, on the other hand, is associated in the plays with the pursuit of power and an increase of wealth. Shakespeare imbues this pursuit with a large moral scope, emphasizing the morality by a class-distinctive speech that valorizes the rich-poor divide, making it seem a natural and even desirable reality. But also, in the examples discussed above, the fusion of patrician with legitimate interests produces ideological and practical complexity. *Macbeth* opens with the presumption of the need for the state not merely to control violence but to use violence against its own citizens. In the play Shakespeare draws a distinction, Alan Sinfield proposes, 'between violence the state considers legitimate and that which it does not.'[12] What follows the legitimate killing of Macdonwald is a drama built around the confusion that results from the indeterminacy of the ideological formation of what is legitimate.

The patrician use of the poor to commit crimes on its behalf helps to keep the two poles of the social formation apart. Hence, Macbeth's indignantly righteous disgust at the murderers he feels compelled to use is a paradoxical and darkly comic reflection on himself, a sign of abjection as he attempts to take the murderousness from his own body and to emblazon it on another. Having convinced his messenger-murderers that it was Banquo, not himself, who thwarted them in some or other evil designs, and having thus provided them with a motive to kill Banquo, Macbeth elicits from the first of these (nameless) villains, the declaration, 'We are men, my Liege' (3, 1, 90), a statement that is reminiscent of the Captain's remarks about 'man's work' in *Lear*. Macbeth's response to this simple declaration is astonishing:

> Ay, in the catalog ye go for men
> As hounds, and greyhounds, mongrels, spaniels, curs,
> Shoughs, water-rugs, and demi-wolves, are clept
>
> . . . .
> All by the names of dogs ...
> Now if you have a station in the file,
> Not i'th' worst rank of manhood, say't;
> And I will put that business in your bosoms,
> Whose execution takes your enemy off,
> Grapples you to the heart and love of us,
> Who wears our health but sickly in his life,
> Which in his death were perfect.   (91–3, 101–8)

The very essence of the messenger is one who carries his business in his bosom, and the understanding between Macbeth and his hired men depends upon the secrecy of their contract. The speech intensely and wittily represents the social distinction between the murderous monarch and his agents. Macbeth, quite unlike Bolingbroke, is brutally direct, appealing to his hirelings on the most basic level of self-interest in a manner that indicates his knowledge of the misfortunes that have apparently dogged these two. His mistrust of them and his own abrogation of his contract with them is revealed in his secret employment of the Third Murderer, whose job is to witness the contract being fulfilled.

Macbeth's murderers are eloquent in their rough way. The blackly humorous response of the First Murderer to Banquo's 'It will be rain tonight' (3, 4, 16) expresses rage, violence, and finality: 'Let it come down' (17). The phrase, an ugly and ironic riposte, nevertheless has power and passion in it, and, for a moment, limns a killer who is larger and more human than the simple job he has to do. Not everyone who reads this passage sees the murderers as working ruffians. Marvin Rosenberg, for example, writes that these two 'are not the dregs of society. [Shakespeare] could have designed the killers at the Porter's level, lewd greedy fellows; instead he presented men of some feeling and with the verbal agility to give their feeling expression.'[13] The association of feeling and the verbal agility to express it conforms neatly to the paradigm to which Shakespeare himself sometimes seems to subscribe, although I would not regard the Porter as lacking in that particular gift. Class, in other words, and its accoutrements, such as an extensive vocabulary and rhetorical models of expressions of feeling, determine the human capacity for fine feelings such as compassion, sympathy, and an appreciation of refinement. This kind of nonsense, still alarmingly extant, as I think Rosenberg's remarks demonstrate, helps to marginalize social groups lower on the scale.

The killing of Lady Macduff and her son reveals a tense ambiguity about the reality of subornation. It is noticeable in *King Lear* that the Captain sees the killing of his captives as mere work, a matter of course. The murderer who kills Macduff's son meets resistance – as Exton met resistance. Paradoxically, resistance by the victim seems to make the murderer's task easier, not, as one might expect, more difficult. The boy stands up to the killer:

Son. Thou liest, thou shag-hair'd villain!
Mur. What you egg! [*Stabbing him*]
   Young fry of treachery!   (4, 2, 81–2)

The boy's abuse of and resistance to him gives the murderer a pretext for attacking the child on his own as well as Macbeth's behalf. 'You egg!' does not come from the job; it puts rage and motive into the murder. The presence of resistance is a challenge to services that require subterfuge and ingenuity as well as those that call for the violent taking of innocent life. The servant-messengers of drama are always at their best when they are in danger of being exposed. We might recur to Hermes himself, who displayed sufficient talent after the commission of his crimes to fool even Apollo by his appearance of innocence back in his cradle.

The dying words of murder victims carry considerable dramatic weight. In death, the character is often allowed access to new and powerful dimensions of his or her self. Life is not always so kind to dying men and women. Even Macduff's son transcends his preciosity, dying in a blaze of courage and compassion. His murderers fly from the stage in pursuit of Lady Macduff, while the heroic child occupies the stage fully. The murderers are the mere messengers of tyranny, while the child takes a place in the pantheon of Shakespeare's heroes. Perhaps, in this play about kings who are either terminally weak or terminally morally ill, and about soldiers who are at first praised for heroism in killing and later condemned as dead butchers, the disorder of the world is most vividly demonstrated in the fact that true courage is left to a child to display. Cordelia, on the other hand, has no dying words. She is murdered offstage and her murderer is killed by her father. The whole burden of her death is borne by Lear and the whole of his final appearance is moulded by the experience and memory of her death. We note, however, that he begs her to speak, to leave him something of herself, a message that connects them. The Captain's purpose as an agent of a greater power has been served. True, he is killed, but as a mere captain, he is also allowed to disappear like most other hired killers of lower social class. The murderers of *Macbeth* disappear altogether, with no history following them to penitence or, indeed, no other sign of consciousness.

VII

We may look to Exton and his ilk for the morality play of conscience acting upon crime. Richard's last words sear Exton to the brains, but that is largely because he is patrician and, according to some of the stereotyping in the plays and the critics, he has brains. Hubert, only a would-be assassin, after one encounter with Arthur becomes a quivering mass of sensitivity and fine feeling, leaving us with the impression that to further his ends John should have looked lower on the social scale to find a man who could do the job properly. Hubert and Exton have in common that patrician virtue, lauded by Marvin Rosenberg, that nicely complements their elevated discourse – a viable and active conscience that is set into trembling motion by moral eloquence. The man who would have blinded and then murdered a child at the behest of his superior is transformed by the child's eloquence and furthermore, unlike so many rough villains, has the capacity to be so transformed. More apocalyptically, Exton realizes the wages of his sin and wanders disconsolately into exile, his heart heavy with the knowledge of his crime and his mind, presumably, reeling with the treachery of his employer.

Several politics of power are at play in these constructions of murder by messenger. One is the way in which the plays seem to collaborate in and advance social myths about the moral implications of class. The somewhat skewed image of the social world that the plays present indicates a social formation dominated numerically and relationally by the upper classes. The plays also make the issue of the hiring of murder a measure of the depths of cynicism to which tyranny can sink. The use of messengers of all kinds, from note bearers to surrogate killers, has the effect, usually by design, of keeping a distance between the hirer and the recipient of his message, with the messenger mediating that distance at all times. Thus, Bolingbroke's wriggling away from the responsibility of killing Richard, while successful, is possible only because of the mediation of Exton. The power of the messenger as a political tool is the underlying truth that tyrants recognize. In these and other plays in which Shakespeare employs messengers of death we see something of the consequences of embarking on this particular course of action to resolve conflict. The inevitable moral consequences to the murderers of their acts of murder remain, however, part of the imaginative fantasy of drama.

CHAPTER NINE

'Noseless, handless, hack'd and chipp'd':[1] Broken Human Bodies

I

The cohesion of the group is a necessary precursor of political action. Group action implies and depends upon bonds of common interest uniting the body of people who make it up. Such interest, while normally understood to be constituted by self-interest – such as a desire for change or, equally, a desire for things to remain the same – can also be wrought from negative desire, such as a shared dislike or abhorrence for those things that the group perceives as a threat to its unity as a group. Sometimes such perceptions may be justified by rational group fear – the threat of invasion or war, spreading epidemics, mass starvation, and so on – and sometimes these fears may take the form of commonly felt antipathies that lack any real basis in evidence or reality, but that nevertheless have the power to take hold of the imagination of the group and induce fear and loathing, through which it then becomes united. A palpable reality of political life is the recognition that group action may be driven and manipulated by reference to external threats to the group's cohesiveness. The group is, by definition, a single body of differentiable individuals united – more or less – by overriding common interests and values. Thus, while it is not necessary, desirable, or even possible for a complete unanimity of value, certain significant values need to be agreed upon for the group to survive as a group.

There are, however, certain basic feelings that, while overlaid with cultural connotations and implications, are nevertheless universal and, as such, transcend the interests and forces that distinguish the group as a political entity; that is, they are common to almost all individuals and therefore to almost all groups. One such feeling is disgust, a powerful emotion that, disgust theorists like William Ian Miller tell us, is produced in human beings by similar conditions – substances, fears, feelings – in all cultures. Miller points out that the facial expression that registers disgust is the same in all cultures and that the object or spectacle that causes it has common sources. Disgust, he goes on to remind us, 'is a feeling *about* something and in response to something, not just raw unattached feeling.'[2] To unite a group of people in disgust, which is a feeling of physical revulsion, is a potentially powerful means of uniting the group. Disgust, in other words, is not ideological but is a spontaneous physical reaction. We can learn to mime disgust when imagining notions that we disapprove of; but real disgust is an involuntary physical response. Moral revulsion has less force than the intestinal, instinctual, and spontaneous revulsion produced in the group united by sheer visceral aversion.

The overwhelming source of disgusting matter in human life is the human body. When its contents are safely enclosed and protected by the skin, the body is not normally disgusting, but the reality of its capacity to produce and expel disgusting substances makes it a ready source of disgust and, for us all, the most immediately available such source. When bodily substances and parts are separated from the body, disgust is most strongly felt. While the body is whole, and its life-sustaining matters are safely enclosed by the skin, disgust is kept at a distance; once the substances and the body parts are separated from the body, however, they and the body itself – producer of these substances and objects – acquire the power to disgust. The disgusting has a paradoxical and troubling additional power: it can attract us just as it repels us, often possessing an allure equal to that revulsion. The disgusting produces a fear of contamination; for while fear without disgust 'sends us fleeing to safety and to a sense of relief ... disgust puts us to the burden of cleansing and purifying.' We have, Miller continues, 'a name for fear-imbued disgust: horror.'[3] And few things more rapidly produce this kind of horror than evidence of human partibility. The demonstration that human body parts are separable from the human body usually arouses feelings of horror; horror at the spectacle of the disordered body and at the demonstration of the simple ease with which partibility is accomplished: it could happen to any of us. Then, to further complicate matters, the maimed or mutilated and therefore re-formed body itself can inspire disgust.

It should be clear by now that I am referring to visceral disgust at the apprehension via the senses of things that arouse the emotion, not mental apprehension through ideas and notions of that which we find disgusting. A disgusting idea may inspire the facial expression that registers disgust, but more powerful than the idea is the sight, sound, smell, tangible feeling, and spectacle of disgust. In other words, the engagement of the senses produces a sensation of disgust that is, probably in all human beings, stronger than that sensation produced by words alone. I think it has been fairly said that the spectacle of the eye-gouging of Gloucester produces a far stronger reaction in an audience than the spectacle of Lear at his most fraught – that is to say, of course, a far stronger visceral reaction. The reason is clear: the *sight* of eyes being gouged and the possible engagement of other senses in production, like sound, have a direct and visceral effect that produces horror and disgust in equal proportions. If well executed, the representation of this kind of horror on the stage has the effect of uniting an audience in an immediate and visceral way. When audiences act as though they are united in feeling, they express themselves with laughter, groans, gasps, usually – although not always – produced by dramatic representations more than by words. The power of the visceral lies in its spontaneity. Horror is horror for all. So, while philosophers may quarrel about the meaning and moral power of a moral point of a narrative, there is little to quarrel about in the response to the obviously disgusting when it is given spectacular form. The surround of why, how, who, and what lose currency in the immediacy of the audience's experience effected in unison. One of the attractions for Shakespeare of the Senecan example is the capacity that certain forms of violence possess to galvanize an audience simultaneously in this one potent feeling. When Medea murders her children onstage, as occurs in several of the many versons of this story, the question may be asked whether we are more horrified by the act of child-murder or the half-hidden bags or robes containing the mutilated remains of children. I would argue that the horror felt at the sight of already dead, bloody child bodies is the more potent reaction. The presence onstage of a simple sack containing the head of a man, if it is used effectively – that is, treated with carelessness and, say, dropped with an audible thump – produces a kind of uniformly felt disgust and horror. On the other hand, what we can absorb theoretically can arouse feelings of disgust and horror, but within the bounds of the mental capacity. The disgusting onstage must be parcelled out by degrees and portions, like laughter. An audience to horror onstage can easily be satiated and react with what the writer may not have wanted: laughter, which becomes a refuge from excess of horror. There is, it seems, a limit to how much of the disgusting we desire in our aesthetic diets.

The language and spectacle of Shakespearean plays richly exploit the particular power possessed by drama to unite an audience emotionally by calling up images of the damaged body to produce horror through disgust. An audience, united momentarily in horror, is a congregation whose emotional energy is for that moment concentrated on a single object. Gloucester's eyes, plucked from his body, held in the naked hands of Cornwall and Regan, and then presumably discarded like vile jelly, as partible eyeballs, produce a far stronger reaction than Othello's hypothetical but ugly threat to chop Desdemona's body into bite-sized morsels. This threat to cut a woman into bits is a common trope in Shakespeare and in the drama of his contemporaries. The idea shocks us, but I don't think it disgusts us.

In an age when public mutilations were carried out by officials of the state, violence against the human body such as the punishment visited on Philip Howard, Earl of Arundel – whose treachery brought him to be 'hanged until he were half dead, his Members to be cut off, his Bowels to be cast into the Fire, his head to be cut off, his Quarters to be divided into four several parts and to be bestowed into four several Places'[4] – would have given a chilling resonance to the quite common and popular theatrical performances of dismemberment. It is unlikely that the public mutilations would have lessened the response of disgust that such actions have the power to bring. Dismemberment as practised on the stage and off has at least two sources of disgust: the thing severed or gouged – the hand, nose, or eye of the subject; and the remaining human body, dead or alive – the once whole person now disfigured, the symmetry of his or her body thrown out of order. It is well established that the first apprehension of that disordered body, while it can and often does come to seem ordinary with familiarity, arouses our disgust. Shaking hands with a person whose hand is deformed may be initially uncomfortable, but the discomfort can ease over time; the sight of a missing finger can become familiar; those first impressions are compounded of pity and disgust. The politics of disgust refers to the common human reaction – a force that unites the spectators and marginalizes the object of that spectatorial gaze. The sight of the object or what one allows oneself to imagine is the sight of the object – the thing onstage that stands in for the severed part, eye, head – is crucial. That is, the possibility and the apparent fact of partibility are partners in the provocation of disgust. Consider, by way of contrary example, the fact that the broken hymen of the violated virgin does not provoke disgust: it must, indeed, provoke strong reactions, but disgust is not among them. (We are disgusted and horrified by Lavinia bleeding from hands and mouth because of the dismemberment. We are not disgusted by knowing that she has been raped.) The reason for this is, surely, that the broken part of the virgin's body remains within her body, the evidence of violation being the very predictable blood flow; but externally, the victim remains intact in appearance, her skin apparently whole. It is the cutting off or away of what is visible that produces the emotion of disgust.

What becomes of a body part once it is separated from its host, the human body? On the stage, unlike the hospital where we may have left our tonsils, appendixes, and even prepuces, the body part never simply becomes garbage. It has the solidity of an identifiable thing – even if we cannot see it – that has been violently torn from its natural place. It is like newly created matter: a thing is made from the human body that had no prior independent existence. In other words, as a part of the human being literally becomes a useless, functionless piece of garbage, it simultaneously acquires new and original significance.

The Renaissance stage is littered with severed, gouged, and mutilated parts of human bodies. Hieronimo's tongue, Piracquo's finger, Annabella's heart, Lavinia's hands and tongue, Gloucester's eyes, the heads of countless victims, and even Hotspur's thigh, to name a few, all possess a powerful presence on the stage. These are a few of the visible human remains endowed with the function of producing dramatic, spectacular, and ideological effects. As each piece of human flesh is brought into existence by violence, it is absorbed into the dramatic moment by emotions of shock frequently intensified by disgust. These moments, because of the violence that produces them, engage emotion at the expense of reason. They are those authentic moments of dramatic excitement that every playwright and director aims for – an audience powerfully embraced by their words and spectacle. And that is the point. However often we might watch the scene in which Gloucester's eyes are plucked from his head, we are never quite prepared for it or able to watch it without horror – always supposing, of course, a good production or an engaged reading. The concrete reality of actual stage mutilations are differentiable from the linguistic imagery through which Shakespeare so frequently presents isolated parts of the human body as metonymic equivalents for actions and states of being and by which we are never quite so shocked as we are when we see noses, ears, and lips made gorily concrete. Thus, for all that *Hamlet*, in John Hunt's memorable image, 'looks like a dissecting room, stocked with all of man's limbs, organs, tissues, and fluids,'[5] it doesn't really, and nothing in it produces the visceral disgust and horror that we find so vividly in the charnel house of *Titus*.

In *Hamlet*, Hunt argues, Shakespeare portrays the body as 'a collection of pieces whose morbidity intimates their ultimate violent dissolution.'[6] This is, of course, a metaphor. Some plays practise the literal production of these 'pieces,' methodically performing the actual deconstruction of the human body. Even more ingeniously, and in addition to the literal mutilations in Shakespeare mentioned above, the constantly adumbrated pound of flesh in *The Merchant of Venice* forms a powerful quasi-literal image in the play's dialogic structure. This image, partly because it is not precisely described by Shylock until nearly the end of the play, makes remarkable demands of the audience and impels it to acts of participatory imagination with a relentless persistence not found in any other play. Gloucester's eyes are plucked out while he is tied down, a helpless victim of violence; Macbeth's head is cut off after he is dead, acquiring oppressive hermeneutic weight in the process. Titus allows Aaron to cut off his hand to save his sons and then he goes on to commit some of the bloodiest carnage on the Elizabethan stage. Shylock, however, never acquires that part of Antonio's body he craves, but he describes it almost lovingly and hankers after it with obsessiveness bordering on monomania, dragging the fascinated audience with him into his game of imagination of his prize, its shape and form.

The body part taken from a living body comes into existence in its own right simultaneously with the experience and expression of terrible physical pain. The excruciating and disabling agony that accompanies the bringing into being of, say, an eye as an eye, a tongue as a tongue, or a hand as a hand is an inevitable and essential part of its identity. Worse still, the thing dies as it is created, and the cry of pain that usually accompanies its creation is also a cry of recognition of an irrecoverable loss. As the part is separated from the body, and because that body can never again be whole or complete, the victim is both physically and mentally transformed.

The accumulation by soldiers of 'enemy' body parts, such as ears, genitals, scalps, noses, and hands, is a practice as old as warfare itself. Frowned on though it is, the act of mutilation of enemy corpses is a ritualistic, sometimes deliberately sacrilegious act of desecration, which proclaims the triumph of the mutilator and the evidence of his victory. Seen as a rite of passage for some soldiers, it is the transcendence of disgust that makes the act difficult and the difficulty itself that makes it a rite. The sexual mutilation by the Welsh women of the English soldiers, referred to in *1 Henry IV*, which so disgusts the English nobles for whom the acts are described, is evidently a ritual mutilation intended to prevent the ghosts or spirits of those soldiers from rising against the Welsh in the future. A thousand of Mortimer's men were killed,

> Upon whose dead corpses there was such misuse,
> Such beastly shameless transformation,
> By those Welshwomen done as may not be
> Without much shame retold and spoken of.   (1, 1, 42–6)

The nature of the mutilation unites the hearers in the kind of revulsion that mere killing does not. Mutilation of corpses is a different order of violence than the mutilation of living persons. It is a deliberate desecration, an act of superstition, or one of violent contempt, which argues the presence of fear in the mutilator. Severing the hands of the enemy is more than a ritual, it has practical meaning, since it can prevent reprisal: thus, the mutilation is made as disabling as it is deforming. If René Girard is correct in arguing for the imitative nature of violence, the mutilator typically tries to ensure, by the nature and kind of mutilation he inflicts, that the imitation of his crime lies outside his victim's power.[7]

All instances of bodily mutilation in Shakespeare involve power relations at their most basic and crude; these include moments when the subject is completely under the physical power of another, a prisoner whose body seems to belong to his captor. He or she can be transformed, with an audience watching, into an object of disgust, a deformed, broken being whose physical nature is violently reconfigured. For all the pity and sympathy elicited by the plight of this victim of violence, he or she nevertheless becomes contaminated by the brutal act that has been committed against him or her. The victim of mutilation arouses horror and disgust as well as pity. But even then, the horror and disgust and pity have the paradoxical effect of rendering the victim even more fascinating. Normally, instead of making us avert our gaze, we are captivated by the very sight that repels us. This paradoxical function of disgust is part of the sensation of dread that pulls us in two directions at once, not unlike the alarming desire to jump off cliffs and tall buildings that most of us seem to have felt at one time or another. The fascination of dread, the desire to look and avert the gaze at the same time, is often produced by the disgusting – attraction and revulsion tugging the observer in contrary directions. The good dramatists recognize and exploit that paradox.

II

The excision of Gloucester's eyes is probably the most notorious piece of brutality in Shakespeare, made more ugly and evil by the taunting that accompanies the act of eye-gouging by two villainous characters, whose capacity for evil is nowhere better illustrated than in this act of blinding the old man. The first eye is prised out by Cornwall to the horror of all watchers except his wife. Marvin Rosenberg describes various methods of intensifying the horror that have been used, including a production in which Cornwall gives the plucked eye to Regan, who smashes it in her cupped hands, imbricating in the action the sense of touch, which so often complements the disgusting sight.[8] Following the plucking out of Gloucester's first eye is a sixteen-line dialogue, which includes a violent fight between Cornwall and his servant in which Cornwall is fatally wounded and that Regan ends by running the servant through from behind. During this interruption of his blinding, Gloucester sits tied to a chair, writhing and groaning in pain and watching the terrible events with his remaining eye. Then follows the appalling moment when that eye is torn out to the accompaniment of the words, 'out vile jelly!' (3, 7, 82). Significant here is Cornwall's recognition of the disgusting properties possessed by these organs. He plucks the eyes out, but his own revulsion is evident in his description.

Eyes are eyes; they have no inherently moral or attractive or repellent properties in or of themselves, but they have utility. Yet, as Gloucester's eyes are torn from their sockets, they instantaneously become objects of horrible revulsion: their innate properties are gruesomely exposed – they are glassy, bloody, venous, and squishy. Removed from their proper places in Gloucester's head, the man's two eyes become repulsive objects, while minutes before (possessing precisely the same properties) they were merely his eyes and lacked any power to harm or contaminate us. Now, as disgusting, dead, and misplaced organs, they possess an almost magical power to galvanize an audience in a common feeling of horror and revulsion, a feeling that is

shared with Cornwall himself. The metamorphosis of eyes into vile jellies is immediate, and the feeling of disgust that the process produces
marks the power by which an audience can be united in feeling and,
hence, in power. We become complicit with Cornwall's powerful
authority in our shared revulsion towards the vile things that Gloucester's eyes and, by extension, Gloucester himself have become. The old,
eyeless man is contaminated by his own terrible plight and in that
plight possesses, we believe, the power to contaminate us by it; hence
our disgust at Gloucester himself. The expression or even simply the
feeling of our own revulsion in the form of a facial expression connot-
ing disgust – and I know no one who does not recoil in disgust at this
point in the play – is a talismanic gesture that we seem to suppose will
ward off the effects of that contamination.

The plucked eyes become dead flesh, while the body goes on living.
This is a crucial part of the equation. Mutilation that does not produce
immediate death is the creation of deformation. To Girard, mutilation
becomes a reciprocal action; it takes the direct form of a 'loss of differences, a "becoming the same" at the hands of those whom violence has
already made identical ... Mutilation ... must be viewed as the creation
of fearfully deformed beings and as the elimination of all distinguish-
ing characteristics.'[9] While Regan and Cornwall in this scene become
monstrously changed and morally irredeemable by the mutilation they
perform on the old man, it is he, the wounded survivor, whose new
and suddenly produced physical deformity produces a disgust that is
more visceral, and hence more fully felt by the audience than the moral
disgust it feels for his attackers. As Gloucester's eyes become part of
the ghastly detritus of the drama's violence, so Gloucester himself becomes reconstructed as one of the play's human physical wrecks, a
helpless lurching blind man with blood and ghastly ooze seeping from
his sockets. He has been virtually annihilated. From his position of
proud independence, he is thrust into a landscape of misery and desti-
tution. More than that, his blindness turns him into one of the grotesques and pariahs who people that landscape; Gloucester has been
made useless. Without his eyes, he lacks one of the essential coordinates of the human being. The effect of his mutilation is almost to
dehumanize him, or at least to deeply change his humanity. The play's
imagery of monstrous transformation applies with apt literalness to
the reshaped, monstrously altered Gloucester, now consigned to that
circle of his world where monstrosity exists; he is the realized deformity of Lear's imagination.

The cruel reality of the physical mutilations upon living human beings is that their victims are transformed into physical grotesques, people in whom the order of nature has been artificially distorted. As their severed parts become detritus, what is left of their bodies becomes the object of revulsion, pity, fear, and trepidation. The virtually universal fascination with the likes of Mother Teresa or St Catherine of Siena is that they *seem* immune to the shaming, but real, revulsion most of us experience in the presence of deformity and visible disease – that is, the kinds of mutilation of the external body that nature or other people (mutilators or surgeons) produce. Mutilation is one way in which human beings actually turn other human beings into 'others,' that is, into human beings whose lot it becomes to be regarded as monsters. Usually we assume human monstrosity to be an element of physical appearance that one is born with. Marie-Hélène Huet, however, on the subject of monsters and people who are often called 'freaks,' discusses the social basis for the traditional explanation of monstrosity. Monstrosity was initially thought to reside in the *unlikeness* of the monster to his or her legitimate parents: 'More specifically, monsters were the offspring of an imagination that literally imprinted on progeny a deformed, misshapen resemblance to an object that had not participated in their creation. They were products of art rather than nature.'[10] While Huet is here describing the superstition that once explained monstrosity as the product of a pregnant woman's imagination, there remains the practice of actual artificial production of monstrous deformation in human beings through art (tattooing or piercing) and violence (the practice, for example, of deforming children to be more effective street beggars). Kathryn Schwarz discusses the production of monstrosity by artificial means. Writing on the missing breast in Amazonian literature, she talks of the effects of mutilation: 'Diseases of the breast threaten to literalize the Petrarchan process of fragmentation, displacing the tropes of aestheticized desire with a horrific actuality. In midwives' manuals and anatomical texts, loss of the breast seems to inspire a horror matched only by the loss of the womb; aesthetic and medical preoccupation converge in the certainty that such a mutilation can produce only monstrosity.'[11] Depending on the extent and kind of deformation, the victim of deformation remains a social being, more or less marginalized – sometimes in proportion to his or her deformity. Mutilated humans are often regarded and treated in much the same way as naturally deformed persons, and like them, can be relegated to the social margins. While this marginality can be

explained as a manifestation of unsympathetic superstition, the fascinated disgust of the spectator likely precedes the mythology with
which monstrosity and deformity are surrounded.

Indeed, Miller explains how monstrosity unsettles us with its capacity to produce chaotic disturbance of our assumptions and expectations. Monstrosity, with its power – well understood by Shakespeare –
to force us to look at it or suffer self-consciousness in forcing ourselves
not to look, is disturbing: 'Something pre-social seems to link us to a
strong sense of disgust and horror at the prospect of a body that
doesn't quite look like one, either grotesquely deformed by accident or
disorganized by mayhem.'[12] He explains this disgust as an emotional
reaction, provoked by visual stimuli that have their own aesthetic. It is
not, he argues, that we fear intimacy with the monstrous, the hideously
ugly, or the deformed, or their intimacy with others, but that we know
how we see them and could not bear to be seen thus ourselves: 'The
horror then is not in being intimate with them (though that too), but in
being them.'[13] In short, it is the fear of contamination that provokes our
fear of difference and monstrosity and that gives rise to the disgust by
which that fear is expressed. The disfigured form of Gloucester is a site
of the contending impulses of pity and revulsion; for him there is apt-
ness in being under the care of a madman, one in whom rational
responses have no place, in whom, that is, disgust has died; he is a man
who 'eats the swimming frog ... [and] in the fury of his heart, when the
foul fiend rages, eats cow-dung for sallets; swallows the old rat and the
ditch-dog; drinks the green mantle of the standing pool' (3, 4, 132–5).
In reality, of course, the love and care of Edgar for his blind father with
the bleeding eye sockets teach us how disgust can be overcome by
love, revulsion tamed by its healing power.

III

The partibility of the fragile human body – and the horror we feel at its
evidence – is nowhere in Shakespeare more vividly represented than in
Titus Andronicus. The violent mutilations of the play powerfully test
the dialectical oppositions of disgust and pity – frequent partners of
horror; this drama is a crucible for the conflict of these emotions, challenging both its internal and external audiences. Tragedy, we are
reminded, almost always includes violence against the human body.
Francis Barker argues convincingly for the existence of a 'more inter-
nally robust connection between the dramatic scene and the seen body

than one merely of perversity of taste.'[14] To Barker, the 'visibility of the body in pain ... is systemic rather than personal; not the issue of an aberrant exhibitionism, but formed across the whole surface of the social as the locus of the desire, the revenge, the power and the misery of this world.'[15] The visibility of the body in pain, however, can be both systemic and personal. Indeed, the excruciating but precisely detailed violations of various bodies effectively personalize the pain and bring what is political into the realm of the personal, effectively enforcing the two realms of experience into a single, painful reality largely by the agency of feeling.

That reality finds expression in the aesthetics of excess that underlies the actions of *Titus Andronicus*. The relentless carnage of the play is a violent assault on the private and public sensibilities of its audiences; social and personal categories become confused in the sheer volume of violence – the quantity of blood shed, limbs lopped, body parts cast away, the killings and physical desecrations. In the process, Gillian Murray Kendall argues, language plays as vital a part as the physical actions of maiming and dismembering.[16] She writes, 'Perhaps language is always more effective when used destructively in a world where language is something that inevitably fragments and distorts that which it seeks to convey.'[17] The play's multifarious acts of brutality against the body are made the central focuses of a verbal drama of horror that derives its power from rhetorical and spectacular displays of human horror. But spectacle, it has been argued, is more disturbing than language, and this play satisfies on both levels. It produces body parts with abandon: a tongue, four heads, three hands and several corpses are some of the properties of the play. Carla Mazzio has made the point that 'the rupture and consequent scattering of heads, hands, and eyes can be seen to thematize multiple anxieties about integrity and fragmentation, the severing, wounding or symbolic elaboration of the tongue is a particularly charged form of mutilation.' In particular, she adds, the loss of the woman's tongue is linked to the birth of a voice, resisting the notion, therefore, that 'agency is located in a body part.'[18] The dramatic excuse for such excesses those of *Titus Andronicus* is simply excess, which, paradoxically, has its own limits. Indeed, this play is notorious for its testing of these limits and often strays, in the views of many of its audiences, outside the realms of its genre. The language is, of course, a crucial part of the process; its literalizing metaphors, its repetitions and accumulations function with a force similar to the relentless expanding spectacle of excess. Albert Tricomi notes that the language of the play, 'self-consciously focuses upon itself so as to demonstrate the manner in which figurative speech can diminish and even transform the actual horror of events.'[19]

The complementarity of excess in both speech and spectacle is captured in the moment when the messenger returns Titus's severed hand with the severed heads of his two sons. The dialogue focuses extensively on the severed hand. Verbal flourishes surround the object as it becomes the obsessive focus of a series of speeches that have the effect of putting the victim several removes from the object itself. That is, the episode of Titus's severed hand and the words with which it is constructed seem an attempt to neutralize horror by language. An audience might normally be galvanized and united in disgust by the horrible spectacle of a hand being cut from a man's arm. This spectacle, horrible though it is, is so overlarded with hyperbole and grotesque action as to inspire ridicule. Shakespeare releases the audience from the responsibility of its own disgust by making a joke out of the horror, by forcing laughter out of cruelty. Indeed, 'horrid laughter' has become a critical term for the risibility that Titus's antics evince in the observers of his almost ludicrous distress.[20] The excess overcomes the impulses of compassion and alienates the viewers of pain and the disgusting sight of the handless arm. There are some gruesome flourishes, including the ghoulish injunction to the handless, tongueless Lavinia to 'Bear thou my hand, sweet wench, between thy teeth' (3, 1, 282).

This repulsive grossness is made palatable by its own excess and made absurd by its sheer implausibility, and culminates in a kind of hermeneutic hysteria as Titus overloads the object with more meaning than it can bear; the efficacy of the disgusting sight is carried to the brink of the absurd by spectacular and linguistic hyperbole and reiteration:

What violent hands can she lay on her life?
And wherefore dost thou urge the name of hands,
To bid Aeneas tell the tale twice o'er,
How Troy was burnt and he made miserable?
O, handle not the theme, to talk of hands,
Lest we remember still that we have none.
Fie, fie, how franticly I square my talk,
As if we should forget we had no hands,
If Marcus did not name the word of hands! (3, 2, 25–33)

Titus's hand thus acquires an existence separate from Titus himself. It becomes an object of discussion and bitter, ironic reflection; it exists in its disembodied form to stimulate awareness of itself and to function reflexively as an index of the ruthless criminality of his enemies. Thus the hand, before it is cast onto the growing heap of body parts, is given powerful symbolic existence within the play, although it has been robbed of its power to disgust by the superogatory attention to which it is subjected. Katherine Rowe concludes that Lavinia and Titus, 'in their complex relation to their missing hands, test the seamlessness of physical metaphor, question the "natural" associative logic in the fact of being a body and having a hand. If dismemberment symbolizes loss of effective action in the world, it is clearly the condition of political agency in the play.'[21]

The disgusting objects that Gloucester's eyes become lose significance as they hit the boards, as the focus turns to the eyeless man. On the other hand, the picture of Titus holding his severed hand produces an effect of horror simply through the display of his own dead flesh. The existence of the hand as a prop, brandished like a trophy on stage, is the sign of unalterable change in Titus. Like Gloucester, his adjustment to his new role as a deformed and maimed and monstrously changed man requires adaptations that make demands on his internal and external audiences. In him we discern, perhaps, a newly charged, even manic energy, which contradicts the apparent enfeeblement to which he has been reduced.

It is Titus's killing of Lavinia that most completely recognizes the extent of the deformation that the mutilations have wrought. The sexual pollution of his daughter is one of the reasons he gives for her murder. But the implication remains that the appalling and disgusting object she has become since, a handless, tongueless, disfigured counter-example of a useful and beautiful woman, has made her more of burden than her father can bear to consider. Simply, she is an irrecoverably hopeless, somewhat repellent, and useless member of community, and her death is a kindness to all – including, evidently, herself. In her maimed state, Lavinia has no social function. While she lives, she remains the delirious focus of attention, the image and evidence of the damaged world of this play. Bate writes that Lavinia's body 'is at the centre of the action, as images of her pierced and wounded body are central to the play's language.'[22]

Die, die, Lavinia, and thy shame with thee;
And with thy shame thy father's sorrow die!
     [*He kills her*].   (5, 3, 46–7)

Mutilation is the visible demonstration of human fragility. The horror of the spectacle of mutilation, and the human monstrosity that it
can produce, is the inevitable recognition that it can be worse than
death. Lavinia's death comes as a relief, not because she has been
raped or that she is 'impure' and unmarriageable, but because the sight
of her, of her pathetic and, yes, her disgusting, bleeding, suppurating
human flesh – of her mouth that oozes and does not speak, of her arms
that end in horrible, unsightly stumps that wave helplessly and revolt-
ingly around in the desperate desire to be expressive, has been
removed. The wounded Lavinia is a reproach to us all. She is a tragic
victim of violence, but also a visible sign of our own partibility, and as
such – against our wills, perhaps – she disgusts us. Her death comes as
a relief partly because it kills our own disgust with her and with ourselves in whom servitude to disgust seems, as we watch the horror of
her deformed life, greater than servitude to pity. When Lavinia is alive,
we are repelled by her deformities; when she is dead, we are consoled
by our pity for them.

IV

The most notorious of all Shakespearean body parts is the one that
never actually materializes: the pound of flesh. While it is true that
Shylock specifies only late in the play that the pound of flesh is Antonio's heart, this is not articulated initially and, as a result, has led
criticism into strange and interesting conjectures. Eventually, Shylock
reveals what he and Antonio have known from the outset but Shakespeare has withheld from his audience until the trial:

> Ay, his breast,
> So says the bond, doth it not noble judge?
> 'Nearest his heart,' those are the very words.   (4, 1, 24–51)

The vagueness up to this point has left open the possibilities of the
nature of that pound of flesh. James Shapiro points to the frequently
used phrase in which the flesh is 'cut off' Antonio's body, rather than
the heart 'out' of it; and Shapiro speculates that 'an occluded threat of
circumcision informs Shylock's desire to cut a pound of Antonio's
flesh.'[23] He goes on to propose that the pound of flesh, somewhat mys-
teriously alluded to until the trial scene, is a hidden but threatening
reference to castration, citing sources and precedents for this confusion

that the play's vague references encourage. One such reference is the suggestive and ambiguous and ominous

> An equal pound
> Of your fair flesh, to be cut off and taken
> In what part of your body pleaseth me.   (1, 3, 145–7)

The phrasing carries implications that disgust. A piece of a man's flesh, Salerio asks Shylock, 'what's that good for?' (3, 1, 46). And that is the point: it is good for nothing, but the man dies or is mangled in the process. While we are left uncertain as to the part of the human body from which the flesh is to be taken, our imaginations are free to wander around that body and conjure up the disgusting spectacle. We are not allowed to be certain whether the man is to be permitted to live after this ghoulish surgery – until, that is, Shylock tells Tubal, 'I will have the heart of him if he forfeit' (3, 1, 117). From the moment he signs the agreement, Antonio seems a doomed man; not only in the sense in which he lives in the shadow of his own death, but rather in the sense that his whole being becomes subordinate to this piece of his flesh. His body is whole, but his identity includes a piece of that body outside itself.

Shapiro argues that the pound of flesh, especially with its genital connotations, follows and contributes to a tradition of anti-Semitic writing that goes back to the Middle Ages. It refers somewhat obliquely, he says, to the ritual practice of circumcision and hence to a mythical power to threaten gentile sexuality. This putative, but quite compelling example of genital mutilation, which is later transformed more specifically into cutting out a heart, is a reference to a body part whose cutting off carries powerful symbolic connotations and cross-cultural inferences. The sexual mutilation of men is a practice as old as warfare; its implication in The Merchant of Venice is proportional to the mystery of the meaning of the pound of flesh. The pre-Romantic Shylocks, who were mere caricatures of villainous Jews with their sharp knives, Judas-like red hair, hooked noses and alien manners, would have terrorized audiences with their evident thirst for a pound of human flesh severed from a Christian body; and if the Jewish practice of circumcision made Christian men quail for fear of the safety of their own genitals through identification with Antonio's plight, so much the better for the drama.

From the moment Antonio's masculine wholeness is threatened, he is under sentence of mutilation and the concomitants of mutilation. In the eyes of the audience, his body has changed. Thus, every glance at him by us or his friends becomes almost prurient, as though our gaze includes a proleptic disfigurement. The pound of (missing) flesh, like Gloucester's missing eyes, becomes an element of his persona, with a separate identity from the man from whom it is to be taken. Its image haunts the play quite as powerfully – in an imaginative sense – as the vile jellies that are Gloucester's eyes possess their stage, but it does so without producing the visceral disgust that accompanies the plucked out eyes. Body parts possess a context in the play's most famous speech: the Jew is anatomized, but not literally, and we see the difference: 'Hath not a Jew eyes? Hath not a Jew hands?' (3, 1, 52–3). The contrast is brutal and devastating. The brilliant fullness of Shylock's awareness of what it is to be human, the completeness of his picture of the means and ways in which we are alive, make his catalogue of body parts sinister. He deeply wishes to commit murder by the literal severing or gouging of flesh from the body of another.

Potentially, the violent act of cutting out Antonio's heart is one in which the state is to conspire with an individual in the legitimate murder of one of its own citizens. In forcing this pass, Shylock is seeking validation for murder by the use of social sanction. He is on the verge, he thinks, of making fools of all of Venice, forcing its citizens to conspire with him in the performance of an illegal act, sanctioned by the highest state authority. The trappings of religious ritual are brilliantly travestied, with Shylock playing the role of a priest/ritual slaughterer and the Venetians standing by as his reluctant acolytes and witnesses. The sacrificial ritual adumbrated here is a travesty of the blood sacrifice, but its very perversity lends an objective perspective to the process of sudden violent dismemberment occurring elsewhere in the plays. Collectivities in which sacrifice is practised concentrate their social pathologies in the victim as a substitute for intra-social hostility and destructive urges. That is why, as Girard reminds us, in societies where blood sacrifice is practised, the victim is always taken from that society's margins – typically prisoners of war are used – so as not to exacerbate social tension within the group. Girard points out that the ritual victim must come from outside the community, and that if the ritual of sacrifice did not 'limit itself to appropriate sacrificial victims, but instead ... vented its force on a participating member of the community—then it would lose all effectiveness, for it would bring to pass the very thing it was supposed to prevent: a relapse into the sacrificial crisis.'[24]

A measure of Shylock's power and intelligence is the extent to which he, an outsider, forces the hostile community to conspire in the sacrifice of one of its most valued members. Even Antonio cooperates in the inverted ritual by slipping obligingly into the role of sacrificial victim through his compliant construction of himself as 'a tainted wether of the flock' (4, 1, 114). The fact that a wether is a castrated ram contributes to the hidden imagery of genital mutilation throughout the first three acts of the play.

The pound of flesh, like the body parts cut and torn from other Shakespearean victims, is living tissue about to become waste matter. The potential dead flesh of *The Merchant of Venice* is charged with implication and meaning. Its existence is precisely coeval to and concomitant with the death of Antonio. The exact moment when the pound of flesh is expected to come into existence is the moment when Antonio will die. Thus, it looms obscenely over the actions involving Antonio and Shylock, a disgusting figment of the mind, inchoate but bloody, always bloody and always standing for human violence, like all other severed body parts in the plays. The phrase, 'pound of flesh,' and the image it invokes are a curious amalgam of the exact and the amorphous. Shylock is vicious in his determined scrupulosity in bringing a set of scales to the execution. What we have brandished before us by the sight of the scales is the idea of one pound of human flesh, of bleeding skin, muscle, and fat. Yet, as the phrase is repeated, reiterated, contemplated, the thing that it is becomes increasingly present and evident in the texture of the play's discourse. To each person who uses the phrase, except Shylock, it has a vivid and repellent meaning. Its gross materiality is its overwhelming truth; what it stands for in legal, juridical, personal, or historical terms seems inconsequential in relation to the brutal means by which it must be exacted.

IV

Body parts in Shakespeare's plays are one means of galvanizing an audience in a common emotion of disgust. They function individually as horrible objects that have the power to unite an audience in revulsion. They can be aids to strong sensation by exploiting the simple but real fact of the object itself as a piece of the human body that is suddenly defined by its redundance. Out of the complete human body is produced something terrible but, in an inevitable way, fascinating as well: a thing that has no proper place has been brought into existence.

It is a paradox made concrete; for it acquires being as it simultaneously acquires inutility and lifelessness, except, like Lavinia's tongue or Antonio's pound of flesh, as the symbolically charged object that can be a conduit or guide to meaning. We respond differently to severed body parts than we do to dead bodies. Dead bodies, ubiquitous in the plays, do not produce the powerful, sudden, emotional revulsion that body parts do. Hotspur's body as a body arouses little interest until Falstaff hacks at it with his sword and reminds us of its partibility and his own capacity for brutality.

One of the significant achievements of *The Merchant of Venice* is its manner of withholding the sight and fact of the piece of Antonio's body while simultaneously supplying it with continuous, powerful resonance as an imagined object whose merely conceptual existence dominates the drama. Once the pound of flesh has been given imagined life, it achieves an ineradicable presence in the play as a determinant of juridical and ethical action. The literal presentation of objects such as Titus's hand and Gloucester's eyes radically interrupts their narratives; the parts, being actualized through violence, have a fragmenting effect on the dramatic flow, producing the spectacle of sheer horror.

The stage presence of an object, including a severed, useless body part, is never independent of its political and moral context. Indeed, few objects exist on the stage that as forcefully and violently recall the immanent contextuality of subjects and objects as vividly as the body part that has been severed from a human being. Whatever the motive of the character who inflicts mutilation, the fact remains that a social basis for the mutilation surrounds it. That basis can be as plain as the desire or need to render another person harmless in the context of relations of power, and it can be as complex – psychologically, socially, and politically – as the desire to inflict pain and suffering on another while reaffirming the power of the inflictor of the wound. Thus, the violence of dismemberment has dimensions not associated with assault alone: it produces loss in many forms. In addition to the physical, the loss can be complete social death for the maimed victim, as she or he is marginalized by his or her literal disfigurement to become an object of disgust or revulsion.

Notes

1: Tragedy and the Nation

1 Edwards, *Threshold of a Nation*, 243.
2 Vaughan, *Othello*, 16.
3 Greenfeld, *Nationalism*, 65.
4 Vaughan, *Othello*, 22.
5 Helgerson, *Forms of Nationhood*, 198. See also Weimann, *Shakespeare and the Popular Tradition*, and W. Cohen, *Drama of a Nation*.
6 Helgerson, *Forms of Nationhood*, 198.
7 Greenfeld, *Nationalism*, 49–50.
8 Gellner, *Nations and Nationalism*, 7.
9 Ibid., 57.
10 Hobsbawm, *Nations and Nationalism*, 37.
11 It is noteworthy and unsurprising that the word appears with greatest frequency in *Henry V*.
12 Helgerson, *Forms of Nationhood*, 195–245. Describing the uniqueness of *2 Henry VI*, he writes that in the play, 'Against the negative and exclusionist strategy of noble self-aggrandizement stands the positive and inclusionist ideal of the king and commonwealth ... [But] what Cade's rebellion does is to push that inclusionist ideal towards its own exclusionist extreme' and thus undermine it (207).
13 Neill, 'Broken English and Broken Irish,' 3.
14 Ibid., 10.
15 The term 'culture' is used here in what Gellner calls its anthropological sense; that is, 'the distinctive style of conduct and communication of a given community' (*Nations and Nationalism*, 92).
16 John Keegan discusses the sharp division among 'pre-historians' on

whether 'pre-men' were aggressive towards each other in *History of Warfare*, 115–26.

17 Benedict Anderson defines the nation as 'an imagined political community'; it is imagined because, he says, it is only in the minds of its members that the image of their communion lives (*Imagined Communities*, 6). Furthermore, I would suggest, it is imagined because the notion of communion is based upon a set of impossibly purist assumptions and goals.

18 Ignatieff, *Blood and Belonging*, 5.

19 Ibid., 5.

2: History and the Nation

1 Rackin, *Stages of History*, 4–8.
2 Lyotard, *The Postmodern Condition*, 81.
3 Holderness, Potter, and Turner, *Shakespeare*, 19.
4 Greenfeld, *Nationalism*, 36.
5 Belsey, 'Making Histories,' 44.
6 Greenfeld, *Nationalism*, 47.
7 Weimann, *Shakespeare and Popular Tradition*, 166.
8 Axton, *The Queen's Two Bodies*, 114.
9 Berger, 'Psychoanalyzing the Shakespeare Text,' 215.
10 Belsey, 'Making Histories,' 35.
11 Pugliatti, *Shakespeare the Historian*, 108.
12 Greenblatt, 'Invisible Bullets,' 41.
13 Belsey, *The Subject of Tragedy*, 6.
14 Pugliatti, *Shakespeare the Historian*, 119.
15 Ibid., 130.
16 See, especially, Holderness, *Shakespeare Recycled*, 130–78.
17 Belsey, 'Making Histories,' 44.
18 Rackin, *Stages of History*, 206.
19 Smidt, *Unconformities in Shakespeare's History Plays*.
20 Holderness, *Shakespeare Recycled*, 54.
21 Axton, *The Queen's Two Bodies*, 112.

3: Slave Voices

1 Skura, 'Discourse and the Individual, and Vaughan and Vaughan, *Shakespeare's Caliban*.
2 Fiedler, *The Stranger in Shakespeare*, 208–9.
3 See Davis, *The Problem of Slavery*, 133–7.

4 Patterson, *Slavery and Social Death*, 100.
5 Hegel, *The Phenomenology of Mind*, 228–40. See also Fukuyama, *The End of History.*
6 Hegel, *The Phenomenology of Mind*, 228–40.
7 Hindess and Hirst, *Pre-capitalist Modes of Production*, 113; emphasis in original.
8 Ibid.; emphasis in original.
9 Voss, '"The Slaves Must Be Heard,"' 64.
10 Patterson, *Slavery and Social Death*, 101.
11 Hindess and Hirst, it must be noted, declare that Hegel's argument, though justly famous, 'has nothing to do with slavery and establishes no special relation of domination between master and slave. Hegel's object is the genesis of self-consciousness not the dynamics of slave systems' (*Pre-Capitalist Modes of Production*, 114).
12 Hegel, *The Phenomenology of Mind*, 239.
13 Berry, *Shakespeare in Performance*, 135–6.
14 Patterson, *Slavery and Social Death*, 1–14.
15 Ibid. See Jonathan Bate's lucid discussion of the adaptations of the Caliban figure in literature of the Third World (*The Genius of Shakespeare*, (240–7).
16 These readings are numerous; a comprehensive list is provided by Skura. Of historic interest are two books in particular: Mannoni, *Prospero and Caliban*, and Fanon, *Black Skin, White Masks*, especially 83–109, which constitute a radical's rebuttal of Mannoni's 'conservative' position.
17 Miner, 'The Wild Man through the Looking Glass,' 95.
18 Hendricks and Parker, *Women, 'Race,' and Writing*, 2.
19 Brown, '"This thing of darkness,"' 59; emphasis in original.
20 White, 'The Forms of Wildness,' 15.
21 One of the reasons for the importation of African slaves to the northern hemisphere was their physical hardiness, relative to the native populations. These, usually 'Indian' peoples, proved susceptible to diseases and died in such numbers as to render them uneconomical. Transportation from Africa proved to be the more efficient method of acquiring and keeping slaves. See Bean, *British Trans-Atlantic Slave Trade*, 8–20.
22 Hindess and Hirst, *Pre-Capitalist Modes of Production*, 112; emphasis in original.
23 Skura, 'Discourse and the Individual,' 60.
24 Patterson, *Slavery and Social Death*, 315.
25 Ibid., 319
26 Shakespeare, *The Tempest*, 193n.

4: The Scapegoat Mechanism

1 Bristol, *Big-Time Shakespeare*, 175.
2 Girard, *Violence and the Sacred*, 96.
3 Shapiro, *Shakespeare and the Jews*, 4.
4 The issue of the complicity in the oppression of Jews in Nazi Germany has been addressed most recently in Daniel Goldhagen's controversial study, *Hitler's Willing Executioners*.
5 Genovese, *Roll, Jordan, Roll*, 98.
6 Dawidowicz, *The War against the Jews*, 29.
7 Appiah, *Critical Terms*, 274–87. Appiah notes that during the Renaissance both Moors and Jews were considered unbelievers whose physical differences were signs but not causes or effects of their unbelief.
8 Shapiro, *Shakespeare and the Jews*, 72–4.
9 Wolf, 'Jews in Elizabethan England.' Shapiro, in *Shakespeare and the Jews*, contends that Wolf's claims were inflated, deriving from an apparent need in turn-of-the-century Anglo Jewry to 'ground itself in this most celebrated period of Protestant England's cultural and political past' (66).
10 Dunbar, *Poems of William Dunbar*, 106.
11 Hall, *Things of Darkness*, 19, 128.
12 De Grazia, Quilligan, and Stallybrass, *Subject and Object*, 2.
13 Vaughan, *Othello*, 58.
14 Shapiro, *Shakespeare and the Jews*, 114–30.
15 Hegel, *The Phenomenology of Mind*, 228–40.
16 Kureishi, 'Intimacy,' 92.
17 Neill, *Issues of Death*.
18 Hawkins, *Likenesses of Truth*, 74.
19 Shakespeare, *The Tempest*, 62.
20 This much-discussed problem is profoundly informed by the 'racial' difference between Caliban and Miranda, complicated by the fact that the threat of rape is the overwhelming image formed by the racist imagination. See Hall, *Things of Darkness*, 140–8.
21 For a comprehensive treatment of this subject see Vaughan and Vaughan, *Shakespeare's Caliban*.
22 For a good account of the 'representation of Caliban as popular demagogue and revolutionary' (250) see Bate, *The Genius of Shakespeare*, 240–50.
23 The Vaughans supply a useful history of the reception of the play in *Shakespeare's Caliban*.
24 Hall, *Things of Darkness*, 142.

25 Ibid., p. 143.
26 Thus the General Assembly of the Presbyterian Church in 1861. See Genovese, *Roll, Jordan, Roll*, 187.
27 See Cohen, *The Politics of Shakespeare*, 38–54.

5: The Self-Representations of *Othello*

1 De Grazia, Quilligan, and Stallybrass, *Subject and Object*, 17.
2 Maus, *Inwardness and the Theater*, 26.
3 Ibid., 29.
4 Greenblatt, *Renaissance Self-Fashioning*, 234.
5 To Paul Smith the phrase 'individual subject' is not a contradiction but a dialectical construction in which 'the subjection which the subject inhabits is always partial' (*Discerning the Subject*, xxxiii).
6 Ibid.
7 Bristol, *Big-Time Shakespeare*, 175–6.
8 See Brower, *Hero and Saint*, 1–29.
9 Maus, *Inwardness and the Theater*, 121.
10 Greenblatt, *Renaissance Self-Fashioning*, 245.

6: *King Lear* and Memory

1 Bowers, 'The Structure of *King Lear*,' 16.
2 Reibtanz, *The Lear World*, 15.
3 Girard, *The Scapegoat*, 24–45.
4 Girard, *Violence and the Sacred*, 49.
5 Catherine Belsey writes, 'Since meaning is plural, to be able to speak is to be able to take part in the contest for meaning which issues in the production of new subject positions, new determinations of what it is possible to be' (*The Subject of Tragedy*, 6).
6 Smith, *Discerning the Subject*, xxxiii.
7 Danson, *The Tragic Alphabet*, 166
8 Rackin, *Stages of History*, 123.
9 Dollimore, *Radical Tragedy*, 202.
10 Girard, *The Scapegoat*, 33.
11 Kernan, '*King Lear*,' 14.
12 Jackson, '"These same crosses ...,"' 387.

7: The Past of *Macbeth*

1 Stevenson, '*Virginibus Puerisque*,' 106.
2 As will become evident, it is hard to be specific as to number, some of the 'experiences' being rather vague and allusive, while others are quite precisely remembered events.
3 Holderness, Potter, and Turner, *Shakespeare*, 144.
4 Mullaney, *Place of the Stage*, 133.
5 Mullaney comments that this episode sets the traitor at an uncertain threshold of Renaissance society, 'athwart a line that sets off the human from the demonic, the natural from the unnatural' (ibid., 116).
6 Girard, *Violence and the Sacred*, 41. John Turner addresses the issue of Macbeth's contamination via Girard in Holderness, Potter, and Turner, *Shakespeare*, 137.
7 Mullaney, *Place of the Stage*, 31.
8 Holderness, 'Radical Potentiality and Institutional Closure,' 259–60.
9 Weimann, *Shakespeare and Popular Tradition*, 217.
10 Wills, *Witches and Jesuits*, 128.
11 Girard, *Violence and the Sacred*, 102.
12 Wills, *Witches and Jesuits*, 30.

8: Messengers of Death

1 Hammond and Scullard, *Oxford Classical Dictionary*, 503.
2 Brown, *Hermes the Thief*, 68.
3 Parker, *Shakespeare from the Margins*, 233.
4 Wiggins, *Journeymen in Murder*, 29.
5 *2 Henry VI, Richard III, Richard II, Romeo and Juliet, King John, Much Ado About Nothing, Henry V, As You Like It, Othello, King Lear, Macbeth, Anthony and Cleopatra, Pericles, Cymbeline, The Tempest.*
6 Wiggins describes how contemporary accounts differ. He cites R. Fabyan and *The Mirror for Magistrates*, where it is proposed that the king sent for Exton, while Holinshed sees the murderer as a self-motivated opportunist. See Wiggins, *Journeymen in Murder*, 97–8.
7 Dollimore, *Radical Tragedy*, 203.
8 Girard, *The Scapegoat*, 14. Girard distinguishes between conscious and unconscious scapegoating; that is, between those who know of the innocence of the scapegoat and those who sincerely believe him to be responsible for the social discord he is accused of causing.
9 Mahood, *Bit Parts*, 175.

10 Rackin, *Stages of History*, 147.

11 Mahood, *Bit Parts*, 176.

12 Sinfield, *Faultlines*, 95.

13 Rosenberg, *Masks of Macbeth*, 398.

9: Broken Human Bodies

1 *Troilus and Cressida*, 5, 5, 34.

2 Miller, *Anatomy of Disgust*, 8.

3 Ibid., 26.

4 Quoted by editor Jonathan Bate in Shakespeare, *Titus Andronicus*, 23.

5 Hunt, 'A Thing of Nothing,' 29.

6 Ibid., 30.

7 Girard, *The Girard Reader*, 9–19.

8 Rosenberg, *Masks of King Lear*, 242.

9 Girard, *Violence and the Sacred*, 245.

10 Huet, *Monstrous Imagination*, 5.

11 Schwarz, 'Missing the Breast,' 156.

12 Miller, *Anatomy of Disgust*, 82.

13 Ibid.

14 Barker, *Tremulous Private Body*, 21.

15 Ibid, 22.

16 Kendall, '"Lend me thy hand,"' 298.

17 Ibid., 316.

18 Mazzio, 'Sins of the Tongue,' 62–3.

19 Tricomi, 'The Aesthetics of Mutilation,' 13.

20 Brooke, *Horrid Laughter*.

21 Rowe, 'Dismembering and Forgetting,' 303.

22 Bate, 'Introduction,' in Shakespeare, *Titus Andronicus*, 36.

23 Shapiro, *Shakespeare and the Jews*, 121.

24 Girard, *Violence and the Sacred*, 102.

Works Cited

Anderson, Benedict. *Imagined Communities: Reflections on the Origin and Spread of Nationalism.* New York: Verso, 1991.

Appiah, Kwame Anthony. *Critical Terms for Literary Study,* ed. Frank Lentricchia and Thomas McLaughlin. Chicago: University of Chicago Press, 1990.

Axton, Marie. *The Queen's Two Bodies: Drama and the Elizabethan Succession.* London: Royal Historical Society, 1977.

Barker, Francis. *The Tremulous Private Body: Essays on Subjection.* London: Methuen, 1984.

Bate, Jonathan. *The Genius of Shakespeare.* London: Picador, 1997.

Bean, Richard Nelson. *The British Trans-Atlantic Slave Trade, 1650–1775.* New York: Arno Press, 1975.

Belsey, Catherine. 'Making Histories Then and Now: Shakespeare from *Richard II* to *Henry V.*' In *Uses of History: Marxism, Postmodernism and the Renaissance,* ed. Francis Barker, Peter Hulme, and Margaret Iverson. Manchester: Manchester University Press, 1991.

– *The Subject of Tragedy: Identity and Difference in Renaissance Drama.* London: Routledge, 1985.

Berger Jr, Harry. 'Psychoanalyzing the Shakespeare Text: The First Three Scenes of the *Henriad.*' In *Shakespeare and the Question of Theory.* New York: Methuen, 1985.

Berry, Ralph. *Shakespeare in Performance: Casting and Metamorphoses.* London: Macmillan, 1993.

Bloom, Harold. *Shakespeare: The Invention of the Human.* New York: Riverhead Books, 1998.

Booth, Stephen. *'King Lear,' 'Macbeth,' Indefinition, and Tragedy.* New Haven, Conn.: Yale University Press, 1983.

Bowers, Fredson. 'The Structure of King Lear.' *Shakespeare Quarterly* 31, 1 (Spring 1980) 7–20.

Bristol, Michael D. *Big-Time Shakespeare*. London: Routledge, 1996.

Brooke, Nicholas. *Horrid Laughter in Jacobean Tragedy.* London: Open Books, 1979.

Brower, Reuben A. *Hero and Saint: Shakespeare and the Graeco-Roman Heroic Tradition*. Oxford: Clarendon Press, 1971.

Brown, Norman O. *Hermes the Thief: The Evolution of a Myth*. Great Barrington, Mass.: Lindisfarne Press, 1990.

Brown, Paul. '"This thing of darkness I acknowledge mine": *The Tempest* and the Discourse of Colonialism.' *Political Shakespeare: New Essays in Cultural Materialism*, ed. Jonathan Dollimore and Alan Sinfield. Ithaca, N.Y.: Cornell University Press, 1985.

Cohen, Derek. *The Politics of Shakespeare*. Basingstoke: Macmillan, 1993.

Cohen, Walter. *Drama of a Nation: Public Theatre in Renaissance England and Spain*. Ithaca, N.Y.: Cornell University Press, 1985.

Cunningham, James. *Shakespeare's Tragedies and Modern Critical Theory.* London: Associated University Presses, 1997.

Danson, Lawrence. *The Tragic Alphabet*. New Haven, Conn.: Yale University Press, 1974.

Davis, David Brion. *The Problem of Slavery in Western Culture*. Harmondsworth, U.K.: Penguin, 1970.

Dawidowicz, Lucy S. *The War against the Jews, 1933–1945*. New York: Holt Rinehart & Winston, 1975.

De Grazia, Margareta, Maureen Quilligan, and Peter Stallybrass. *Subject and Object in Renaissance Culture*. Cambridge: Cambridge University Press, 1996.

Dollimore, Jonathan. *Radical Tragedy: Religion, Ideology and Power in the Drama of Shakespeare and His Contemporaries*. Brighton, U.K.: Harvester Press, 1984.

Dollimore, Jonathan, and Alan Sinfield, eds. *Political Shakespeare: New Essays in Cultural Materialism*. Ithaca, N.Y.: Cornell University Press, 1985.

Dunbar, William. *The Poems of William Dunbar*, ed. James Kingsley. Oxford: Clarendon Press, 1979.

Edwards, Philip. *Threshold of a Nation: A Study in English and Irish Drama*. Cambridge: Cambridge University Press, 1979.

Fanon, Frantz. *Black Skin, White Masks*, trans. Charles Lam Markmann. New York: Grove Press, 1967.

Fiedler, Leslie. *The Stranger in Shakespeare*. New York: Stein and Day, 1973.

Fukuyama, Francis. *The End of History and the Last Man*. New York: Avon Books, 1992.

Gellner, Ernest. *Nations and Nationalism*. Oxford: Basil Blackwell, 1983.

Genovese, Eugene D. *Roll, Jordan, Roll: The World the Slaves Made*. New York: Vintage Books, 1976.

Girard, René. 'Mimesis and Violence,' *The Girard Reader*, ed. James G. Williams. New York: Crossroad, 1996.

– *The Scapegoat*, trans. Yvonne Freccero. Baltimore, Md.: Johns Hopkins University Press, 1986.

– *Violence and the Sacred*, trans. Patrick Gregory. Baltimore, Md.: Johns Hopkins University Press, 1977.

Goldhagen, Daniel. *Hitler's Willing Executioners: Ordinary Germans and the Holocaust*. New York: Knopf, 1996.

Green, Douglas E. 'Interpreting "her martyr'd signs": Gender and Tragedy in *Titus Andronicus*.' *Shakespeare Quarterly* 40 (Fall 1989) 317–26.

Greenblatt, Stephen. 'Invisible Bullets: Renaissance Authority and Its Subversion, *Henry IV* and *Henry V*.' In *Political Shakespeare: New Essays in Cultural Materialism*. Ithaca, N.Y.: Cornell University Press, 1985.

– *Renaissance Self-Fashioning: From More to Shakespeare*. Chicago: University of Chicago Press, 1980.

– gen. ed., *The Norton Shakespeare*. New York: W.W. Norton, 1997.

Greenfeld, Liah. *Nationalism: Five Roads to Modernity*. Cambridge: Harvard University Press, 1992.

Hall, Kim F. *Things of Darkness: Economies of Race and Gender in Early Modern England*. Ithaca, N.Y.: Cornell University Press, 1995.

Hammond, N.G.L., and H.H. Scullard, eds. *The Oxford Classical Dictionary*. Oxford: Clarendon Press, 1970.

Harbage, Alfred. *Shakespeare and the Rival Traditions*. Bloomington: Indiana University Press, 1970.

Hawkes, Terence. *Meaning by Shakespeare*. London: Routledge, 1992.

Hawkins, Harriet. *Likenesses of Truth in Elizabethan and Restoration Drama*. Oxford: Clarendon Press, 1972.

Hegel, G.W.F. *The Phenomenology of Mind*, trans. J.B. Baillie. New York: Harper and Row, 1967.

Helgerson, Richard. *Forms of Nationhood: The Elizabethan Writing of England*. Chicago: University of Chicago Press, 1994.

Hendricks, Margo, and Patricia Parker, eds. *Women, 'Race,' and Writing in the Early Modern Period*. London: Routledge, 1994.

Hindess, Barry, and Paul Q. Hirst. *Pre-Capitalist Modes of Production*. London: Routledge and Kegan Paul, 1977.

Hobsbawm, E.J. *Nations and Nationalism since 1780: Programme, Myth, Reality*. Cambridge: Cambridge University Press, 1990.

Holderness, Graham. 'Radical Potentiality and Institutional Closure: Shake-speare in Film and Television.' In *Shakespeare, Macbeth: A Casebook*, ed. John Wain. Rev. ed. Basingstoke, U.K.: Macmillan, 1994.
– *Shakespeare Recycled: The Making of Historical Drama*. Hemel Hempstead, U.K.: Harvester Wheatsheaf, 1992.
Holderness, Graham, Nick Potter, and John Turner. *Shakespeare: The Play of History*. London: Macmillan, 1988.
Huet, Marie-Hélène. *Monstrous Imagination*. Cambridge: Harvard University Press, 1993.
Hunt, John. 'A Thing of Nothing: The Catastrophic Body in *Hamlet*.' *Shakespeare Quarterly* 39 (1988) 27–44.
Ignatieff, Michael. *Blood and Belonging: Journeys into the New Nationalism*. Harmondsworth, U.K.: Penguin, 1993.
Jackson, James L. '"These same crosses ..."' *Shakespeare Quarterly* 31 (Autumn 1980) 387–90.
Keegan, John. *A History of Warfare*. New York: Random House, 1994.
Kendall, Gillian Murray. '"Lend me thy hand": Metaphor and Mayhem in *Titus Andronicus*.' *Shakespeare Quarterly* 40 (Fall 1989) 299–316.
Kernan, Alvin B. *King Lear* and the Shakespearean Pageant of History.' In *On King Lear*, ed. Lawrence Danson. Princeton, N.J.: Princeton University Press, 1981.
Kureishi, Haniff. 'Intimacy.' *New Yorker*, 11 May 1998, 92.
Lyotard, Jean-François. *The Postmodern Condition: A Report on Knowledge*, trans. Geoff Bennington and Brian Massumi. Minneapolis: University of Minnesota Press, 1984.
Machiavelli, Nicolo. *The Portable Machiavelli*, trans. and ed. Peter Bondanella and Mark Musa. Harmondsworth, U.K.: Penguin, 1979.
Mahood, M.M. *Bit Parts in Shakespeare's plays*. New York: Cambridge University Press, 1992.
Mannoni, O. *Prospero and Caliban: The Psychology of Colonization*, trans. Pamela Powesland. New York: Praeger Publishers, 1964.
Maus, Katharine Eisaman. *Inwardness and the Theater in the English Renaissance*. Chicago: University of Chicago Press, 1995.
Mazzio, Carla. 'Sins of the Tongue.' In *The Body in Parts: Fantasies of Corporeality in Early Modern Europe*, edited by David Hillman and Carla Mazzio. New York: Routledge, 1997.
Miller, William Ian. *The Anatomy of Disgust*. Cambridge: Harvard University Press, 1997.
Miner, Earl. 'The Wild Man through the Looking Glass.' *The Wild Man Within: An Image in Western Thought from the Renaissance to Romanticism*, ed. Edward

Dudley and Maximillian E. Novak. Pittsburgh: University of Pittsburgh Press, 1972.

Mullaney, Steven. *The Place of the Stage: License, Play and Power in Renaissance England*. Chicago: University of Chicago Press, 1988.

Neill, Michael. 'Broken English and Broken Irish: Nation, Language, and the Optic of Power in Shakespeare's Histories.' *Shakespeare Quarterly* 45 (1994) 1–32.

– *Issues of Death: Mortality and Identity in English Renaissance Tragedy*. Oxford: Clarendon Press, 1997.

Parker, Patricia. *Shakespeare from the Margins: Language, Culture, Context*. Chicago: University of Chicago Press, 1996.

Parker, Patricia, and Geoffrey Hartman, eds. *Shakespeare and the Question of Theory*. New York: Methuen, 1985.

Patterson, Orlando. *Slavery and Social Death: A Comparative Study*. Cambridge: Harvard University Press, 1982.

Pugliatti, Paola. *Shakespeare the Historian*. Basingstoke, U.K.: Macmillan, 1996.

Rackin, Phyllis. *Stages of History: Shakespeare's English Chronicles* Ithaca, N.Y.: Cornell University Press, 1990.

Reibtanz, John. *The Lear World: A Study of King Lear in Its Dramatic Context*. London: Heinemann, 1977.

Rosenberg, Marvin. *The Masks of King Lear*. Berkeley: University of California Press, 1972.

– *The Masks of Macbeth*. Berkeley: University of California Press, 1978.

Rowe, Katherine A. 'Dismembering and Forgetting in *Titus Andronicus*.' *Shakespeare Quarterly* 45 (Fall 1994) 279–303.

Schwarz, Kathryn. 'Missing the Breast: Desire, Disease, and the Singular Effect of Amazons.' In *The Body in Parts: Fantasies of Corporeality in Early Modern Europe*, ed. David Hillman and Carla Mazzio. New York: Routledge, 1997.

Shakespeare, William. *King Lear*. The Arden Shakespeare, edited by Kenneth Muir. London: Methuen, 1966.

– *The Tempest*. The Arden Shakespeare, edited by Frank Kermode. London: Methuen, 1966.

– *The Tempest*. The Oxford Shakespeare, edited by Stephen Orgel. Oxford: Oxford University Press, 1987.

– *Titus Andronicus*. The Arden Shakespeare, 3rd Series, edited by Jonathan Bate. London: Routledge, 1995.

Shapiro, James. *Shakespeare and the Jews*. New York: Columbia University Press, 1996.

Sinfield, Alan. *Faultlines: Cultural Materialism and the Politics of Dissident Reading*. Berkeley: University of California Press, 1978.

Skura, Meredith Anne. 'Discourse and the Individual: The Case of Colonialism in *The Tempest*.' *Shakespeare Quarterly* 40 (1989) 42–69.

Smidt, Kristian. *Unconformities in Shakespeare's History Plays*. London: Macmillan, 1982.

Smith, Paul. *Discerning the Subject*. Theory and History of Literature, Vol. 55. Minneapolis: University of Minnesota Press, 1988.

Stevenson, Robert Louis. *'Virginibus Puerisque': Familiar Studies of Men and Books*. London and Toronto: J.M. Dent, 1929.

Tricomi, Albert H. 'The Aesthetics of Mutilation in *Titus Andronicus*.' In *Shakespeare Survey 27*. Cambridge: Cambridge University Press, 1974.

Vaughan, Alden T., and Virginia Mason Vaughan. *Shakespeare's Caliban: A Cultural History*. New York: Cambridge University Press, 1993.

Vaughan, Virginia Mason. *Othello: A contextual history*. Cambridge: Cambridge University Press, 1994.

Voss, A.E. '"The Slaves Must Be Heard": Thomas Pringle and the Dialogue of South African Servitude.' *English in Africa* 17 (May 1990) 59–71.

Weimann, Robert. *Shakespeare and the Popular Tradition in the Theater: Studies in the Social Dimension of Dramatic Form and Function*, ed. Robert Schwartz. Baltimore, Md.: Johns Hopkins University Press, 1978.

White, Hayden. 'The Forms of Wildness: Archaeology of an Idea.' *In The Wild Man Within: An Image in Western Thought from the Renaissance to Romanticism*, ed. Edward Dudley and Maximillian E. Novak. Pittsburgh: Pittsburgh University Press, 1972.

White, R.S. *Innocent Victims: Poetic Injustice in Shakespearean Tragedy*. London: Athlone Press, 1986.

Wiggins, Martin. *Journeymen in Murder: The Assassin in English Renaissance Drama*. Oxford: Clarendon Press, 1991.

Williams, Gordon. *A Glossary of Shakespeare's Sexual Language*. London: Athlone Press, 1997.

Wills, Gary. *Witches and Jesuits: Shakespeare's Macbeth*. New York: Oxford University Press and the New York Public Library, 1995.

Wilson, J. Dover. *The Fortunes of Falstaff*. Cambridge: Cambridge University Press, 1943.

Wolf, Lucien. 'Jews in Elizabethan England' *Transactions of the Jewish Historical Society of England* 11 (1924–7) 1–91.

Yates, Frances A. *The Art of Memory*. London: Routledge and Kegan Paul, 1966.

Index